Claire Elise Katz is Professor of Philosc
Studies at Texas A&M University. A specialist in contemporary
Jewish thought, philosophy of religion, feminist theory, and French
philosophy, she has written and edited *Levinas, Judaism, and the
Feminine: The Silent Footsteps of Rebecca* (2003), *Emmanuel Levinas:
Critical Assessments, vols 1-4* (2005) and *Levinas and the Crisis of
Humanism* (2013).

"'With an engaging and probing approach to Jewish concerns, from education to prayer, Claire Elise Katz gives us a fresh new look at some of the most influential Jewish philosophers of modern times. Written in an engaging and easy style, this is a wonderful way to introduce students and all learners to the rich and fascinating world of modern Jewish thought."

Susannah Heschel,
Eli Black Professor of Jewish Studies, Dartmouth College

"What is modern Jewish philosophy? Claire Katz, in answering this question, has crafted a perceptive essay in intellectual history centred on the philosophy of Emmanuel Levinas. Her book traces all of the major themes in Levinas' writings from their literary sources in the writings of Moses Mendelssohn, Hermann Cohen, Lev Shestov, Martin Buber, and Franz Rosenzweig through the writings in ethics and politics by some of Levinas' peers, notably Abraham Joshua Heschel and Emil Fackenheim. The book touches on most of the major themes of Jewish thought in the twentieth century: especially the meaning of the Holocaust, the problems with Jewish education in liberal secular societies, and the challenges to Jewish self-understanding from both modernism and post-modernism. Despite its title, the book is much more than an undergraduate introductory textbook in modern Jewish philosophy: though at this it performs its task well. Claire Katz is herself an important post-modernist feminist Jewish thinker whose writings successfully integrate, as they do in this volume, her academic knowledge of modern philosophy with her personal passion for Judaism."

Norbert Samuelson,
Harold and Jean Grossmann Professor of Jewish Philosophy,
Arizona State University

"Jewish philosophy is viewed by Claire Elise Katz as the voice of the other: as an internal point of difference and limit without which western philosophy cannot be truly critical. Reshaping the conceptual contours of the western philosophical tradition, as Katz does here, means that something happens to Jewish philosophy in the process. The author places the latter more squarely in the history of western philosophy and thus brings it into conversation with Descartes, Locke, Hobbes, Kant, Hegel, Husserl, Sartre, and de Beauvoir. She imaginatively draws Jewish philosophy out of its own self-enclosure, thereby transforming it into something more cosmopolitan, more rigorous, more curious, and more conceptually generative than perhaps has been previously imagined."

Zachary Braiterman,
Professor of Religion, Syracuse University

AN INTRODUCTION TO
MODERN JEWISH PHILOSOPHY

CLAIRE ELISE KATZ

I.B. TAURIS
LONDON · NEW YORK

Published in 2014 by I.B.Tauris & Co Ltd
6 Salem Road, London W2 4BU
175 Fifth Avenue, New York NY 10010
www.ibtauris.com

Distributed in the United States and Canada Exclusively by Palgrave Macmillan
175 Fifth Avenue, New York NY 10010

Cover illustration: Andy Warhol's *Martin Buber* (1980), from *Ten Portraits of Jews
of the Twentieth Century*, portfolio, screenprint, 40 x 32 inches.
Image courtesy of Scala, reproduced by permission (©2013 The Andy Warhol
Foundation for the Visual Arts, Inc. / Artists Rights Society (ARS), New York).
Courtesy Ronald Feldman Fine Arts, New York / www.feldmangallery.com

ISBN: 978 1 84885 488 8 (hb)
       978 1 84885 489 5 (pb)

A full CIP record for this book is available from the British Library
A full CIP record is available from the Library of Congress

Library of Congress Catalog Card Number: available

Typeset in Caslon by Free Range Book Design & Production Limited

Printed and bound in Great Britain by T.J. International, Padstow, Cornwall

For my students.

I learned much from my teachers, more from my
colleagues, but most from my students.
R. Hanina (Talmud: Ta'anit 7a)

Contents

Acknowledgements

This book project began in fall 2008 with an email from Alex Wright, the editor at I.B.Tauris, asking if I would be interested in writing *An Introduction to Modern Jewish Philosophy*. I was interested but at first I hesitated. I had several other projects on my table, and even though I was tenured, I was only into my second year at a new university, which came with its own set of demands and responsibilities. Taking on this project would have also meant returning to material that in my current position I have not had an opportunity to teach. This point was both exciting to me in that it offered me the excuse to return to material I love to read; but it was also daunting since it would mean re-familiarizing myself with material I had not read or taught in several years. I eventually agreed to the project and I am deeply grateful to Alex for this opportunity—not only to return to the material but also to do so in a way that allowed me to reconsider how I had previously read it. I initially balked at his suggestion to include literature in the book and I now think that discussion is central to the final chapter. Most importantly, I am grateful for his patience in waiting for the completion of the project when several obstacles to finishing it were thrown in my path. My gratitude also to Pear Fosh and Amy Himsworth at I.B.Tauris, and to Paul Tompsett at Free Range Book Design & Production who smoothly moved this manuscript through production. Finally, a special thanks to Hila Ratzabi whose editing skills helped me clean up these files so I could finally send them to press.

Several sections of this book appeared previously in print in a different form. I am grateful to Indiana University Press for permission to reproduce in whole or summary, the discussions of education by Franz Rosenzweig (Chapter 3), Emmanuel Levinas (the education section of Chapter 4), and Abraham Joshua Heschel (Chapter 4). Hila Ratzabi provided excellent copyediting suggestions. Zachary Braiterman caught a few infelicities.

There are several other people to acknowledge. During the 2011/12 academic year, I was in residence at Amherst College through the Copeland Colloquium, without which this project would simply not have been finished. My engagement with Jewish philosophy that year was enhanced by conversations with Catherine Epstein, Daniel Gordon, Maria Heim, Leah Hewitt, Premesh Lalu, Karen Remmler, Austin Sarat, and Susan Shapiro. The Cornerstone Faculty Fellowship, awarded to me by the Texas A&M College of Liberal Arts, provided financial support that enabled me to travel to conferences, meet with other scholars, purchase books, and contributed to my ability to accept the residential fellowship at Amherst College. The Cornerstone fellowship also provided financial assistance for use of the cover art. The community of scholars that works in Jewish studies, and in particular modern Jewish philosophy, has provided extraordinary intellectual support in addition to invaluable friendships over the past fourteen years. In particular, I would like to thank Deborah Achtenberg, Annette Aronowicz, Leora Batnitzky, Andrew Benjamin, Jeffrey Bernstein, Bettina Bergo, Miriam Bodian, Zachary Braiterman, Jerome Coplusky, Oona Eisenstadt, Matthew Menachem Feuer, Randy Friedman, Sandor Goodhart, Robert Gibbs, Lewis Gordon, James Hatley, Susannah Heschel, Leah Hochman, Dana Hollander, Jonathan Judaken, Gregory Kaplan, Martin Kavka, Steven Kepnes, Shaul Magid, Peter Ochs, Monica Osborne, Sarah Pessin, Randi Rashkover, Elliot Ratzman, Tamar Rudavsky, Carl Sachs, Norbert Samuelson, Susan Shapiro, Martin Shuster, Jules Simon, Hava Tirosh-Samuelson, Elliot Wolfson, Michael Zank, and Laurie

Zoloth. My students who challenged my thinking in the Modern Jewish Philosophy classes I taught at Penn State were a source of joy that I am lucky to have experienced. I thank in particular Alex Stehn and Mariana Alessandri. Mitchell Aboulafia, Daniel Conway, Theodore George, Joe Golson, Emily Grosholz, Cathy Kemp, John and Patricia McDermott, and Kristi Sweet generously indulged my need to discuss the Enlightenment—and this project. Matthew Wester provided excellent suggestions regarding the Hannah Arendt sections. A special thank you to the Melbern G. Glasscock Center for Humanities Research, the Texas A&M Honors and Undergraduate Research program, and my 2013 Glasscock Summer Scholars students: Christopher Black, Desirae Embree, Michael Gonzales, Jessi Greene, Thomas Sekula. To my Facebook community of friends and colleagues—thank you for the support, encouragement, and suggestions as I worked through this material.

This is a book motivated by my own relationship to teaching and learning. My husband, Dan Conway, to whom I owe everything already, has a real gift as a philosophical interlocutor who can often see the originality of one's project more clearly than we can see it ourselves. Those who are lucky enough to be counted among his students know their fortunes. I am grateful for the intellectual life we share. Our daughters, Olivia and Evie, inspire me every day to be a better teacher.

Abbreviations

DF	*Difficult Freedom*
DS	*The Drowned and the Saved*
EJQ	"The Enlightenment and the Jewish Question"
HO	*Humanism of the Other*
IT	*I and Thou*
JP	"The Jew as Pariah"
JPJP	*Jewish Philosophers and Jewish Philosophy*
JW	*The Jewish Writings*
NT	"The New Thinking"
NTR	*Nine Talmudic Readings*
OJL	*On Jewish Learning*
PW	*Pointing the Way*
RH	*Reason and Hope*
RJ	*Responsibility and Judgment*
RR	*Religion of Reason*
TO	*Time and the Other*

Glossary

Abraham: patriarch of the Israelites who was married to Sarah. He was the father of Ishmael, by his maidservant, Hagar, and Isaac by his wife Sarah. First covenant (b'rit) between God and the Jewish people is made through Abraham.

Alterity: otherness.

Anti-Semitism: hatred directed at Jews simply because they are Jews. Although the hatred of the Jews extends back before the nineteenth century, this term, coined by Wilhelm Marr, is linked with the 1870s because of its racial connotation.

Aporia: an impassable philosophical puzzle.

Assimilation: the process by which a minority group is brought into the dominant culture. Full assimilation would be when the minority group is no longer visible.

Atonement: reconciliation with God for transgressions against God; repenting for wrongdoing. In Judaism, Yom Kippur (the Day of Atonement) is marked as the holiest day of the year for Jews. With its focus on atonement and repentance, it completes the ten days of awe (the High Holy Days).

Bildung: cultivation; education.

B'rit: covenant.

Conservative Judaism: with a focus still on conserving Jewish tradition, it is the branch of Judaism that still views halakhah, or Jewish law, as normative and binding. However, it differs from the Orthodox tradition in that it believes there is historical justification for making changes in Jewish law.

Dasein: a neologism by the twentieth-century German phenomenologist, Martin Heidegger, to denote a particular kind of Being: the kind of Being that has as its concern its own being.

Deuteronomy (*Devarim*): the fifth book of the Torah. It takes its name from the first word of the book: Words.

Dreyfus Affair: a political scandal in the late nineteenth century in France involving the French military officer, Alfred Dreyfus, who was falsely accused of treason. The affair came to its resolution in 1906, but the effects of the Dreyfus affair were to divide France between those who defended Dreyfus (Dreyfusards) and wished for a stronger secular society and those who wished for a stronger role of religion in government. Dreyfus was eventually acquitted.

Election: the term is associated with the concept of "chosenness," the view that Jews were "chosen" to form a covenant with God. Election refers to "elected to responsibility" to uphold the commandments. Insofar as some ways of reading "responsibility" privilege that concept, the term has frequently conveyed a privileged status.

Emancipation, of the Jews: emancipation refers generally to the freedom accorded particular groups of people. Within Jewish history it refers to the level of citizenship and rights accorded to the Jews living in parts of Europe. The specific dates and the specific rights vary but in general, Jewish emancipation took place primarily between the eighteenth and twentieth centuries.

Enlightenment: an intellectual period spanning roughly the mid-seventeenth century through the eighteenth century marked by dramatic developments and changes in science, philosophy, and political thought. It has been noted that there were several different Enlightenments each marked by distinct characteristics and thinkers, most notably Scottish, French, and German.

Epistemology: the philosophical study of knowledge, which incorporates such questions as: what can we know and what counts as truth?

Eretz Israel: the land of Israel.

Ethics: traditionally this has been the philosophical study of right and wrong action and incorporates the question, how should we treat others? Post-modern philosophy has questioned the traditional way this field has been defined.

Existentialism: although the term applies to the philosophies of nineteenth-century philosophers, Søren Kierkegaard and Friedrich Nietzsche, it is most closely identified with a set of philosophers in post-war France: Jean-Paul Sartre, Simone de Beauvoir, and Albert Camus. This philosophical movement responded to the philosophical position that human being, human existence could be understood through science and scientific method by claiming this was inadequate to human experience. It argues that a further set of categories that are better able to capture what human experience is like is needed.

Ezekiel: Hebrew prophet, viewed as author of the Book of Ezekiel.

Gandhi, Mahatma: born in 1869, he was a prominent leader in British-ruled India who led Indians in the protest against the national salt tax (1930). He is known for both practicing and advocating the use of non-violence to protest injustice. He died in 1948.

Gemara: the commentary on the oral law known as the Mishna. Together, the Gemara and the Mishna form the Talmud.

Halakhah: Jewish law. It is viewed as the legal side of Judaism to be contrasted with the aggadah, or the non-legal material.

Haskalah: or Jewish Enlightenment. A movement among European Jews toward the end of the eighteenth century and into the nineteenth century, which advocated Jews adopting enlightenment values and taking their place in Western society. Those who followed this movement were called *maskilim*.

Hebrew, biblical or classical: language in which Jewish prayers are said; language in which the Torah is written.

Hebrew, modern: one of the official languages of Israel.

Hegel, Georg Wilhelm Friedrich (1770–1831): Hegel was a German philosopher associated with German Idealism. A systematic philosopher, he is best known for offering a teleological account of history, which influenced Karl Marx's theory of historical development.

Heidegger, Martin (1889–1976): Heidegger was a German philosopher and part of the phenomenological tradition whose ideas had a substantial impact on the development of French and German philosophy in the twentieth century. In the 1930s and 1940s he and his ideas were closely associated with Nazi Germany raising questions about the meaning of some of his writings at that time.

Hitler, Adolf (1889–1945): Austrian born politician who became the leader of National Socialism (Nazi Party), which promoted racial purity and racially motivated policies, leading to the extermination of close to eleven million people in Europe. His memoir, *Mein Kampf* (My Struggle), written while he was in prison for a failed coup, details his deep anti-Semitic feelings.

Israel: Jewish nation-state established in 1948.

Judaism: a monotheistic religion that is also one of the three Abrahamic religions. The other two are Islam and Christianity.

Jerusalem: capital city of Israel. Home to the holy sites of the three Abrahamic religions: The Western Wall (Judaism); the Dome of the Rock (Islam); the Church of the Holy Sepulcher (Christianity).

Jesus of Nazareth: He was a Jewish rabbi (teacher). His mother is Mary and he is believed by Christians to be the son of God. His teachings are central to Christianity.

Kant, Immanuel: eighteenth-century German philosopher central to the German Enlightenment who was also a contemporary and friend of Moses Mendelssohn. He was a systematic thinker whose work continues to have a significant impact on the development of all areas of Western philosophy, including, epistemology, aesthetics, moral theory, social and political philosophy, and logic.

Kierkegaard, Søren: nineteenth-century Danish philosopher known for his critique of modernity. Considered to have inaugurated the philosophical tradition known as existentialism, Kierkegaard is most well known for his book, *Fear and Trembling*, which offers an extended meditation on the Hebrew Bible story, The Binding of Isaac.

Liberalism: political philosophy closely associated with the Enlightenment period that is founded on the principles of liberty and equality. See John Locke.

Locke, John: seventeenth-century British philosopher and contract theorist whose book, *Two Treatises of Government*, inaugurates political liberalism.

Maimonides: medieval Jewish philosopher, rabbi, and physician who lived in the geographical region now known as Spain. He is the author of the Mishneh Torah.

Marburg School: a school of neo-Kantian philosophy founded by Hermann Cohen. Later, prominent neo-Kantian's included Ernst Cassirer.

Marx, Karl: nineteenth-century German philosopher known for formulating the philosophical/sociological theory of communism.

Maskilim: followers of the Haskalah movement (see Haskalah).

Messianism, Jewish: belief in the Messiah or savior who will redeem the people of Israel.

Metaphysics: branch of philosophy concerned with the study of reality—nature of being and the world. Some questions that concern metaphysics: What is real? Are we free? Is there a God?

Midrash: interpretation. In this case, it refers to the commentary and body of interpretation that accompanies the Jewish sacred texts (the Torah, the Prophets, and the Writings).

Mishna: the written account of the oral law (see Talmud). It is one part of the Talmud.

Moses: figure in the Hebrew Bible (Exodus) who received the Ten Commandments and led the Israelites out of slavery to freedom, though he himself was not able to join them in the promised land.

Napoleon Bonaparte: credited with emancipating the Jews as he made his way across Europe. The Jews who were emancipated under Bonaparte were often given citizenship rights they had not previously enjoyed.

National Socialism: see Hitler, Adolf.

Nietzsche, Friedrich: nineteenth-century German philosopher included in the existentialist tradition.

Noahide Commandments: set of commandments given to Noah that are considered to be applicable to all of humanity regardless of religious affiliation.

Orthodox Judaism: one of the branches of Judaism considered the most traditional in its approach. Although comprising myriad movements within this category, the different movements that would refer to themselves as "Orthodox" all share an adherence to Torah—both written and oral—which they believe is the exact word of God.

Paganism: a term typically used to apply to religious traditions that are polytheistic, often associated with nature, as opposed to monotheistic religions, which are often associated with a transcendent God.

Palestine: name for much of the geographical territory now known as Israel; a contested name still used by people who do not recognize Israel as a legitimate nation-state.

Prophets (Jewish): those who were viewed as a spokesperson for God in order to convey a message, lesson, teaching, or warning. They are often considered role models.

Protestant: a division in Christianity, closely associated with the sixteenth-century German theologian, Martin Luther, that includes Christians who protested Roman Catholicism leading to the Reformation, although this group was not originally referred to as Protestants.

Quota: a number that limits the number of people who can be admitted into a country, university, job, occupation, and so forth.

Reform Judaism: beginning in the nineteenth century, it is the branch of Judaism that differs from the more ritually observant branches—Conservative and Orthodox—in its belief that traditional Judaism can and should be reconciled with modern life. Although still anchored in Jewish thought, most notably the Jewish prophets, Reform Judaism believes that Judaism has changed and adapted over time and will continue to do so.

Rosh Hashanah: literally—head of the year. The Jewish new year marking the beginning of the ten days of awe, ending with Yom Kippur.

Rousseau, Jean-Jacques: eighteenth-century Swiss philosopher whose writings were thought to have influenced the French Revolution. His writings included, *The Social Contract*, *Discourse on the Origin and Basis of Inequality*, and *Emile*.

Shabbat: within the Jewish religion, it is the seventh day in the Jewish week—Friday sundown until one hour after Saturday sundown. It is the day of rest where work, and weekday concerns can be set aside. It is often observed through worship, Torah study, visiting with friends, and a festive meal on the Shabbat evening.

Shoah (Holocaust, Catastrophe): the Hebrew word for calamity. It is used to name the mass murder (six million) of the Jews during World War II. The mass murders included other groups also: those with disabilities, homosexuals, the Romani, and Polish and Soviet civilians. Including these other groups, scholars believe that the number of those killed through extermination is between ten and eleven million.

Social Contract: a theory in political philosophy that states that an individual's rights and responsibilities emerge out of the agreement first made between/among the individuals and the government when the society was formed. Although associated most closely with the Enlightenment period, one can find traces of the social contract in the speech Socrates gives to Crito (in "Crito") in which he explains to Crito why he must stay in prison rather than escape.

Socialism: an economic system defined by social or collective ownership of the means of production. In a more contemporary sense, it has come to mean the distribution of certain goods and services via the government, e.g., public schools and national healthcare.

Socrates: ancient Athenian philosopher (469–399 BCE). Teacher of Plato. His teachings, life, and character are thought to have shaped the formation of Western philosophy.

Talmud: considered the central text in rabbinic Judaism, the Talmud comprises two parts: the Mishna, or the oral law (*c*.200 CE) and the Gemara (*c*.500 CE), which contains the commentary on the Mishna.

Theology: systematic study of concepts of God, religious faith, and religious experience.

Torah: Hebrew name for the first five books of Moses, each named for the first word of the book: Bereshit ("In the beginning"—Genesis), Shemot ("Names"—Exodus), Vayikra ("He called"—Leviticus), Bamidbar ("In the desert"—Numbers), and Davarim ("Words"—Deuteronomy). It has myriad translations, including "instruction" or "teaching," central concepts in Judaism. It is occasionally translated as "law," which some believe is misleading.

Yom Kippur—the Day of Atonement: The holiest day of the year for Jews. A twenty-five hour period, consisting of fasting and praying/worshiping in synagogues, it marks the end of the ten days of awe.

Zionism: there are many different types of Zionism but in general, it is a form of nationalism focused on the formation and support of a Jewish state. Although associated with Theodor Herzl, the movement actually predates him.

Preface

At my dissertation defense in February 1999, one of my committee members asked me the following question about my project: "Is this Jewish philosophy?" Like any well-trained philosopher, I responded with a question: "What do you mean by Jewish philosophy?" "Ah," he said, "you had six years to ask me *that* question; now you must answer mine." I am not sure it would be any easier to answer his question today. Let me give a brief sketch of how I came to Jewish philosophy in order to explain why I structured this book as I did.

I came to Jewish philosophy through a back door, so to speak. My path to my research in Jewish philosophy begins when I was an undergraduate. I had been trained primarily in analytic philosophy but through my undergraduate education I developed an appreciation for the history of philosophy and ethics. In my second year of graduate school, I took a course with Tina Chanter called "The Other" (Chanter, 1994; 2001a; 2001b). The course focused on Hegel, Husserl, Heidegger, Levinas, and Irigaray. For the Levinas section, we read large sections of *Totality and Infinity*. The course did not explicitly connect Levinas's philosophical project and his writings on Judaism. Yet, his use of the biblical refrain, "the stranger, the widow, and the orphan," to express his philosophical point that we have an obligation to the most vulnerable among us, resonated with me. I sat in the university library, reading the *Midrash Rabbah* on all the biblical references to this phrase. The one that interested me the most was the reference in the Book of Ruth. As I read the Book of Ruth with the Levinas material in the background, I could see so many points of connection. What does Levinas say about the feminine? How does his Jewish background influence this view? Does it matter? Does philosophy transcend biography, or is it, like Christianity—in particular, Protestantism—another false neutral the way that "man" and "white" have been for women and people of color in the Western philosophical canon.

I found the convergences and divergences in the biblical story to be rich and thought provoking, yielding some answers but also more questions. Yet, my exploration of Ruth required me to push the limits of Levinas's project and consider why these limits were present, what function they served, and if they were structural and thus necessary for his larger project. My initial interest in exploring these themes was connected to the richness of the Jewish sacred texts and the myriad ways they opened up philosophical conversation. I wrote my seminar paper using the Book of Ruth as a point of intersection between Levinas's philosophical/ethical project and his writings on Judaism. The way that Levinas deployed the Jewish texts to do "work" that he could not do with philosophy I found both fascinating and intellectually compelling. My awareness of the obfuscation of Levinas's Jewish identity by not only my graduate student peers but also even more seasoned scholars finally led me from philosophy to Jewish philosophy.

I returned to *Totality and Infinity* and considered Levinas's statement in the Preface that "Rosenzweig's *Star of Redemption* [is] a work too often present in this book to be cited" (Levinas 1969, 28). Although the accuracy of this claim has been disputed, that Levinas believed it to be true and worth highlighting in his Preface is of interest. It means that regardless of whether the statement is actually true, he believed his book to be framed by the ideas of an early twentieth-century German-Jewish philosopher. I read Levinas as a Jewish philosopher in the fullest sense of that term. I view him as a philosopher who was not only Jewish but also as one who advanced a philosophy in a Jewish register.

Yet Levinas's own place in the Jewish philosophical canon still remains suspect. With few exceptions, the vast majority of "Introductions to Modern Jewish Thought/Philosophy" do not include a section on Levinas, or if they do, they pay scant attention to him. In part, this can be attributed to his historical period. He died in 1995 and thus his place in the canon had not yet been determined. But it can also be the case that Jewish philosophy has become subject to some of the same prejudices that dominate the larger philosophical framework. Levinas's thinking, influenced by Edmund Husserl, Martin Heidegger, and the post-modern tradition, is viewed as highly speculative and not as rigorous as "real" philosophical thought. Additionally, comments I hear frequently at conferences or public talks indicate that traditional talmudic scholars believe Levinas to have such an idiosyncratic view of Judaism that they find it difficult to include him in a traditional canon. Thus, his work is often excluded from the traditional canon in modern Jewish philosophy. The major figures in this canon include Moses Mendelssohn, Hermann Cohen, Martin Buber, and Franz Rosenzweig. The canon itself would be determined by how one understands the term "philosophy" and if the canon is referring to "thought" as well as philosophy.

My aim in this book was not to write an exhaustive account—either in breadth or depth—of the subject at hand. Nor was my aim to offer better discussions of the thinkers I included than those already in print; indeed, the many other introductory books on this topic are excellent and should be consulted. Rather, my intent was to offer a new way of thinking about the material that is included in this category that we call Modern Jewish Philosophy—and indeed, a discussion of the category itself could warrant its own book. Additionally, I wished to offer longer discussions of some of the works by the primary figures included in this canon that are often not included in these other introductions.

When I set out to write this book, I considered what has been of help and interest to my own students. When I teach, my students in philosophy are often grateful to discover these other figures and texts, even as they are surprised that my classroom is often the first time that they have heard these names. They suggested a book that would help them see the connections between Jewish philosophy and the canonical figures they are asked to read in their other philosophy classes in addition to one that would help them see how wide the themes are in modern Jewish philosophy. The editors of the press asked me to include a discussion of works by twentieth-century writers that included Levi and Wiesel. Neither Levi nor Wiesel is, strictly speaking, a philosopher. Yet their works ask us to consider philosophical questions and deep ethical problems, and I frequently taught their books in my course "Ethics after the Holocaust." I used this opportunity to draw on the philosophical themes that their respective works ask of us. As a result, this book brings together material from two courses that I frequently taught: "Modern Jewish Philosophy" and "Ethics after the Holocaust."

The question then that organizes this material is the following: "What is Enlightenment?" Thus, while I have followed a standard historical approach to the material, the texts on which I focus and the way in which I treat them varies from these other books. The traditional movements in the history of philosophy can be classified as follows: early modernity (seventeenth and eighteenth century), the critique of modernity (nineteenth century); and post-modernity (twentieth and twenty-first century). I begin with the philosophy of Moses Mendelssohn and focus on two texts, *Jerusalem* and his short essay "What is Enlightenment?," to frame the question of the state and the individual. In the center of the book, Levinas's project functions as a pivot. His work functions like Kant's schematism, which is a bridge between two things that are totally different from each other. Levinas's work sits inside philosophy while also functioning as a critique of philosophy. It is both modern and post-modern. I end with a discussion of the twentieth-century philosophers who position themselves as post-modern, offering a critique of Enlightenment philosophy, the solution to which cannot avoid the Enlightenment itself. I organize the material in this chapter around this question: What are the limits of philosophy?

Finally, in addition to situating these modern Jewish philosophers within the philosophical period in which they lived, my aim was also to consider Jewish philosophy in light of the standard criticisms that are directed at the Western canon. Here I consider whether the Jewish philosophers can offer us a different narrative or set of tools than those shown to be problematic by criticisms found internal to the discipline itself, for example, feminist philosophy. My philosophy of teaching centers on my belief that my job is to provide my students with as many tools as possible. My aim in this book is to help all students of philosophy, not only those in Jewish philosophy classes, see that Jewish philosophy is not marginal to what they study, but central.

Introduction

What is Jewish Philosophy?

In his 1984 essay, "What is Enlightenment?," Michel Foucault takes up the answer Kant provides to the question in his 1783 essay of the same name. In his introductory discussion, Foucault asks, what is modern philosophy?, and he suggests that it is perhaps the philosophy that attempts to answer the question, *Was ist Aufklärung*? If the search for an answer to this question defines modern philosophy, what then defines modern Jewish philosophy? What is Jewish about modern philosophy such that we need to use a modifier? That is, if it is addressing the same set of questions, why use this modifier to limit its explanatory power?

To ask "What is Jewish philosophy?" one might first begin with the question what is philosophy? The etymology of the term, as many of us learned in our introductory philosophy classes, is Love (*philo*) of Wisdom (*sophia*). The philosopher, then, is one who does not necessarily possess wisdom, but rather one who loves it, who pursues it. But what does this tell us about philosophy as a discipline? Not much, really. We could consider the kinds of questions that philosophy asks: What is the good life? What is the best kind of government? What is education? What is right? What is truth? What counts as knowledge? What is art? Does this help us at all? Our pursuit of what philosophy *is* begins to look a little like Potter Stewart's reflections on the definition of pornography. He did not know how to define it precisely, but he knew it when he saw it.

Philosophy has come to mean that which can be applied universally as opposed to idiosyncratically. Thus, some scholars see any philosophy that has a modifier, e.g., feminist, African-American, Jewish and so forth, as by definition not philosophy. To some, the idea of something called "Jewish" philosophy already puts the second part of the title, "philosophy," into question. By modifying philosophy, we limit it, undermining its universality. Thus, can something be both Jewish and philosophy? Indeed, the question can be applied to any number of philosophical areas, e.g., feminist philosophy, that Allan Bloom might have pejoratively labeled "boutique." Yet to lay claim to this universality might in fact be philosophy's most arrogant stance, for to make this claim is not to see the very way in which ideas arise out of situated beings. If we can ask if feminist philosophy can be understood by men, or if Jewish philosophy can be understood by non-Jews, or non-practicing Jews, can we not ask if ancient philosophy can be understood by those living 2,500 years later? Is it not presumptuous to assume that we can understand all the nuance and context that influences Plato's writings? Yet certainly we would not say that even in light of those constraints his philosophy is meaningless or nonsensical to us. Similarly, we can make a parallel claim about those area studies in philosophy that have been forced to use a modifier. Jewish philosophy is one such area.

Jewish philosophy then, as situated inside the Western canon, already experiences a suspect position. Some of modern Jewish philosophy has worked precisely on this question—to show how questions about Judaism can be situated within the larger philosophical project of Western philosophy. The question of Jewish thought is more interesting: where do we locate or position thinkers who appear more theological, such as Abraham Joshua Heschel or Joseph Soloveitchik. Are they Jewish philosophers? If so, are they Jewish philosophers who are similar to or different from a thinker like Moses Mendelssohn who was clearly trying to write within the tradition of the German Enlightenment? Is their philosophy idiosyncratic to Jews? Observant Jews? Judaism? Does this render their thought not philosophy? Or does philosophy itself need to be reimagined and redefined to include thinkers whose work carries this kind of specificity?

It is all the more disappointing when one reads the history of modern philosophy and discovers that some of the marginalization is relatively recent. While it might not be the case that Mendelssohn would be included in a class devoted to the Enlightenment or in a course in modern philosophy, it is the case that he was read by Immanuel Kant and was considered one of the most formidable intellects of the time. Hermann Cohen was a neo-Kantian and Franz Rosenzweig wrote his dissertation on Hegel and the State. The categories that have exiled these thinkers have deprived contemporary students of a significant part of Western philosophy.

More recent divisions in the philosophical landscape—for example, the continental–analytic divide and the marginalization of classical American philosophy—complicate the category we call philosophy and who gets to be included in it. These divisions in turn further marginalize the more contemporary Jewish philosophers on multiple levels. If the philosophers in question are part of the existential/phenomenological tradition of the twentieth century, they are viewed suspiciously by the more dominant tradition in Anglo-American philosophy. For example, how we situate thinkers like Jacques Derrida, Hélène Cixous, and Vladimir Jankélévitch is complicated not only by their connection to contemporary French philosophy but also whether their work would be considered Jewish. Indeed one review of Jankélévitch's book, *Forgiveness*, declares that although he is Jewish and a philosopher, he is not a Jewish philosopher. The work, they claim, relies heavily on the philosophical apparatus of Immanuel Kant (Protestant) and Augustine (Catholic). And yet, his essay, "Should We Pardon Them?," in his book, *L'imprescriptable* (The Unforgiveable), deals exclusively with why it is imperative not to forgive the Germans for their crimes against humanity, rooted fundamentally in their anti-Semitism. Would this be Jewish philosophy? Does writing Jewish philosophy make someone a Jewish philosopher? Alternatively, does one need to be Jewish to be Jewish philosopher—is it the philosophy or the philosopher that identifies the content as Jewish philosophy?

Returning to the question, "What is Jewish philosophy?," we find a different approach in Emil Fackenheim's framing of the question:

"What today, in the age of Auschwitz and the new Jerusalem is Jewish philosophy?" That is, is how can we address that question after the Shoah differently from how we might have defined it before? Indeed it is the case that if there were such a fissure in both thinking and ethics, if timeless truths are non-existent, then how we understand philosophy in general cannot but change. Jewish philosophy will necessarily change also.

Fackenheim on Jewish Philosophy

In his essay, "What is Jewish Philosophy? Reflections on Athens, Jerusalem, and the Western Academy," Emil Fackenheim distinguishes between these two questions: what is philosophy and what is Jewish philosophy? Of the former, Fackenheim says, philosophers ask this question. Of the latter, he says, we might well ask whether it exists at all (*JPJP* 166). That is, the question is not necessarily what is it, but is it anything at all? Of note is that the criticisms come not only from the discipline of philosophy but also from those arguing on behalf of Judaism. He offers as an example the critical reaction to Maimonides' *Guide of the Perplexed* and indicates that Maimonides only narrowly escaped Spinoza's fate of excommunication. In the end, the very Orthodox community that attacked Maimonides when the *Guide* first appeared later embraced the book—and indeed, it is now considered central to Orthodox Judaism.[1]

While Maimonides appears undisputedly inside the category of Jewish philosophy, Fackenheim observes that this is not the case for Spinoza, whose excommunication was approved by Hermann Cohen, a philosopher who himself otherwise disapproved of excommunication. As a result, Fackenheim asks if Jewish philosophy must necessarily be religious. An interesting question in light of philosophy's own aversion to religion! He rightly points out that while there are no obvious answers about what Jewish philosophy is from the Jewish side, the same kind of response ought to be the case from the philosophy side. Yet, philosophy's own inability to welcome Jewish philosophy into its tent might have more to do with philosophy's inability to figure out what counts as philosophy in general—and Jewish philosophy is simply caught in the crossfire. If, as Fackenheim reminds us, philosophy is about non-partisan analysis, objectivity, universal reason, and so forth, then how could Jewish philosophy, with its attached qualifier, count? Is there a Jewish mathematics or a Jewish physics?

Yet, as I mentioned earlier, the same could easily be said of any subfield in philosophy from ancient to medieval to modern. That we categorize these thinkers at all means that we see them as asking a particular set of questions that are peculiar to the time period in which they wrote. It does not mean that their questions are not relevant beyond that time period. Similarly, the questions posited by Jewish philosophy should still be considered relevant beyond the framework from which they arose. Jewish philosophy might not be any more "particular" than any other subfield.

But Fackenheim's point is more interesting. With the exception of what happened during Nazi Germany, we do not call a work "Jewish" philosophy simply because it was written by someone who was Jewish. Works by Henri Bergson or Edmund Husserl, for example, are not works of Jewish philosophy. Thus, Fackenheim says, here are two clear cases of what Jewish philosophy is not. What then do we make of Maimonides and Spinoza—the former is rarely if ever taught in philosophy departments including departments who do offer a course in medieval philosophy (Augustine, Anselm, and Aquinas are the typical figures), while the latter is typically included in mainstream philosophy courses. In this case, Fackenheim asks: does philosophy exclude Maimonides because Judaism still embraces him, while Spinoza is included because he not only "opted out" but also because Judaism kicked him out? Is Spinoza a mainstream philosophical figure because in his "opting out" of Judaism his philosophy can be viewed as transcending a set of beliefs that would otherwise be viewed as tribal or parochial?

Fackenheim rightly points out that even medieval philosophy has had its share of problems being accepted into the canon of philosophy. How are we to view this particular time period? Is it a gap, a developmental stage, an aberration? Is it philosophy at all—any of it, including the

Christian philosophers? Fackenheim identifies three prejudices that have been advanced for keeping Jewish philosophy out: modernist, crypto-Protestant, and neo-Pagan. Here is how he describes them.

A prejudice is modernist when it "rests on the unexamined belief in the superiority of the present wisdom over that of the past" (*JPJP* 169); it is crypto-Protestant when resting on the unexamined belief that a Luther-style belief is superior to all others; and it is neo-Pagan when the "rejection or 'overcoming' of Revelation were a self-evident necessity for modern philosophers" (*JPJP* 169). Indeed Fackenheim points out that many modern philosophers not only did not reject revelation but in fact relied on it for their arguments to work. After exposing these prejudices, Fackenheim argues there is no ground to skip over the medieval period, but if the Christians are going to be included, then why not the Jews? If Aquinas enjoys a secure place in the philosophical canon, why not Maimonides? Certainly one explanation is the way that we see the history of ideas work in Levinas's essay on Hitlerism. Christianity—rightly or wrongly—is viewed in universal terms unlike Judaism. Is Christian philosophy any less particular than Jewish or Islamic philosophy?

If we look more closely at modern philosophy itself, and note the figures who are "in" and "out," the picture we see is much more disturbing. Descartes, Bacon, and Spinoza are always included in courses in philosophy—Descartes and Bacon never renounced their own Christianity. But if we add Mendelssohn to the group, we see more clearly that it is not adherence to religion that excludes a thinker, but adherence to a particular religion. Indeed, the irony of the Enlightenment period is that in the time when reason is supposed to rule, the intolerance toward Judaism and Jewish thought became more pronounced, not less. The Lavater affair, in which the theologian Johann Casper Lavater publicly challenged Mendelssohn either to refute Charles Bonnet's arguments regarding Christianity or else convert, spurred Mendelssohn to write *Jerusalem*, which is viewed ironically as the first book in modern Jewish philosophy. That is, the challenge to Mendelssohn, rather than shutting down or silencing Judaism, motivated its opening as an academic discipline.

Fackenheim continues his evaluation of the history of philosophy through late modernity (Hegel and Kierkegaard) and into the twentieth century with figures like Sartre. But here is where I diverge slightly from his analysis. Kierkegaard is not taught as widely as Fackenheim might have thought, and while Sartre does acknowledge the Christian existentialists, he also undermines them with the claim that existentialism runs counter to any religious belief that views a creator as having an idea of the created beforehand. Yet, Fackenheim is correct that when Sartre mentions the religious existentialists, the absence of Buber among them is striking.

As I mentioned above, the problems with particular figures as we approach the twentieth century are complicated and over-determined by myriad factors that are internal to the philosophical discipline. With the rise of Anglo-American philosophy as the dominant tradition, what counts as philosophy has become an increasingly exclusionary conversation. For example, the Jewish question with Emmanuel Levinas's work is less an issue for analytic philosophy than Levinas's own philosophical lineage, which includes phenomenology and then advances into the category we call post-modernism. Rather than seeing these different bodies of thought, which emerged out of twentieth-century French and German philosophy, as part of philosophy proper, analytic philosophy denies them entry into the canon. Thus, being a "Jewish" philosopher is the least of Levinas's concerns here.

That said, Fackenheim is nonetheless correct, for even inside the tradition of philosophers that travel under the label "continental" philosophy, not only has Jewish philosophy been historically excluded, but there has been explicit rejection of Levinas as a Jewish philosopher. Only recently, quite literally in the past few years, has this begun to change among the philosophers who read his work. Much of that change can be traced to the persistence of philosophers who work in philosophy departments who have actively and repeatedly argued this case. What Fackenheim points out almost in passing, but I think crucially, is what the years 1933–45 mean for philosophy in general and Jewish philosophy in particular.

For Fackenheim, those years *ought* to have been a rupture to philosophy itself; and they certainly were for Jewish philosophy. That is, Jewish philosophy after the Catastrophe will never be the same as it was before those years. But why is that not the case for philosophy itself, and is this a reason that whatever relationship Jewish philosophy might have had to philosophy proper before the Holocaust, it might never have a "normal" relationship with it now? If in ancient Greece philosophy began in wonder, it will still do so today, but that wonder, as Fackenheim says, will now be mixed with horror. He ends this essay by asking after the possibility of post-modern philosophy demanding this meeting between Athens and Jerusalem. Maybe it is time for philosophy to give up its claim to the universalist myth to which it has clung and which allowed it to dispense with what it perceived as particular. Indeed, Fackenheim reminds his readers that the vision to end war ("And they shall beat their swords into plowshares and their spears into pruning hoods. Nation shall not lift up sword against nation, neither shall they learn war any more" [Isaiah 2:4]) came not from Athens, but from Jerusalem.

At the end of the day, Fackenheim does believe that there are themes that are truly philosophical and yet idiosyncratically Jewish. They are: Jewish identity, a Jewish state (as a problem for political philosophy), and the Holocaust. These are themes that even if of particular interest to Jews can be taught in such a way that clearly engage larger philosophical questions. As we will see with Mendelssohn, the pressing question became what does it mean to be Jewish in a non-Jewish nation? What boundaries are there and should there be between state and religion? What rightfully belongs to each and under what circumstances might their respective interests and authority transgress these boundaries? In the post-modern period, we see the fissure in moral theory as the result of its inability to respond to the events of the Holocaust. Given the fundamental anti-Semitism that grounded Nazi ideology and in light of Levinas's retracing of the history of ideas as birthing anti-Semitism, we can ask if the Holocaust is a theme in Jewish philosophy. The questions raised by Wiesel, Levi, Arendt and Levinas, among others, certainly put philosophy on notice.

Spinoza

In light of the questions raised above, we can ask after Baruch Spinoza's position as a Jewish philosopher. I place him here in the Introduction since the questions he raises about the state and religion cannot be ignored in a discussion of modern Jewish thought. Yet, the question of whether he is a Jewish philosopher remains unclear. He is almost always taught in courses focused on the history of modern philosophy, yet he is taught in the tradition of the rationalists that extends from Descartes with little or no mention of his Jewish background or what bearing that background might have had on his thinking. The debate over Spinoza as a Jewish philosopher is the subject for an entire book. I do not typically teach the *Theological-Political Treatise* (*TTP*) as a book that fits into the canon of Jewish philosophy. However, the questions Spinoza raises in this book are not only relevant to Jews and Jewish thinkers, but also to the concerns raised by Mendelssohn and those who followed him. In many respects, Spinoza provides the transition between the medieval period and the Enlightenment. For that reason, placing him in the Introduction seemed appropriate.

Spinoza was born in 1632 in Amsterdam. He enjoys an infamous reputation in the philosophical world for his excommunication from the Sephardic Jewish community in Amsterdam (1656), but his fame came with a price. Although the exact reasons for this act are not known for certain, it is not an unreasonable speculation that he was speaking his "dangerous ideas" before they were published. What were these dangerous ideas? In his philosophical works, Spinoza denies the immortality of the soul, rejects a transcendent God (the God of Abraham, Isaac and Jacob) and rejects that God gave the law. Although on the verge of the Enlightenment, religious thinking still held power, and thus Spinoza's ideas were considered too dangerous to allow him to continue living within that community. At the time that Spinoza wrote the *TTP*, he had already left Amsterdam. Yet, the United Provinces were still in the throes of debate about the political authority of the Church. The apparent task of the *TTP* was to demonstrate that reason was not a threat to religious piety, and in fact that the latter might be strengthened by it. Yet, by most accounts, when one reads this text closely, the aim of the text, or at least the method of the text, demonstrates an undermining of religious authority in the realm of the state.

Anticipating worries that Rousseau had with regard to the vanity and greed that might lead someone to make faulty political decisions, Spinoza identifies a similar kind of thinking within the clergy. This kind of superstitious thinking and behavior plays on ordinary emotions to attract followers. People guided by this thinking organize their lives around these superstitions: they pray, sacrifice and so forth with the hope of gaining goods that are promised if one in fact prays and sacrifices in this way. Using this faulty method of thinking as his guide, Spinoza argues that if we are to correct this thought, we must begin anew, reading the Bible closely and examining what it says. Thus begins his journey to demonstrate the inconsistencies and contradictions that define the Hebrew scriptures.

By using this method, Spinoza denies the status of the prophets, claiming instead that they are simply people who are potentially morally superior, but not gifted philosophers. Thus, in matters pertaining to the intellect, prophets are not necessarily able to deliver truths regarding history, science, or philosophy. Along with debunking the authority of the prophets, Spinoza also raises questions about Moses as the author of the Torah (Pentateuch). What would it mean for Moses to have narrated his own death? By debunking beliefs that are central to Judaism, Spinoza undermines its religious authority. He argues that the first five Books of Moses were written by someone other than Moses, and further that there is no evidence that these particular books carry the special status accorded to them. Taken together, his rereading of the Hebrew Bible for these rational errors upends the authority of this text as a governing set of beliefs. What is the core of religious belief? "To know and love God, and to love one's neighbor as oneself." The message is universal and it lies at the heart of Spinoza's argument for religious tolerance. We can see how Spinoza's view of religion, then, would lead him to a view of the state that relies less on religious authority. That is, a state that circumscribes religious authority and emphasizes or supports individual freedom, and in particular freedom of belief and freedom to express those beliefs. The argument, however, is more strongly put—it is not simply that Spinoza promotes political freedom; rather, he argues that freedom is essential to political well-being. Just as we will see in Mendelssohn's argument, religious belief is private; it is inward worship and thus belongs exclusively to the individual. As such, it cannot be legislated by the state or anyone/anything else. Mendelssohn makes a similar claim when he describes how futile it actually is to control belief—indeed, it is a nonsensical position to hold.

How does this view cohere with a view of state authority? This argument relies on a view of freedom. Insofar as we obey state authority, we have assented to do so by recognizing as legitimate an authority that we have freely authorized. Democracy, which extends directly from the people, is the most stable since the rules emanate from the people's ability to self-govern. By contrast, monarchy, which he believes will ultimately devolve into tyranny, is the least stable. Because it rules with a heavy hand, this kind of government is most likely to evoke rebellion. With freedom and reason lying at the center of Spinoza's argument, he is often thought to have ushered in the Enlightenment. As Steven Nadler notes, in a passage that foreshadows John Stuart Mill's utilitarian defense of liberty nearly two centuries later, Spinoza says that "this freedom is of the first importance in fostering the sciences and the arts, for only those whose judgment is free and unbiased can attain success in these fields" (*TTP*, ch. 20, G III.243/S 226).

The Enlightenment

We can situate the intellectual period known as the Enlightenment between the mid-seventeenth century and through the eighteenth century. As we approach the nineteenth century, we also encounter the beginning of the intellectual movement known as Romanticism, thus those figures positioned in this transition are not as easily classified. Additionally, as we approach the end of the eighteenth century, the philosophers in this period were beginning to see the philosophical problems associated with the Enlightenment, thus reflecting on its efficacy, culminating in a number of philosophers trying to address the question, "What is Enlightenment?"

To be clear, it is a misnomer to characterize this period as the Enlightenment as if there were only one. There were in fact many, each with its own characteristics, concerns, questions, and thinkers: British, French (Diderot, Montesquieu, Voltaire), German (Immanuel Kant, G. E. Lessing, Moses Mendelssohn, Christian Wolff), Scottish (David Hume, Thomas Reid, and Adam Smith) and so forth. Nonetheless these dates help us consider the primary figures associated with this movement and the major questions that occupied them. For the purposes of this book, I will simply refer to the Enlightenment as that period that oversaw dramatic changes in how we think about science, philosophy, politics and so forth, as differentiated from the medieval period that preceded it.

With its emphasis on reason as an equalizing characteristic, the Enlightenment is often viewed as culminating in the French Revolution (1789). In this revolution, rule by nobility, by the hierarchy of the church and so forth is overturned in favor of a governing system that would recognize freedom and equality, and ultimately be founded on a political and social order rooted in principles of reason. Ironically, though philosophy concerned itself with what is "really" real, it was unable to compete with the new science. Thus, during this period, science, now informed by scientific method, split off from philosophy. But the defining features of the Enlightenment include the ability to think for oneself, a reliance on one's own understanding, the power of and confidence in reason to deliver truth in areas of scientific, political and ethical realms. Thus, it is the Enlightenment that offers a foundation for self-governance and our ability to make ethical decisions in a process that is believed to be separate and distinct from religious authority and religious scriptures. Although a course in the history of modern philosophy would focus primarily on the development of epistemology and metaphysics, the Enlightenment's most powerful legacy is the radical change in the political—the ability to self-govern and the development of the democratic state. We see these changes marked most clearly in various revolutions of the time: English, American and French. The French Revolution is often associated with the writings of Jean-Jacques Rousseau, and the American Revolution finds its roots in the writings of John Locke. From here it is a short step to the way this plays out in ethical theory. If reason can aid us in self-governance, so too can reason aid us in making moral decisions. Additionally, the liberalism that pervades, for example, Locke's political theory tells a story about who we are in relationship to others—insofar as we are all equal by virtue of reason, all human beings stand universally in a moral relationship to each other. Though the parameters of this book do not allow for a detailed discussion of this point, it should not be lost on us that this phrasing was not quite accurate in the formation of varying states—the American Revolution, for example, and the ensuing state that was built did not initially eliminate slavery nor did it provide equal rights for women. Indeed, a citizen was defined as land-owning, thus even a white male of a different class could initially be excluded. One can abstractly declare that all by virtue of reason are equal, but if one also declares that some are not able to reason, then the universal rule applies universally to those who fit the definition, and the rule is not immune to a different kind of exclusion. Thus, as we will see in Mendelssohn's writings, reason alone was not enough to counter a state that had particular interests and that ironically saw reason as linked to the Christian subject.

Although later we will see how Emmanuel Levinas redefines both ethics and politics, for the purposes of discussing the Enlightenment, it is worth looking at how philosophers emblematic of this intellectual moment regard ethical theory. The most important ethical theorist of this time is the Scottish philosopher, David Hume. Although reason is the trademark of the Enlightenment, Hume is often regarded as the most 'enlightened' moral theorist for allowing emotions to play a role in ethical decision-making. An empiricist, Hume attempted to ground ethics in a science of human nature that was free from religion and theological assumptions. Hume is also credited with one of the most interesting (and humorous) responses to unreflective religious belief.

Contrary to the view that the Enlightenment was the enemy of religion, it was instead critical of certain of its features—superstition, intolerance, political authority, coercion of belief, and so forth. Hume's response to religion as expressed in his *Dialogues Concerning Natural Religion* remains one of the most effective responses to the so-called empirical arguments for belief in God. Voltaire's *Candide*, which uses the Lisbon earthquake and the tremendous suffering that resulted, raises questions about Leibniz's claim that this is "the best of all possible worlds." For both Hume and Voltaire, among others, theodicy, or the justification of God's existence in light of so much human suffering, is simply an untenable argument. As we will see later, this argument does not change and indeed comes to a head in reflections on the Holocaust. This period is identified closely with a kind of philosophy that explicitly challenged religious authority in the state—in belief, thought, ethics, morality, politics, knowledge and so forth. It is not that religion needed to be discarded but rather reined in.

The Crisis of the Enlightenment

If the Enlightenment marks a period that emphasized the role of reason to govern oneself, Kant's moral philosophy exemplified such a position. His *Groundwork for a Metaphysics of Morals* emphasized not only our own freedom to make moral decisions but also the role of freedom in understanding what was morally right. Morality not only accentuated our own freedom but the freedom of others. Writing at the end of the Enlightenment, Kant's writings are also on the cusp of the time when the intellectual period underwent a crisis of sorts. A fundamental belief about the Enlightenment and the role of reason in it centered on a belief that with reason, human life could tell a story of progress—we would learn from our mistakes and continue to develop toward an ultimate end. However, various views that both informed and proceeded from the Enlightenment ultimately came into direct conflict. On the one hand, the Enlightenment was informed by the development of science that put into doubt the ability of both philosophy and religion to tell a story about what is real, what is nature and what is right.

On the other hand, the very reliance on reason that tells a story about the human ability to govern oneself was based on a view of freedom that ran counter to the mechanistic model that made science plausible. Thus, the Enlightenment produced two views—one about nature and one about the human—that were directly in conflict with each other and with no real way to reconcile this tension. Kant's philosophy attempted to resolve this tension by reconciling the empiricist and rationalist trends that pervaded this time period. His extraordinary work, *The Critique of Pure Reason*, attempts to resolve this problem. In short, he accomplishes this task by demonstrating that there are a priori conditions of knowledge—namely, space and time—and these conditions are the mind's way of structuring our experience. He thus paves the way for demonstrating the possibility of metaphysics without undermining the "truth" of the sensible world. From here, he can provide an argument for a morality based on reason that accentuates the role of human freedom.

Kant's philosophical system, which includes the three critiques, among other writings, is undisputedly brilliant. Even with Hegel's scathing critique in his *Phenomenology of Spirit*, Kant's moral philosophy remains one of the most influential theories well into the twenty-first century. Along with the emphasis on freedom and reason, Kant's moral philosophy emphasizes duty over inclination. One acts in accordance with the moral law because it is one's duty to do so; not because one feels like doing so. But the criticisms that accompany Kant's moral philosophy cannot be ignored and they persist today. In particular, the very emphasis on duty becomes the primary target. As has become famous, Adolf Eichmann sat at his trial in Jerusalem and proceeded to tell a story about how he had simply done his duty—and "just doing one's duty" has now become another way of saying that one blindly followed an order and therefore should not be held morally accountable for the consequences of that action. Kant's moral system seemed to allow no place for nuance, for placing one moral obligation above another or for deciding between two competing moral obligations. The classic example offered in an introductory class in moral theory would be the following: The Nazis come to your door and you are hiding a

Jew in the attic. They ask for the Jew. What do you do? Kant held out lying to be among the greatest of moral lapses. Would lying be worse than turning the Jew over to the Nazis? On Kant's account it would seem so.

Similar criticisms can be found in the Utilitarian approach to ethics, which, put crudely, simply calculates the good and the bad that will result from any particular moral decision. For some, Kantian moral theory is a sophisticated version of Utilitarianism, which accounts for consequences, but in an oblique way. Regardless, what we see through much of modern philosophy is a set of moral theories, all reliant on reason, and thus all reduced to a kind of calculation or justification. The space that was opened for all acts, no matter how heinous, cannot be closed and it was not until the events of the Holocaust that it became apparent exactly what reason, if pressed, could justify. The Holocaust, coming at the end of a time when reason appeared to progress, seemed to signal the degeneration of reason. The Holocaust exemplified the worst of what reason could allow insofar as it justified why the particular could not live with the universal. It used science to identify a group as sub-human and then used reason to justify the annihilation of that group.

The Fissure/The Shoah

After the Holocaust, many philosophers took a long hard look at the intellectual development that might have contributed to these events. These philosophers, grouped mostly within the European philosophical traditions such as Critical Theory (the Frankfurt School), Deconstruction, Post-Modernism, Post-Structuralism came to believe that certain features of modern philosophy contributed to a kind of thinking that led to the Holocaust. They no longer believed that there was a grand narrative or a story about moral progress that could be told. In fact, moral theory, with its emphasis on rules, calculation, deliberation, justification, duty and so forth could now be seen as the culprit. Reason rather than allowing us to flourish had become the cause of our own undoing. Philosophy needed to tell a different story and that story needed to begin with a good long look at itself. Thus, another way to consider these "post" philosophies is to think about them as philosophy of philosophy—philosophy reflecting on itself. It is at this point that I consider where contemporary Jewish philosophy enters the conversation. What might it contribute to the way that philosophy examines itself? What might it offer to this reflection? These are questions similar to the questions Fackenheim raises and it is how I end this book.

Layout of the Book

In the first few sections of the book I examine how Mendelssohn and Cohen utilize the Enlightenment to engage their own questions regarding Judaism. In Mendelssohn's case, the challenge to him to convert, or rather, the challenge put to him to explain why he is still a Jew opens up the discussion of the particular in the universal: what does it mean to be a Jew living in a Christian state? In what ways can the language of the Enlightenment help him respond to this challenge? I use his short essay, "What is Enlightenment?," and his more developed thought in *Jerusalem* to address these questions. In Chapter 2, I use Hermann Cohen and Hannah Arendt as figures who signal a transition from modernity to post-modernity. I examine several sections of Cohen's long work, *Religion of Reason, Out of the Sources of Judaism*. Additionally, I examine the ways that Cohen takes up the Kantian framework—how that coheres with Judaism and the ways that this framework is limiting. I then turn to Hannah Arendt, a philosopher and political theorist not typically characterized as a Jewish philosopher. Yet, her work in political theory is informed not only by thinking of the Jew as the outsider but also herself as the Jew who was an outsider. In Chapter 3, I turn to existential philosophy and consider the Russian philosopher, Lev Shestov, along with Franz Rosenzweig and Martin Buber. I examine themes related to freedom, education, humanism, ethics and the state, using this discussion as a transition between Enlightenment thinking and the fissure that reveals the limits of the Enlightenment.

In Chapters 4 and 5, I turn to Emmanuel Levinas's work and situate him as a pivot between the philosophy that comes before the Holocaust and the philosophy that comes after. If Jewish philosophy is the critic of Western Protestant philosophy, then Levinas is the critic of the critics. Writing as a phenomenologist after the Shoah, he witnessed the spectacular failure of the Enlightenment. Levinas is both modern and post-modern, enabling him to be both the Jewish philosopher and the critic of modern Jewish philosophy. Contra Mendelssohn and Cohen, for example, who were largely supportive of the Enlightenment project and who situate the Jew within the Enlightenment and ask why not, Levinas presses us to ask if "why not" is still possible and to consider what is at stake in this pursuit. Why shouldn't the Jew have full rights under the law? What are the boundaries of state authority? Is secular society really secular? Is it really secular for Jews? Similar to how Mendelssohn called out the unfairness of the quotas imposed on Jewish citizenship, Levinas is able to see that what appears as secular to Christian society is not secular to those who sit at its margins. When national exams are given on Saturdays, for example, the observant Jewish population is excluded from taking them.

Levinas has the benefit of hindsight. Looking back over the eighteenth and nineteenth centuries, he can see how history has developed. And he can see where philosophical ideas were successful and where they fell short. I am sympathetic to the intellectual position that rejects defining Jewish Studies around the Holocaust as the only significant event in Jewish history. But it is nonetheless a significant event in the story of the Enlightenment and the failure of ethical theory that was produced by modernity's thinkers. We can speculate about how Levinas's thought or philosophy would have developed had the Holocaust not happened, but we do not know for sure. In philosophy, we call that a hypothesis contrary to fact. The fact that the Holocaust did happen shaped Levinas as a teacher and a philosopher (Levinas, 1946, 1994; Katz, 2013). That event brought into relief the spectacular failure of the Western ideal of the power of the intellect—that the intellect, the power of rationality, will be enough to confront evil. Additionally, it questioned the view that by virtue of our intellects (a secular exchange with the religious view of the soul) we are all equal under the law. The philosophy that guided Hitler, and indeed that was not new to Nazi Germany, returned us to a view of materialism and the body that rendered enlightenment thinking powerless.

With regard to these questions, Emmanuel Levinas occupies an interesting position—if one invokes his Jewish writings to supplement his philosophical thought, he is viewed by "mainstream" continental philosophers as "too Jewish" and thus not really a philosopher. And it needs to be noted that "mainstream continental philosophy" is already viewed suspiciously by many scholars who align themselves intellectually with twentieth-century analytic philosophy, the dominant trend in the discipline. Consequently, he is an interesting marginal figure whose voice calls us to examine the failure of what the Enlightenment promised regardless of who promoted it, e.g., Mendelssohn or Kant. Over the past ten or so years, we can see an increase in the scholarship on Levinas's writings on Judaism.[2] These writings had been absent from most of the secondary philosophical literature on Levinas (Critchley 1992; Peperzak 1993; Perpich 2008). Most recently, we can see philosophers who once eschewed this body of work now taking it seriously, even arguing that this work is significant for a robust understanding of Levinas's thought.

Yet Levinas nonetheless remains marginal within the Jewish philosophy canon. Ironically, this might be the case precisely because of the way he calls philosophy itself into question. I see him in a task parallel to what Husserl called on philosophy to do. In "Philosophy as a Rigorous Science," Husserl suggests that the task of philosophy is to become a philosophy of philosophy, to examine philosophy itself. Levinas, taking Husserl seriously, responds to this request, only he uses the perspective of Jewish philosophy to accomplish this task.[3] One can certainly worry that as his writings on Judaism are taken more seriously, he will be taken less seriously by continental philosophy, leaving him without an intellectual home.

As a result, Levinas's thought, in particular his critique of the Enlightenment, which he advances not only because of his experiences as a Jew but also because he was subjected to the horrors of Nazi

Germany, is significant not only within the canon of Jewish philosophy but also within "mainstream" political theory. His thinking then provides a fresh way of examining questions that cannot be answered adequately by other modern thinkers. His ethical project provides new tools to reconsider not only old questions but also contemporary problems with which we are currently faced.

In the last chapter, "The Limits of Philosophy," I turn to several figures—some philosophers and some non-philosophers—in order to consider the limits of philosophy. If the Holocaust is viewed as a rupture that reveals not only the limits of Western philosophy but also the limits of moral theory, then where are we to turn? First, we must be able to explore and express what the problem is. Although the philosophers can talk about the fissure, they cannot necessarily provide an answer to it, nor are they necessarily able to express what happened—or rather, they cannot express the rawness of the suffering and anguish, the cruelty and the pain. For this, we need to turn to literature, to the first-person accounts that tell us what happened, that raise the existential questions but that do not offer any answers. Using the Holocaust as the example, I turn to the moral and political question of forgiveness and explore different philosophical accounts of the problem. Finally, I turn to Fackenheim's essays that consider what Jewish philosophy is and why it might still be relevant to us now, even more so in the twenty-first century.

I take the intellectual task of modern Jewish philosophy, then, to function as the voice of the critic. Today, Jewish philosophy is frequently positioned outside the boundary of modern Western philosophy, as this topic is taught in philosophy departments, which have been dominated by thinkers of Protestant background. This marginal position allows Jewish thought to expose the myth of philosophy's neutrality and objectivity. If that is the case, then Levinas's position in relationship to Jewish philosophy is similar to Husserl's position in relationship to philosophy. Their methods allow them to critique their own lineage. That is, where philosophy has historically enjoyed being the critic of all other disciplines, now philosophy's eye turns on itself.

Those whom we classify as Jewish philosophers ask questions and utilize methods that characterize the discipline of philosophy. Before continuing, I should note that not surprisingly who is included among that cast of characters in Jewish philosophy is also contested. My aim in this book is not settle the question of what is Jewish philosophy or who counts as a philosopher, much less a Jewish one. The question, "What is philosophy," is as old as philosophy itself. The answer to this question almost always depends on who is answering the question and what academic power they have to settle the issue.

This question continues well into the twenty-first century, though it takes many different forms—sometimes the question targets a particular figure and sometimes it questions the methodologies of a particular subfield. My point is that we are not going to settle the question here. Instead, I present the philosophers who are most commonly associated with modern Jewish philosophy and situate them within the larger, canonical, philosophical thought in which they lived and wrote. Thus, we will be better able to see their ideas, questions, and methods within that context, better equipping us to consider them not only as Jewish philosophers, but also simply as philosophers. As I mentioned in the Preface, I have organized the material around the question, "What is Enlightenment?," and I use this theme to explore the ways in which the Enlightenment both helped and hindered the Jews living in the diaspora.

1

Mendelssohn and
the Enlightened Mind

In the opening sentence of his compact essay "What is Enlightenment?," the eighteenth-century German philosopher, Immanuel Kant, asserts, "Enlightenment is man's emergence from his self-imposed immaturity."[1] He then adds that the motto of the Enlightenment is to have the courage to use one's understanding—to know what reason tells us to do, and then to act in accordance with that reason. Kant explains that men and women have been convinced that it is far more dangerous to go out on one's own, to learn to walk by oneself than to let others be our guardians. Like the British philosopher, John Stuart Mill, who will argue a similar point eighty-five years later in England, Kant describes our state as a learned domesticity—indeed one where we have been shown the risks of learning to use our own reason without also having been shown the advantages. As a result, moving out of our own immaturity is a difficult task, requiring strength to go against received wisdom and the force of the community. Only a few succeed in doing so.

Kant's essay is a call for freedom, a call to throw off the shackles of immaturity that keep one confined. The danger that would result from this freedom, however, is not the danger that the protectors claim threatens those whom they hope to confine. Rather, the danger would result from the knowledge those freed now have of those who kept them in intellectual chains. Enlightenment, then, Kant says, must be attained slowly.

What, then, is this freedom for which Kant calls? It is the freedom to use reason publicly, what we would now call "freedom of speech" or "freedom of expression." He cites examples where the common phrase of the day instructs not to argue, but to drill, not to argue but to believe, not to argue but to pay (e.g., the tax collector). Our lives are structured so that if we go against what those in positions of authority tell us—and the one thing they tell us is not to question them—then we put ourselves at risk, even if the risk is simply imagined. The freedom of thought that Kant promotes is not simply freedom of conscience, though it includes that as well. It is also the freedom of thought to express that thought publicly—to argue with those who claim to have authority over us. It is only when we exercise this freedom that we can bring about the enlightenment of all humankind.

Addressing church authority, Kant says

> would not a society of clergymen, such as a church synod or a venerable classis (as those among the Dutch call themselves) be justified in binding one another by oath to a certain unalterable symbol in holding an unremitting superior guardianship over each of their members, and by this means over their people, and even to make this eternal? [...] Such a contract, concluded for the purpose of closing off forever all further enlightenment of the human race, is absolutely null and void, even if it should be confirmed by the highest power, by parliaments, and by Imperial Diets, and by the most solemn peace treaties.[2]

Speaking about the time in which he lives, Kant says that although we are not enlightened, we do live in an age of enlightenment, where these acts, where the steps out of immaturity are made possible by those who in positions of authority do not prescribe others' behavior but allow them freedom in, for example, religious matters. He tells us at the end of the essay that he focused on religious matters specifically because on the one hand, our rulers have no interest in governing matters of the arts and sciences (if only that were true today!) and because the form of immaturity that characterizes those under the protective sway of religious leaders Kant finds the "most pernicious and disgraceful of all."

We can take Kant's worry, then, as the starting point for Mendelssohn's motivation to respond to a variety of critics: some who wanted him to convert to Christianity and some who wished for him to explain the more philosophical question, "Can one be both a Jew and also hold the position Mendelssohn holds with regard to religious authority?" That is, are there limits to religious authority, and if so, what are they? This question will take many forms over the course of the next few hundred years, but in short, the question originates from an assumption that there is a fundamental contradiction in being both Jewish and being "something else," whether that something else is a citizen of a nation (not Israel) or simply an "enlightened" human being, however we understand that term. Put more generally, the question is: can one be particular (read here as not Protestant) when living in a state governed by a people viewed as universal? The question is not much different from the one we ask today regarding the Muslim or the Jew living in France, a country which considers itself to be governed by secular laws. In response to a similar question, Mendelssohn published his landmark book, *Jerusalem; or, On Religious Power and Judaism*, in 1783, just one year before Kant's aforementioned essay. In light of the popularity that Mendelssohn enjoyed as a scholar of the German intellectual community, the response to this book was less enthusiastic than what one might have expected. It is worth noting some of Mendelssohn's biographical details in order to place this work into its proper context.

Mendelssohn's Life

Moses Mendelssohn was born in 1729 in Dessau, Germany, and at the age of 14, he moved to Berlin to study under Rabbi David

Fränkel. During this time Friedrich II (the Great) succeeded to the Prussian throne in 1740. In 1753, Mendelssohn began work as a clerk in the Bernhard family silk factory and in 1761 he became the manager. On a trip to Hamburg in 1761, his first trip away from the city since moving there, he was introduced to Fromet Gugenheim. The introduction, made by Sarah Bernhard, the daughter of the owner of the factory where Mendelssohn was employed, led to a romantic relationship. His letters about the affair reveal a deeply romantic love story, which culminated in their wedding in the summer of 1762. Even before they were married, Mendelssohn encouraged his beloved "to acquire an education befitting a philosopher," yet when it appeared she was spending too much time on her studies he urged her to limit her intellectual investment.

Yet even during the age of Enlightenment, a permit was needed for Mendelssohn and his wife to live inside the city of Berlin, which at the time was resistant to increasing its number of Jewish residents. On March 26, 1762, Mendelssohn was able to inform his fiancée that permission was granted. Although a seemingly minor inconvenience, this incident points to the fragile status of and the careful balance in Mendelssohn's life as an intellectual Jew in the German intellectual community. Certainly these points appear to be operating in the background while Mendelssohn is writing both *Jerusalem; or, On Religious Power and Judaism* (1783) and his much shorter essay "What is Enlightenment?" (1784).

In spite of Friedrich II's own intellectual engagement and the view of him as an enlightened monarch, he nonetheless penned several edicts that prevented Jews from becoming fully integrated citizens. The most "draconian" of these edicts was that of 1750: *Revidierte General Privilegium und Reglement* declared Jews inferior and "tolerated only by the grace of the royal house".[3] The edict divided the Jews into "six groups according to their economic benefit to the state" (Feiner 38). Mendelssohn, because of his status as a private tutor, was lumped together with the servants, "the least privileged order. People in his category were expressly forbidden to marry within the city limits under penalty of expulsion" (Feiner 39).

These edicts notwithstanding (or maybe because of them, since they inspired resistance from those who were more tolerant) and the anti-Semitism that persisted in Europe, Mendelssohn enjoyed respect and popularity as both a scholar of philosophy and a Jewish sage. He was part of the Berlin intellectual community and maintained a deep friendship with the philosopher Gotthold Lessing, from 1753 until Lessing's death in 1781. One of his greatest admirers, Lessing wrote the play *Nathan der Weise* (Nathan the Wise), an homage to his friend in which he modeled Nathan on Mendelssohn. Mendelssohn's publishing career spanned over thirty years, literally until his own death in 1786, and included essays and books on Plato, Rousseau, metaphysics, logic, the emotions (or sensual feelings), the Enlightenment, and of course, religion. We can now turn to Mendelssohn's writings to see how he handles the question of religious authority understood within the context of the Enlightenment.

"On the Question: What is Enlightenment?"

Although written one year after *Jerusalem*, Mendelssohn's essay "What is Enlightenment?" provides an interesting context for his longer work on Judaism. In light of the prejudice that Mendelssohn and his fellow Jews continued to experience, engaging the question of what is Enlightenment could not have been more pressing. How, in the age of Enlightenment, which prized reason and truth, could such religious prejudice still exist? In *Jerusalem*, Mendelssohn identifies the boundaries of state and religious power, and his essay on enlightenment ties together themes regarding both a virtuous disposition (based on moral or religious upbringing) and the intellect. Just as *Jerusalem* challenged the view that one could be a German citizen and also maintain a Jewish identity—a discussion that continues well into the twentieth century—"What is Enlightenment?" also engages the question of truths and their relationship to deeply held prejudices, whose shattering might rock the very foundations of religion and morality. When Mendelssohn's friend, Herz Homberg, was rejected by the Emperor for a university post because he was a Jew, Mendelssohn is reported to have said in response, "Very infrequently extraordinary people do what ordinary people expect of them, for they are extraordinary people. What His Majesty [the Emperor] has decided in your case is therefore not exceptional" (Feiner 189).

The irony that Mendelssohn's biographer notes—that Homberg was working to implement the Emperor's toleration laws regarding Jewish education, which required a balanced curriculum combining religious study and general subjects in the humanities, natural sciences, and foreign languages—is particularly poignant in this age of Enlightenment (Feiner 154). The educational reform was made in exchange for greater Jewish acceptance as citizens within Prussian society. That Emperor Josef II issued edicts that were to increase tolerance of the Jews made his resistance to this university appointment all the more troubling. If the emperor who mandates increased Jewish tolerance will not make such an appointment, then who will?

In a letter to Homberg, Mendelssohn expressed his sentiment that hypocritical toleration was more of a concern than open persecution (Feiner 190). Thus, in the last years of his life, Mendelssohn was left with the most fundamental of problems facing the enlightenment: religious prejudice. He writes, "The prejudices against my nation are too deeply rooted as to enable their easy eradication," and he wondered if this inability to free oneself of religious prejudice raised questions for the Enlightenment project as a whole. If one could not use reason to free oneself of the deepest prejudices, then what extraordinary power did reason hold? In his letter to the Swiss physician, Johann Georg Zimmermann, dated September 1784, Mendelssohn wrote:

> We dreamed of nothing but the Enlightenment and believed that
> the light of reason would illumine all around it with such power

that delusion and inflamed fanaticism would no longer be able to be seen. But as we can see, from beyond the horizon the night rises once more with all its specters. Most frightening of all is that evil is so active and influential. Delusion and enthusiasm [*Schwärmerey*] act, and reason makes do with words. (Feiner 191)

Two things haunted Mendelssohn during these last years. The first was the continued presence of an oppressive establishment religion that threatened religious tolerance. The second was a new intellectual movement, *Sturm und Drang* (storm and stress), that threatened the Enlightenment by replacing reason with emotion, spontaneity, naturalness, and so forth (Feiner 191). What becomes clear in Mendelssohn's concerns is that the success of the Enlightenment, indeed the truth of the Enlightenment, is its ability to overcome religious prejudice through reason. Robust religious tolerance, then, becomes the litmus test of an enlightened individual and an enlightened nation.

In response to what Mendelssohn saw as the breakdown of the Enlightenment, he published a short essay in 1785 in which he placed the blame for the Enlightenment's unraveling in its own lap. Because Mendelssohn's project was to negotiate the relationship between religious belief and reason, rather than replace one with the other, he saw any extreme, on either side, as both potentially dangerous and also potentially false. He took issue with the extreme disbelievers, like Voltaire, as he did with the religious fanatics. Each extreme was dangerous to the Enlightenment in its own way. Thus, if one uses this point as a frame, then looking back to the essay at hand, "What is Enlightenment?," we see that his aim in this essay is to circumscribe not only the limits of the Enlightenment but also its dangers (Feiner 192).

Mendelssohn opens this essay by engaging in a discussion of semantics. The words enlightenment, education, and culture are new, he says, but does this mean that society did not have these attributes before they were named? Could not an attribute be present even if there is not a word to name it? At the time of his writing this essay, the boundaries between these concepts were not yet clear. Education was synonymous with enlightenment, and both were synonymous with culture. They were all modifications of social life and they were the result of man's diligence to better his circumstances. For Mendelssohn, the more social conditions were brought into harmony with man's calling, the more we could say that a particular group was educated (53).

Although Mendelssohn claims that at the time of this writing, there is no distinct boundary between these terms, his goal in this essay is to discern what those distinctions are. His claim is that education comprises both culture and enlightenment. He then proceeds to distinguish between *culture* and *enlightenment* and then explain how they both contribute to what is meant by *education*. He observes that *culture*

> appears to be more oriented toward practical matters: (objectively) toward goodness, refinement, and beauty in the arts and social mores; (subjectively) toward facility, diligence, and dexterity in the arts and inclinations, dispositions, and habits in social mores. The more these correspond in a people with the destiny of man, the more culture will be attributed to them, just as a piece of land is said to be more cultured or cultivated, the more it is brought, through the industry of men, to the state where it produces things that are useful to men. Enlightenment by contrast seems to be more related to theoretical matters: to (objective) rational knowledge and to (subjective) facility in rational reflection about matters of human life, according to their importance on the destiny of man. (53–54)

What Mendelssohn refers to as the "destiny of man" for him is the "measure and goal of all our striving and efforts," the end to which we should always have our sights set (54). Mendelssohn claims that language attains enlightenment through sciences, that is through theoretical endeavor, but it gains culture through actual use: social intercourse, poetry, and so forth (54). Both are necessary for the language to be considered "educated."

Significantly, Mendelssohn emphasizes the role of both theory and practice in education. He maintains this distinction and the importance of both throughout this essay. He asserts that language is the best indicator of education, of both culture and enlightenment (54).

The essay then moves to a discussion of the destiny of man, which can be separated into two different discussions: the destiny of man as *man* and the destiny of man as *citizen*.[4] Because culture is already the application, or the practice, of the individual, with regard to culture, then, the destiny, or calling of man as both man and citizen coincide. Man as man has no need of culture. It is only man as a citizen, as an individual who *lives* with others, who needs the practical value. Yet, while Mendelssohn believes that man qua man needs no culture, like Rousseau's wild child, he does need enlightenment (54). Insofar as culture is a practice, or a practical expression, its success is determined by how well one's vocation and the respective rights and duties that accompany that vocation correspond. Additionally, each individual requires different theoretical insights and different corresponding skills to acquire those insights based on his/her status and vocation. That is, each individual requires a different degree of enlightenment. For Mendelssohn, the enlightenment of man as man is universal and does not change regardless of status or vocation. However, the enlightenment of man as citizen is contingent on status and vocation. Thus, in this case, the destiny of man remains the gage for what that enlightenment should be.

What, then, does it mean to say that a nation is enlightened? For Mendelssohn, the enlightenment of a nation is proportional to four criteria:

1. the amount of knowledge
2. its importance—that is, its relation to the destiny a) of man and b) of the citizen
3. its dissemination through all estates
4. its accord with their vocations.

Thus, the degree of a people's enlightenment is determined according to at least a fourfold relationship, whose members are in part composed out of simpler relations of members. Mendelssohn acknowledges that the enlightenment of the man can come into conflict with the enlightenment of the citizen. The truths that would prove useful to men as men might be harmful to the man as citizen. Thus, the following should be considered: "The collision can arise between the (1) essential (matter of existence) or (2) accidental destinies (matter of improvement) of man and the (3) essential or (4) accidental destinies of citizens" (55). He then proceeds to discuss what happens in each possibility of conflict.

Without an essential vocation toward which man is aimed, he sinks to the level of an animal; without an unessential vocation, man is "no longer good and splendid as a creature." That is, without the essential destiny, man becomes indistinguishable from a beast, but without the accidental destiny, man does not improve. A similar description can be applied to man as a citizen. Without the essential destiny for man as a citizen, there can be no constitution of the state. But without the accidental destiny for man as a citizen, "the state no longer remains the same in some ancillary relationships" (55).

For Mendelssohn, that state is unhappy that cannot bring into harmony the essential destiny of man with the essential destiny of its citizens. That is, that state is unhappy that cannot allow "the enlightenment that is indispensible to man to be disseminated through all of the estates of the realm without risking the destruction of the constitution" (55). When this happens, the state might prescribe laws that are applied to mankind to keep them down. Yet if the unessential destiny of man comes into conflict with the essential or unessential destiny of the citizen, rules must be established that are not fixed but which allow for exceptions and for conflicts to be decided.

What happens if the essential destiny of man comes into conflict with the unessential destiny of man? That is, what if certain useful and adorning truths may not be disseminated without destroying certain prevailing religious and moral tenets? In this case, Mendelssohn says, the virtue-loving bearer of the enlightenment will proceed, but with caution. That individual will endure prejudice rather than drive away the truth (55). But it is here in this tension that we find the complexity of the Enlightenment period and of enlightenment itself. What do we do when truth appears to be in conflict with religion? What do we do when truth appears to be in conflict with morality? What is enlightenment? Is it to know when to pursue the truth in the face of the conflict? Is it to know how to pursue this truth? How do we know when enlightenment transgresses its own boundaries and itself falls into the category of dogma and prejudice? When is enlightenment subject to the very misuse that its wisdom allows us to see about that which emerges from superstition and prejudice?

Therein lies the danger of that which is intended to elevate both man as man and man as citizen. Invoking the phrase that that which decays most ghastly is that which is most noble in its perfection, the misuse of enlightenment can be particularly harmful, particularly grotesque. Indeed to take that which is aimed at the truth, at the good, and misuse it can precisely lead to "hard-heartedness, egoism, irreligion, and anarchy. Misuse of culture produces luxury, hypocrisy, weakness, superstition, and slavery" (56). When enlightenment and culture, i.e., education, are in harmony, they create the best shield against corruption. Thus, an educated state would be much less susceptible to corruption.

Mendelssohn ends the essay with this statement:

An educated nation knows of no other danger than an excess of national happiness, which, like the most perfect health of the human body, can in itself be called an illness, or the transition of an illness. A nation that through education has come to the highest peak of national happiness is just for that reason in danger of collapse, because it can climb no higher. (56)

Jerusalem

Before turning to an examination of the themes in *Jerusalem*, the background on how Mendelssohn came to write this book must be presented. In response to the increasing hostility toward the Jews, Mendelssohn had staked out a protected space for himself. However, in 1769 that safety came to an end when Johann Casper Lavater challenged him on this very front: his citizenship as a Jew. In spite of the clergy belonging to intellectual circles that took the Enlightenment as their brand, these clergy often seemed no more tolerant of Jews than non-Jews had been prior to the Enlightenment. Indeed, in some instances it was as if the ideals of the Enlightenment enlivened the question, why remain a Jew, especially if reason and Christianity were now seen as intermingled. In this instance, Lavater had become a friend of Mendelssohn, visiting him on several occasions. He was impressed by Mendelssohn's intellect and on one occasion pressed Mendelssohn to share his own views of Christianity. After being assured that their conversation would be held in the strictest of confidence, Mendelssohn confided that he had no ill regard for Christians or Christianity. But Lavater held an eschatological position that propounded the Millennium would only come after all the Jews had been converted. With Mendelssohn's confession that he had no ill will toward Christianity and respect for the moral character of Jesus, Lavater had his ammunition:

> Five years after the conversation Mendelssohn received by mail a copy of *Philosophical and Critical Inquiries Concerning Christianity*, a newly published and as yet unbound book by Charles Bonnet, a naturalist and philosophical writer from Geneva, that had been translated into German by Lavater. Bonnet's work held less interest for Mendelssohn than did Lavater's preface, where, on the first page, the translator in effect publicly challenged the "German Socrates," anticipating nothing less than his conversion to Christianity. (Feiner 85)

Mendelssohn was stuck. Lavater clearly had exploited Mendelssohn's generous spirit and betrayed his trust. But Mendelssohn also worried that any response to resist Lavater's challenge would be damaging to the Jewish community. What should he do? Should he attack Lavater personally? Should he refute the evidence? He eventually decided to draft an open letter in response. Rather than be persuaded by Lavater's challenge, Mendelssohn rose to the occasion and penned an essay that would be a centerpiece of Enlightenment religious tolerance. That is, contrary to the view that the Enlightenment ideals are a call to the Jews to give up their particularity, Mendelssohn turned the tables. In his "Letter to Deacon Lavater of Zurich," which he completed writing on December 12, 1769, Mendelssohn explains that the Enlightenment calls for religious tolerance and he uses his defense of Judaism, in light of enlightenment values, to make a subtle dig at Christianity. Judaism, aligned with the Enlightenment, is not a missionary religion, unlike Christianity. Judaism is binding only on the Jews and the Jews do not expect others to abide by their laws, with the exception of the Noahide commandments, which are laws for all humanity. All who respect these laws have a share in the world to come.

The response to Mendelssohn's public letter was itself interesting. He received a note from Bonnet who explained that the preface had been written without his knowledge or consent and he was deeply sorry for this offense. Additionally, Prince Karl Wilhelm Ferdinand of Braunschweig begged him to reveal his true thoughts about Christianity. Breaking a promise to himself to keep silent on matters of religion, Mendelssohn wrote a letter to the prince asking him to promise not to share his thoughts publicly. Once assured of this, Mendelssohn did not hold back his true beliefs. What emerged was a view of Christianity that not only explained why he did not believe in Christianity but which also served to question why anyone would. Even Lavater wrote him begging for his forgiveness. Yet, anti-Jewish sentiment had real consequences, and in spite of the academic praise and respect Mendelssohn enjoyed there were civic limits to what he was able to accomplish and circles he was able to enter. Ironically, these events confirmed for him that at its root, the Enlightenment was about nothing if it was not about religious tolerance. These events drove him harder to press that particular argument, the fruit of which we see in *Jerusalem*.

Part I

What is the relationship between religion and the state? Even today, this question leaves us perplexed. We can, however, trace many of the themes that we discuss today back to the modern period, and in particular to the thought of Moses Mendelssohn as presented in *Jerusalem*. Mendelssohn opens his discussion with the following statement:

> State and religion—civil and ecclesiastical constitution—secular and churchly authority—how to oppose these pillars of social life to one another so that they are in balance and do not, instead, become burdens on social life, or weigh down its foundations more than they help to uphold it—this is one of the most difficult tasks of politics. (33)

Mendelssohn observes that the boundary between the state and religion is an uneasy one. Although it is necessarily blurred, this lack of precise definition contributes to the easy transgression of one side into the other. Either the church intentionally moves into the domain of the state or the state encroaches on the church. Mendelssohn considers both of these actions violent, and the inability for church and state to get along produces any number of evils. Yet, when church and state do agree, this rare collaboration can be the most dangerous, since it is frequently for the purposes of suppressing *liberty of conscience* (33). Mendelssohn outlines the historical extremes of the Roman Catholic Church as the example of supreme church authority and Thomas Hobbes's political theory as the extreme for state authority. The church has no mechanism to decide doctrinal differences and Hobbes wished to preserve some semblance of liberty of thought. For the latter, Hobbes distinguishes between inward religion, which is the individual's, and the outward expression of religion, which must be governed by civil authority (35).

Although Mendelssohn can see the logical conclusion to Hobbes's extreme position, Mendelssohn also recognizes how such a position becomes the cause of its own undoing. If Hobbes is right that we are not bound by nature to any duty, then what motivates or requires us to keep contracts at all? For Hobbes, in the state of nature, in which men originally find themselves, there is no binding obligation other than that which is based upon fear. Thus, if fear is removed, what happens? We then would fear the removal of fear lest we return to the state of nature. Fear alone does not get us very far. However, for Hobbes, a man must not be able to resist the contract into which he has voluntarily entered. How does this work if the contract is itself based only on fear and not on any other duty or obligation derived independently of fear? The contract is bound by fear of the Omnipotent. Thus, when taken to its logical end, Hobbesian political thought assumes a supreme law that is based on divine being.

Writing during the same period of political upheaval, John Locke argues the point differently from Hobbes. In "A Letter Concerning Toleration" (1689), Locke defines the state as such: "The commonwealth seems to me to be a society of men constituted only for the procuring, preserving, and advancing [of] their own civil interests."[5] The state, then, does not concern itself with religion unless the religious practices interfere with the above aim of the state. If they do not interfere with this aim, the state has no business identifying such differences in religious practice. Indeed in this particular essay, Locke also outlines how he understands the "true business of religion," which is not to exercise compulsive force but rather to guide men's lives according to the rules of virtue and piety ("Letter"). By so doing, Locke outlines the dominion of both the state and religion such that neither should interfere with the other.[6]

Mendelssohn counters Locke by observing that if reason were enough to convince people to be tolerant, then Locke would not have needed to go into exile as many times as he did (38). Moreover, is it really the case that the ends of religion are so different from those of the state? Or might it be that the aim of religion is weightier than the aim of the state? If the state is concerned with the temporal and the church is concerned with the eternal, does not the aim of the state become subordinate to that of the church and thus to ecclesiastical authority? In other words, Mendelssohn questions Locke's rigid separation between state interests and those of the church. Is it not the case that the temporal is related to the eternal? Can one be severed from the other so easily? How one lives in this life is connected to how one lives eternally (who we are now, the choices we make now, will have an impact on the person we are eternally) (39). Mendelssohn observes that many will live an ascetic life thinking that more will be delivered to them in the hereafter; conversely, some live a life of greed or as a bad citizen believing they can redeem themselves in the hereafter. For Mendelssohn, this thinking is delusional, and it is the result of a thinking that severs this world—the temporal world—from the hereafter, the eternal. If these two realms are not separated so rigidly, then neither are state and church.

Our actions comprise the relations men have to each other (the province of the state) and the relations men have to their creator (the province of religion). For Mendelssohn, if our actions serve the common weal, then they are a matter for civil society. If, however, it is our relationship with our creator that provides the source of our actions, then they fall into the realm of "the church, the synagogue, or the mosque" (41). Following this characterization, Mendelssohn then labels *church* those public institutions that concern the formation (*Bildung*) of man's relationship to God; he calls *state* those public institutions that concern the formation of man's relationship to man. Both, according to Mendelssohn, are concerned to educate and govern man (41). For Mendelssohn, the state and the church do not have different aims. Rather, it is one task of the church to demonstrate or persuade people that duties toward men are also duties toward God; serving the state is true service of God (43). If this is the case, how, Mendelssohn wonders, did it come to pass that preachers preach exactly the opposite? Because the felicity of the state is at issue, for Mendelssohn, the person acting need not believe in what he/she does, even if being persuaded to act in a particular way would be best. Rather, it is the outward expression of actions that matters, even if coercion is needed to bring about such actions. Whether or not I believe in or agree with the laws is less relevant than the necessity that I obey them. While the state might allow me freedom of conscience to judge the laws, the state need not grant me permission to act in accordance with that judgment, if that judgment betrays the law.

But here is where religion differs from the state. For Mendelssohn, religion is the outward expression of conviction. Mendelssohn sees the works and deeds that are tied to religion as precisely in conformity with conviction. It is therefore senseless to compel or bribe religion. One's conviction cannot be bought nor can it be compelled via punishment. And this is where religion and state would part company. Religion can do only so much to bring a man to the state. Once the state must bring force to compel action, religion must remove itself. Mendelssohn sums up his point thus:

> The state gives orders and coerces, religion teaches and persuades. The state prescribes *laws*, religion *commandments*. The state has *physical power* and uses it when necessary; the power of religion is *love* and *beneficence*. The one abandons the disobedient and expels him; the other receives him in its bosom and seeks to instruct, or at least to console him, even during the last moments of his early life, and not entirely in vain. In one word: civil society, viewed as a moral person, can have the *right of coercion*, and, in fact, has actually obtained this right through the social contract. Religious society lays no claim to the *right of coercion*, and cannot obtain it by any possible contract. The *state* possesses *perfect*, the *church* only *imperfect* rights. (45)

Mendelssohn calls a right the "authority [moral capacity] to make use of a thing as a means for promoting one's happiness" (45). He calls the capacity moral if it is in accordance with "the laws of wisdom and goodness" (45). The implication, then, is that man has the right to promote his own happiness if this right does not contradict the laws of goodness and wisdom (46). The requirement to act in accordance with goodness and wisdom, or to act contrary to that which would contradict goodness and wisdom, is a moral necessity: "The moral necessity to do or omit doing something is a *duty*" (46). For Mendelssohn, the laws of wisdom and goodness do not come into conflict. If I have a right to do something by implication that means that my fellow man cannot prevent me from doing it. If this were not true, then an action would at once be both morally possible and morally impossible.

To summarize, then, for Mendelssohn, true religion and the state share the same ends. It is their method for achieving those ends that differs. Although a religion might try to persuade one to share its beliefs, it does not have the right to use force. Only the state may use that practice. And here is the salient point: since the state is concerned with actions, not beliefs, the state should not be concerned with the religious convictions of its citizens unless and only if those convictions interfere with the ends of the state. Indeed, the state should even encourage freedom of the mind. As a result, there should be no conflict between being Jewish and being a citizen in a particular nation.

In the middle of this first section, Mendelssohn devotes a long footnote to a discussion of a court case in which two people who were both Jews when they married now share a household with two different religions, the result of the husband having converted to Christianity. Under the view that she entered the marriage with the belief that both she and her future husband would live their lives and raise their children according to Jewish principles, the wife now seeks a divorce. She entered a contract that was based on a set of beliefs she professed. If the court does not grant her a divorce it is as if she is compelled to accept a different set of beliefs, and according to Mendelssohn, no one, especially not the state, has a right to compel beliefs. We will return to this discussion shortly.

What, then, is the relationship between the state and the church? To get at this question, Mendelssohn turns to a discussion of property and binding agreements.[7] Supposing Person A has property that could be used for the sake of benevolence. Person B could request this property from Person A but he cannot compel Person A to turn over the property. This must remain Person A's choice. If Person A does agree to the request, Mendelssohn says, Person A has made a promise. Following in the line of Hobbes and Locke before him, Mendelssohn states that it is these kinds of agreements that move us out of the state of nature and into a state of social relations (56). This movement allows us to move from the pleasure of the immediate moment (like a savage) to plan for the future. How then do property rights and contracts apply to the difference between church and state?[8]

Mendelssohn explains the difference in these terms. Both the church and the state have action as their aim. For the church, actions are based on the relations between nature and God; for the state, relations between man and nature. By the sheer fact that men need each other, they enter into certain kinds of social connections, e.g., contracts. Insofar as men enter into contracts and a relationship with the state, the state has certain prerogatives to regulate or watch over these arrangements. Regardless of what I believe, that is, regardless of whether I might agree with the state, I must still act in certain ways that cohere with the state's rules. To the extent that I do not, the state has a right to intervene, especially as my actions might interfere with what is rightly owed to my neighbor. For Mendelssohn, how the state is allowed to act does not extend to the church. Contrary to the state's need for us to act in certain ways in order for the state to fulfill its duty, God does not need us—God does not need our benevolence, require our assistance and so forth (57).

Mendelssohn believes that this mistaken belief that we "owe" something to God or that we have a duty to God results from a mistaken extension of duties to the state. Indeed, Mendelssohn takes his point further and argues that the conflict that appears to exist between duties to God and duties to others is simply an appearance, a myth based on the original false parallel. Our duties toward others should naturally flow from our relationship to God. The violence that is perpetrated on others in the name of our duty to God is the result of having internalized this false sense of duty and then the ensuing perception that there can even be such a conflict between what is owed to God and what is owed to others (58).[9] Mendelssohn then says the following:

> The system of our duties rests on a twofold principle: the relationship between man and nature and the relationship between creature and Creator. The former is moral philosophy, the latter, *religion*, and to the man who is convinced of the truth that the relations obtaining in nature are but expressions of the divine will, both principles will coincide. To him, the moral teachings of reason will be sacred, just as religion is. (58)

Because it is property that brings about conflict among men, Mendelssohn states that the conclusion to be drawn from this discussion is the following: the church has no right to goods and property (59) and this also means there can be no contract between the church and the citizens, as there is between the citizens and the state. Contracts imply a conflict that might need to be mediated. Following from this conclusion is his further point that the only rights possessed by the church are "to admonish, to instruct, to fortify, and to comfort." Unlike the state, the church has no right to reward or punish.

With regard to convictions, the church and the state come closer to each other. Neither has the right to compel or coerce our beliefs. Yet, insofar as convictions lead to actions, both have an interest in our education. Both must "teach, instruct, encourage, motivate," even though neither may compel, coerce, reward, or punish (which would simply be a version of manipulation). Even though the state has an interest in our actions and has the authority to reward and punish our actions, the state does not have the authority to reward or punish our stated convictions, a right to which is inalienable (61). It is a right that we cannot transfer nor relinquish. As a result, neither the state nor the church has the right to judge in religious matters. Nor do institutions have the right to demand an oath regarding anything that one believes.

The above discussion naturally leads Mendelssohn, at the end of Part I, to address the controversial topic of excommunication. Although the state should be able to exercise the right to banish a citizen, excommunication is diametrically opposed to his understanding of true religion. Indeed he asks his readers to consider the possibility that those who have been excommunicated demonstrate more "true religion" than those who have excommunicated them (73). He further argues that religious excommunication cannot occur without civil consequences since at the very least it would harm the reputation of the individual who has been banished. In response to those who would say that if every society has the right to exclusion then why not also religious societies, Mendelssohn replies that this point is precisely what distinguishes the religious society. Likening the individual who distances himself from his religion, exemplified by morality, belief, etc., to a person who is sick, Mendelssohn concludes that the role of the religion is precisely not to abandon that person but to come to his aid. To do otherwise is to fail in the most fundamental role of religion itself (75).

Before moving to Part II, we should return to the middle of Part I where Mendelssohn offers the long footnote mentioned previously on a particular example of divorce. The footnote comes during a discussion of parental obligations—what do parents owe their children? Mendelssohn writes,

Whoever helps to beget a being capable of felicity, is obligated by the laws of nature, as long as it is not yet able to provide its own advancement. This is the natural duty of education, which is, to be sure, only a duty of conscience. Still by the act itself, the parents have agreed to assist each other in this respect, that is, to discharge together their duty of conscience [...] The parents, through the very act of cohabitation, have entered into a state of matrimony. They have made a tacit contract to render capable of felicity, that is, *to educate*, the being, destined for felicity, for whose coming into the world they are jointly responsible. (50)

Before they reach the age of reason, Mendelssohn says, children cannot be expected to make decisions on their own and thus they have no claim to independence. The responsibility of parents is to "train their children, step by step, in the *art of making rational decisions in cases of collision*, and gradually allow them, as their reason grows stronger, to make free and independent use of their powers" (49). In an interesting twist, Mendelssohn argues that the right to compel education belongs solely to the parents. No third party has the right to coerce or force parents to educate their children. However, the parents of the child have the right compel each other to do so— this stems, Mendelssohn claims, from the agreement that they are presumed to have made. It is worth noting how Mendelssohn's view differs radically from a view we hold today regarding compulsory education, which in the United States is primarily through the public school (state-sponsored) system. The difference here might be attributed to or traced back to the Jeffersonian ideal that with education people could rule themselves. Thus, education takes on a different character when thought in relationship to a democratic political system, as opposed to the political system under which Mendelssohn lived in eighteenth-century Germany.

Linking education intimately to religion, Mendelssohn argues that the duty to educate stems from the decision to have children. This decision yields the obligation to set up a common household in which this education will take place. Marriage then, according to Mendelssohn, is "nothing more than the agreement between two different sexes to bring children into the world." All other rights and duties follow from this agreement (50). At this point, Mendelssohn directs us to the footnote where he analyzes this peculiar case of divorce. Mendelssohn begins his discussion by asking this question: What if a couple that originally shared the same religious principles upon marrying such that these principles were agreed upon insofar as they agreed to be married no longer share the same principles during the course of the marriage? In the case that Mendelssohn examines, the husband who was a Jew at the time the couple married, converted to Christianity but expressed his desire to remain married.

Friedrich Maurer, who wrote about the case, says "that a difference of religion cannot be recognized as a valid cause for divorce [...] Difference of opinion in churchly matters cannot stand in the way of social ties" (51). Mendelssohn disagrees. He reminds his readers that marriage between a Jewish man and a Jewish woman is a civil contract. Because both parties outwardly professed their Jewish religion, then the expectation of both upon entering the marriage was that their household would be informed by Jewish principles, in particular, that the children the marriage produced would be educated according to the laws and principles of the Jewish religion. Importantly, for Mendelssohn, had the woman known that her husband-to-be might have changed religions and had she known that she would be unable to raise her children as Jews, she might very well have not entered into the marriage contract. To force her to live by the principles of another religion, indeed to compel her to raise and educate her children in a religion that runs contrary to her conscience would be an injustice.

And it is important here to focus on Mendelssohn's focus on action as it relates to belief. To compel the woman to accept the conditions of a contract that run contrary to her conscience would be the equivalent of compelling her to believe something that violates her conscience. The state has no authority, indeed, no business allowing beliefs to be imposed on its citizens. Because education and the institutions responsible for this education remain in the province of religion—that is, because education is done with a particular eye toward rearing the child in the religion associated with that education, the person who has retained the religious values she held when she entered the marriage contract is the person whose prerogative it is to educate the children. The state cannot simply assert that marriage is a social issue. Even though the marriage contract is civil, the marriage produces children whose education is inextricably tied to the religion that informs the marriage. When there is a conflict in those principles, for Mendelssohn, the person who stayed true to the religious principles one held upon entering the marriage is the one who has the right to decide how those children will be educated.

The question we are left with in this section is a question that we still face today, even with secular—or non-church related—educational institutions. What is the difference between secular and religious institutions and where do their respective boundaries lie? What might Mendelssohn say about secular and indeed public education? Or, might he see this as an oxymoron? Is education, is the school, for one particular kind of group, if the aim of education is to inculcate moral values that flow directly from the religion? From his discussion of the court case, Mendelssohn seems to believe that the problem that arose in the marriage was directly related to the charge that the couple has to rear their children and that the rearing of the children at the time was the family's and only the family's responsibility. Interestingly, Mendelssohn appears to indicate that this problem might disappear with the advent of a secular or civil moral education, one that is not tied to any particular religion; yet, it is then not clear what would connect moral upbringing, education, and religion. Even a cursory examination of the U.S. public schools reveals how fraught they are with regard to values, moral upbringing, and religion.

A New Twist on Social Contract Theory

As indicated above, Mendelssohn's discussion of state and church authority derives its force essentially from a discussion of social contract theory. The question, then, is how similar Mendelssohn's social contract theory is to those of his peers. Significantly, when modern political theory is taught, Mendelssohn is typically not included in a course syllabus. What might he offer to a discussion of social contract theory?

Social contract theory, in simple terms, is the view that an agreement made between individuals and the state, or rather the authority for the state to govern, is given a normative justification through the consent of the governed. The different social contract theories vary widely in complexity and detail, but the basic premise is the same. Although seemingly a good policy by which to govern, social contract theory has been criticized insofar as the contract never included everyone who is affected by the contract. That is, those who consented consisted of individuals granted a voice to consent while simultaneously excluding other groups of people who were necessary for the contract to work but who did not consent. Indeed, in many cases, the contract made explicit provisions for slavery and the subjugation of women. Thus, the contract—or the success of the society itself—was contingent on a non-contract that assumed the (unpaid) work of these groups of people without their voice in the process. Scholars such as Charles Mills and Carole Pateman criticize social contract theory at its core, arguing that it is fundamentally flawed since these theories assume either a racial contract (Mills) or a sexual contract (Patemen) on which the agreement to be governed is dependent.

Susan Shapiro, a scholar of both feminist theory and modern Jewish philosophy, offers a different approach to social contract theory by examining what Mendelssohn contributes to the discussion.[10] Shapiro pays close attention to the pending court case where a couple's divorce is in the hands of the court. As mentioned above, the case involves a husband and wife who were both Jewish upon marrying. Later in the marriage, and after having children, the husband converts to Christianity and wishes to raise the children in that religion. The wife, unable to comply, seeks a divorce so that she may continue to raise the children as Jews. While this might seem a simple case of religious difference or of patriarchal authority, Mendelssohn sees the situation as a violation of conscience.

He argues that when the couple was married, the wife had every expectation to believe, and indeed no reason not to believe, that the children the couple produced would be raised in the religion and by the principles to which they both consented. Arguing from the position that the purpose of marriage was to raise and educate the children produced by a man and woman, this purpose creates a fundamental obligation, the first promise that the couple made to each other. In this argument, Mendelssohn is also making the claim that the woman's voice carries as much authority as the man's, that her conscience is also fundamental. That is, Mendelssohn is not simply arguing this as a matter of religious freedom, but rather that the man and woman enter the marriage with equal voices and equal expectations of what the promise entails.

When he asserts that this relationship entails the promise and obligation to educate the children even in a state of nature, he is by implication claiming that the marriage contract, with the equal voices of man and woman, founded the social contract that would come later. That is, Mendelssohn's reading of the marriage contract grants men and women an equal voice for entering that contract. There is no reason why this equality could not, then, extend to the social contract that would follow. Thus, by way of religious conviction and precisely because of the promise that was made and assumed in the marriage contract, Mendelssohn is able to argue *for* equality between men and women and for the woman to be granted the divorce so that she is not forced to live in an untenable situation. Mendelssohn is able to base his argument on the situation of the time—the education of children was solely the responsibility of the parents.

Part II

In Part II, Mendelssohn begins with a discussion of religious authority rooted in his opposition to excommunication. Mendelssohn asks, "What if neither the state nor the mother church herself can claim any right to use coercion in religious matters?" We saw previously why Mendelssohn holds the view that the church has no right to religious coercion. Mendelssohn is determined to distinguish between secular civic life and the life of conscience. By making this distinction, Mendelssohn holds that religious life is private; it is about belief and thus is not subject to coercion. This question however was pressed in the letter, "The Searching for Light and Right in a Letter to Mr. M. Mendelssohn" (Berlin 1782).[11] The anonymous author of this letter—later revealed to be August Cranz—asserts that the laws of Moses are fundamentally tied to ecclesiastical power, supported by force, including stoning. If Mendelssohn is to reject such force, is he not rejecting the very cornerstones of Judaism? How can he make these claims and remain a Jew? In other words, the author of this letter cuts to the quick.

Mendelssohn admits that nothing the author says is factually incorrect. Yet, he does not concede the consequences, which the author believes flow from these points. Moreover, he is particularly jarred by the author's claim that perhaps Lavater was correct in his argument that Mendelssohn should convert. Perhaps in his criticism of Judaism, Mendelssohn comes closer to Christianity. In response, Mendelssohn reminds his accuser that Christianity is built on Judaism. The author is misguided if he believes that someone should convert to Christianity if they find Judaism faulty. Isn't that like going to the attic for refuge when the foundation is cracked? Why would climbing to the top be any more secure if the foundation is weak? It will all come tumbling down.

Mendelssohn thus turns to what he believes to be the fundamental error in the author's assessment of Judaism and Mendelssohn's relationship to it. Mendelssohn writes, "It is true that I recognize no eternal truths other than those that are not merely comprehensible to human reason but can also be demonstrated and verified by human powers" (89). He rejects Mr. Mörschel's claim, which had been added as an epilogue to Cranz's letter, that holding this position necessarily means that Mendelssohn must reject Judaism wholesale, or rather that by holding this position,

Mendelssohn implies that Judaism is fundamentally wrong and must be rejected.

Mendelssohn believes that the author's mistake rests on a fundamental and common confusion about Judaism and Christianity, indeed a confusion that Mendelssohn believes points to the characteristic difference between the two religions. Mendelssohn replies:

> I believe that Judaism knows of no revealed religion in the sense in which Christians understand this term. The Israelites possess a divine *legislation*—laws, commandments, ordinances, rules of life, instruction in the will of God as to how they should conduct themselves in order to attain temporal and eternal felicity. Propositions of this kind were revealed to them by Moses in a miraculous and supernatural manner, but no doctrinal opinions, no saving truths, no universal propositions of reason. These the Eternal reveals to us and to all other men, at all times, through *nature* and *thing*, but never through *word* and *script*. (90)

Mendelssohn simply states that he believes that Judaism subscribes to supernatural legislation.[12] This, however, is not to be confused with supernatural revelation of religion, which is the claim of Christianity. Firmly embedded in the philosophical milieu of his time, Mendelssohn uses the distinction between necessary propositions and contingent propositions to make his point.[13] But here Mendelssohn also differs from Locke's epistemology insofar as Locke accepts those propositions that are not contrary to reason but nonetheless above comprehension. Mendelssohn rejects these. Additionally, Mendelssohn draws a distinction between revealed religion and revealed legislation and he adds that Judaism does not see itself as the exclusive bearer of revealed eternal truths that are indispensable to salvation. The event at Sinai was not the revelation of religion but of legislation. The proclamation that says, "I am the Eternal, your God, the necessary independent being" is for Mendelssohn not Judaism but universal religion. For Mendelssohn, the universal statement of religion is that upon which Judaism has been built, but the two are not to be conflated or confused.

Referring to the five books of Moses, he observes that they say many things—they contain laws and religious doctrines, prescriptions for behavior, what to eat and what to wear. On first glance they appear simple and yet reveal complexity with each closer look one gives them. Yet, whatever the books include, Mendelssohn rightly and firmly points out that the books do not ever say, "You shall believe or not believe." Rather, it says, "You shall do or not do." For Mendelssohn, this absence is instructive, for it reminds us that faith cannot be commanded (100). If faith is not commanded by God, then surely it cannot be commanded by clergy, the state or its citizens. Judaism has no articles of faith to which one must commit oneself. Maimonides' "thirteen principles" are just that— principles, but have not "been forged into shackles of faith" (101). Thus, Mendelssohn says, "everything depends on the distinction between believing and knowing, between religious doctrines and religious commandments" (101). Judaism deals with revealed truths, with what it can know.

Mendelssohn then devotes considerable attention to the theme of idolatry, the absence of which he rightfully notes characterizes Judaism. His discussion of language includes drawing a parallel between the confusion of signs with things and the confusion of idolatry with the true notion of God. Judaism is devoid of idolatry, and indeed, the Jew's responsibility is to keep Judaism devoid of idolatrous notions of God. Additionally, Mendelssohn ends *Jerusalem* with an interesting challenge to Christianity. Jews, he says, have not been told by God that they are released from the law. Jews have in their historical past that God made a covenant with them on Sinai, that the law was given. Judaism has no such corollary event that indicates the law was rescinded. So, Mendelssohn says, even if a Jew were to convert to Christianity, nothing in Christianity would release the Jew from the law. Indeed, he says, Jesus of Nazareth observed the laws of Moses and the ordinances of the rabbis. Statements that appear contradictory appear so only at first glance.

A closer examination reveals they are in complete agreement with scripture (134). The challenge to Christianity is to defend its own departure from Judaism.

The question then is not why do the Jews stay Jews but why are the Christians not Jews? Mendelssohn repeats the Jewish view that those born into the law are responsible for upholding that law; they are bound to it and must live according to it. Those who are not born into the law are not bound to it. The question, it seems, is the status of Christianity in relationship to Judaism: if Christianity is built on Judaism and if Mendelssohn is correct that Jesus of Nazareth never renounces the law, then to what are Christians bound? Regardless, Mendelssohn asks his Christian readers how they can find fault with Jews who are simply following the same laws that Jesus of Nazareth, the founder of their religion, followed. It is hard not to see that Mendelssohn is implying that Christians have in fact mistaken the sign for the one true God. They follow Jesus, who followed Judaism. Might it not make more sense to follow Judaism directly?

Mendelssohn ends with a warning to those who wish to make all faiths alike, to those who believe that peace can only be brought about by merging everyone into the same belief system. First, he asks, what would this even accomplish should these people succeed in bringing this state about? At the end of the day, this situation could only be a façade since people could never all believe the same things. Beliefs cannot be forced. Mendelssohn's final statement:

> Let everyone be permitted to speak as he thinks, to invoke God after his own manner or that of his fathers, to seek salvation where he thinks he may find it, as long as he does not disturb public felicity and acts honestly toward the civil laws, and toward you and his fellow citizens [...] Let no one assume a right that the Omniscient has reserved to himself alone! (139)

2

From Modern to Post-modern

Hermann Cohen and Hannah Arendt

Hermann Cohen was born into a devout family in Coswig, Germany, in 1848.[1] Although he originally intended to study at the rabbinical seminary, he decided against that and enrolled in the university in Breslau, eventually receiving his doctorate from the University of Halle. Cohen's major works include several books devoted to commentaries on the eighteenth-century German philosopher, Immanuel Kant: *Kant's Theory of Experience* (1871); *Kant's Foundations of Ethics* (1877); and *Kant's Foundations of Aesthetics* (1889). These three books map onto Kant's three critiques: *Critique of Pure Reason*; *Critique of Practical Reason*; and *Critique of Judgment*. As noted by Cohen's biographers, however, all of his work shares Kant's overarching philosophical orientation. Cohen viewed the entire corpus of his own work as being informed by Kantian philosophy, namely, what Cohen called Kant's "transcendental method"—the philosophical investigation that leads to discovering the conditions of our experience. In this sense, this method is what Kant refers to as the synthetic a priori (see below). Toward the end of Cohen's career, the religious interests he maintained throughout his writing took hold, and he published his most famous work *Religion of Reason Out of the Sources of Judaism* (1919). Although Cohen's presence in the Marburg school—the neo-Kantian school of philosophy that emphasized the theory of knowledge and logic—was prominent, indeed so prominent that the school was said to disband when Cohen's presence was gone, it is only recently that his work has taken hold in Kantian scholarship. His influence on twentieth-century philosophy more widely has not yet enjoyed that same appreciation. His impact, however, on Jewish thought and philosophy can be seen clearly. In addition to the significance of Cohen's own writings, his student, Franz Rosenzweig, and his younger contemporary, Martin Buber, are central to modern Jewish philosophy.

Introduction to *Religion of Reason*

In *Reason and Hope* Cohen writes, "The inner affinities between Kant's philosophy and Judaism are evident in the substantive similarity between the ethics of the Kantian system and the basic ideas of Judaism, though Kant himself neither intended nor was even aware of any such accord" (*RH* 77). Cohen then proceeds to demonstrate how this is the case. One might presume, he says, that this affinity lies solely in Judaism's ethics. But he corrects this impression by claiming that Judaism had already begun to justify its teachings through philosophy—through reason—at least since Saadyah ben Joseph (882–942), Gaon (head) of the Academy at Sura, Babylon in the tenth century. Saadyah asserted that while the Torah is necessary for ethics, it is not sufficient. Reason must accompany the Torah as a source for ethics.

Fundamental to Judaism is the *logos*—reason. Similarly, the Kantian system is based on reason rather than empiricism. If knowledge is to be objective, it must not be subject to the instability of sense perception and empirical knowledge. Kant set out to establish that the synthetic a priori—a statement or truth that while not logically true, e.g., either it is raining or not raining outside—could be established without resorting to experience. The section he titled "the transcendental aesthetic" established this possibility. All experience of objects is subject to space and time, that is, we encounter things before or after, in front of or behind, and so forth. Space and time are the conditions for the possibility of all experience—a statement that is true prior to experience but not a statement that is true based on the logical form of the statement. Having established the role of reason in theoretical knowledge, Kant moved to the application of reason to ethics and developed an ethical system based on reason. Kant's ethics are complicated and there is not space here to provide a full accounting of his project. Suffice it to say that using as the foundation what he called the categorical imperative, Kant established a system of practical ethics where reason and not sense perception or feeling was used to determine what the right and the good were.

Although Cohen acknowledges the important role of revelation in religious matters, he supports the position held by Saadyah ben Joseph. Additionally, Cohen notes that both Judaism and Kantian ethics reject a eudaimonic approach to ethics where happiness is the end result or the determination of the good.[2] Finally, there is the universal applicability of both Kantian ethics and Jewish morality. Derived from the autonomy of reason, Kant's ethics apply to everyone. Similarly, Jewish ethics—not necessarily the 613 commandments, but as we will see, the seven Noahide commandments—have a universal application. The primary difference, as Cohen observes, is that for Kantian ethics, we write the moral law ourselves—the emphasis in Kantian ethics is on individual moral autonomy. In Judaism, God is the source of the moral law. Unlike the philosophers of modernity however, Judaism does not see God and reason as a contradiction— the moral law must be both the law of God and the law of reason (*RH* 81). Cohen believes that this universal equality before God can be found in both Kant and Judaism. In Judaism, we see it expressed in the commandment about how to treat humanity—"You shall love your neighbor as yourself" (Lev. 19:18). The commandment might be best read as, "Love him; he is like you" (*RH* 81). All of this is not to say Kant rejects the existence of God. Rather, God is impersonal, non-material—sublimated into an Idea.

God in Judaism is transcendent and for Cohen, God's transcendence is necessary if morality is to be universally applicable.

Once God and humanity are equated, mysticism arises and morality, rather than being binding because it is based on reason, is grounded in the supernatural. The moral is, then, the supernatural. Like Kant, who expressed a certain reticence regarding immortality—it was not truly knowable but it needed to be posited in order for moral retribution to make any sense—Judaism showed a similar reticence. As Cohen puts it, this view is not surprising for a philosopher shaped by eighteenth-century enlightenment but quite extraordinary for the religious thinkers of the medieval period. Judaism, however, understands the afterlife to be in proximity with God. There is no other good that comes from it.

Identifying another affinity between Kant's philosophy and Judaism, Cohen points to the notion of freedom. Although he affirms God as the moral lawgiver, insofar as God commands that we choose, Judaism affirms our moral freedom. For Kant, freedom was an end in itself and came to be seen as one of the antinomies of morality: to what extent do we care for others when that response might limit the freedom of another? The kingdom of ends for Kant is our expression of individual freedom, and as such we must treat people as ends in themselves rather than solely as means to an end. That means recognizing the freedom of the other person and allowing that person to express that freedom. Cohen points to the prophetic tradition in Judaism as the articulation of a similar view—that the political morality that the prophets taught was about treating people as ends in themselves.

Cohen's most interesting observation is the apparent affinity between Judaism's messianism and Kant's view of history. Cohen points to Kant's essay, "Perpetual Peace," which regards history as being meaningless unless it has a goal. The goal is perpetual peace. For Cohen, this view is not unlike that of the prophets who he believes were the first in the Jewish tradition to articulate this idea of perpetual peace. More interestingly, anyone who believes in perpetual peace believes not only in a messiah, but a messiah who is yet to come (*RH* 87–88). Thus, Cohen concludes that the Jewish philosopher must feel a special affinity with Kant.

God

Cohen opens his section on "God's Uniqueness" with this statement: "It is God's uniqueness, rather than his oneness, that we posit as the essential content of monotheism. Oneness signified only an opposition to the plurality of gods" (*RR* 35). Why does Cohen make this distinction between oneness and uniqueness? Cohen's distinction helps us see that monotheism on its own does not counter polytheism. There is no radical difference between one god and many gods unless there is also a difference in how the one god relates to the universe. Oneness, then, is not simply a number—one as opposed to many—but also a characteristic that qualifies how God relates to the universe, to nature.

This juncture, which asks after God's relationship to the world, is the point at which philosophy rubs against religion. Religion is not philosophy, Cohen tells us, but this is where the problem of philosophy appears. Insofar as Judaism is a religion of reason, by virtue of reason, it has a share in philosophy. Thus, the question of God, while a question for religion, awakens the role of reason.

Cohen argues that monotheism emerges from polytheism rather than being created out of nothing. Yet, although monotheism traces its origins to polytheism, monotheism is a difference of kind. Cohen proceeds to illustrate the differences between the two, noting first that Judaism's sources are literary documents, whereas polytheism erects monuments of "*plastic* art" (*RR* 37). The difference for Cohen is the mode of expression. The literary form allows thought to be exposed. Layers of thought supervene, and interpretation preserves the individual layers and tracks the development of the religion.

Another difference between monotheism and polytheism is that monotheism is a way to express the unity of God, and this unity implies the relationship of God to the world. Yet, while this point is important, "unity cannot be the deepest meaning of monotheism. Unity is always only the negative expression of monotheism, designating only its distinction from polytheism" (*RR* 40). Cohen reads God's response to Moses in Exodus 3:10–14 as God instantiating itself (anthropomorphism becomes necessary). Thus, in God's assertion, God equates itself with Being and thus indicates that no other being can affirm itself in this way. Importantly, Cohen locates philosophy, and if not philosophy, at least reason, in the earliest expression of Judaism: "In such a definite way *being* is named as that element in the name that designates the *person* of God" (*RR* 43). Having read God's being in this way, Cohen concludes that this unique being represented only by the unique God thus negates the being of all other gods (*RR* 43). As such, Cohen affirms that the principle of reason guides Judaism.

We must acknowledge the significance of such a claim given the manner in which religion is often positioned against reason. To believe is normally equated with having faith, which is precisely to believe in spite of reason or in the absence of reason. Cohen's move, on the other hand, is to ground Judaism in reason such that faith and reason are part of the same piece. Both "other gods" and "non-being" are placed in opposition to God's being. The uniqueness of God is this incomparability. Uniqueness also draws the line between existence and being. The former relies on experience, on the senses, on perception. Reason, however, transcends perception and thus "bestows actuality on existence, discovers and elevates the nonsensible to being, and marks it out as true being" (*RR* 44).

Recalling Kant's transcendental aesthetic, which established space and time as a priori conditions of experience, Cohen utilizes these concepts to help us understand the relationship God has to the world. Although God cannot remain without the human world, the human world is limited by both space and time. But where the human world is limited by such things, God is not—indeed, one name for God is space (*ha-makom*). Furthering his argument, Cohen refers to the Shechinah, another name for God which means absolute rest or dwelling. This does not mean that motion is impossible, but rather that through the being of rest "the being of motion becomes possible" (*RR* 45).

Similarly, time is not a limitation for God. In the claim that God is both first and last, the eternity of God is affirmed. Additionally, transcending time also means standing outside of change. At the end of this section, Cohen draws a distinction between messianism and eschatology. Messianism signals the peak of monotheism, which for Cohen implies that the dignity of man is grounded not simply in the individual man but in the idea of humanity. This view will form the basis for the rest of his analysis; indeed, we can see the anticipation of a different kind of ethics when the dignity of man is grounded in humanity and not in the individual.

Discovery of Man as Fellowman

Cohen opens this section by indicating that up to this point, we have come to know man as only a holy spirit, as a being of moral reason: "[M]orality itself denotes up to now only a problem that originates in the correlation between God and man, and which is to be solved through holiness. Therefore man himself is only a problem" (*RR* 113). In this section, Cohen identifies man in two possible ways: the individual and the plurality. Each presents its own problems for thinking about unity, but a special ethical problem emerges when thinking of man as part of the plurality: the problem of the *fellowman* (*RR* 114). Experience tells us that the next man is perceived. Does this not already make him a fellowman? Cohen replies, no, this has been a mistake in thinking. We cannot presume that the "next man" is already our fellowman. How, then, does the next man become the fellowman? For Cohen this change in perception comes about through conceptual knowledge that is based on reason. Since Judaism is a religion with a share in reason, the task of this conceptual knowledge also resides in religion. The claim Cohen makes is indeed striking: "If the correlation between God and man is the fundamental equation of religion, then *man* in this correlation must first of all be thought of as fellowman" (*RR* 114). This correlation however already implies a correlation between man and man. Religion, then, which is the correlation between man and God, thus already also includes the problem of the fellowman.

Therefore, central to both reason and religion is the question of the ethical. The possibility of ethics is fundamentally tied to the problem of the fellowman, above which, Cohen says, there is no greater problem. No other problem takes precedence. Both ethics and religion depend on the concept of the fellowman.

How then does one reconcile the tension between unity and plurality, between the unique nation of Israel, which recognizes the one unique God, and those who would be viewed as enemies of such a people? Cohen answers that this tension between the Israelites and the foreigner is resolved through the stranger. Although it is through monotheism that such a tension first emerges, it is also through monotheism that an ethics to resolve this tension can be found. One example Cohen recites is found in the Noahide commandments and in the covenant God establishes with Noah, a symbol for all humanity. This covenant implies that "every man is already the brother of every other" (*RR* 118). After listing several more examples—the eternal covenant with Abraham, Abraham's insistence on law and justice at Sodom—Cohen demonstrates that the "love of the fellow countryman" implies a love of the fellow man, but the letter though presumed has yet to be established. Referring back to the dispute between Rabbi Akiba and Ben Azai about the commandment "to love your other, as he is you," Cohen says of this misinterpretation, the love of the neighbor must be based on the idea of God's creation of man and not on a "feeling" I might have toward myself or another person. The uniqueness of monotheism is precisely that it does not make a partition between believers and non-believers. The history of monotheism reveals that one is a son of Noah *before* he is a son of Abraham. Thus one is a member of humanity before one is a member of a particular people.

Recalling the analysis that Mendelssohn provided on actions versus beliefs, the former and not the latter being necessary for citizenship, Cohen uses this distinction to argue his point regarding the humanity of man. The Noahide commandments, central to his point, reveal that while monotheism provides the basis for this moral turn to humanity, belief in the Jewish God is not required. That is, in a strange twist of reason, monotheism, which depends on the humanity of man, the idea of the fellowman, thus allows for the non-believer. The only requirement is that the seven Noahide commandments be observed: the prohibitions against incest, murder, robbery, and eating the limb of a living creature, and additionally, the prohibitions against blasphemy of God and against idolatry, which Cohen reads not as a requirement to believe in the Jewish God, but a requirement not to desecrate the land of those in which one resides. The one additional precept that must be followed is to set up a court system. Thus, Cohen argues, the Noahide commandments affirm two things—that we must all view the stranger as a fellowman and that the only requirement of the fellowman when living in a country not his own is to abide by the fundamental moral code that applies to all humanity (*RR* 122–23).

Additionally, the Noahide commandments ground the idea of natural law for the state and also, as we saw in Mendelssohn, the idea of freedom of conscience—no one can be coerced to believe. According to this reading, the stranger should be allowed to join the state because as long as he abides by the seven Noahide commandments, he is a moral person. The equation Cohen writes is Stranger = Noahide = Pious of the Peoples of the World. The Noahide symbolize the harmony possible between religion on the one hand and the state/law on the other. Cohen recalls the early passages in Deuteronomy to make his point that Judaism, a religion of reason, is founded on a view of humanity as that which precedes the particularity of the Jew: there will be one law for you and for the stranger; thou shalt not pervert justice due to the stranger, the widow, and orphan; and support the poor, even if the poor is a stranger. This equality is seen in the commandment that Cohen reads as equality even in the allotment of land. Political equality corresponds to religious equality and is guided by tolerance. All of this, though founded in a reading of the Noahide laws that affirms humanity, is also founded on God's proclamation to love the stranger. Religion, then, Cohen argues, does develop with the state, but with an underlying basic morality that applies to all, even as it does not require all to believe the same way.

In the last part of this section Cohen addresses the problem of poverty, which he believes poses the most difficult question for the concept of man. What are we to make of this difference between men—between rich and poor—who reside in the same land? He cites what appear to be two opposing statements from Deuteronomy 15:4: "There shall be no needy among you" and Deuteronomy 15:11: "For the poor shall never cease out of the land." Though the question could be asked, how could God have created such a world where the suffering of the poor is found, Cohen reads these statements as a claim that God is asking us to correct society such that we respond or care for the poor among us. Although history, even biblical stories, appear to bear out the envy that one man might feel toward another, Cohen warns against this feeling as a justification for the great differences in social class.

Cohen asks us to consider two circumstances—the villain who prospers and the righteous person who does not fare well. It is the latter that presents the problem for God and religion. How is a religious conscience to grapple with the existence of the righteous person who is poor? "How could the misfortune of the righteous be reconciled with God's justice?" Ought we become stoic? Ought we assert that this is the way things are supposed to be? Cohen warns against such justifications and says in response,

> the feeling of *indifference* with regard to well-being and woe cannot arise and assert itself [...] When well-being and ill are actualized objectively in the social differences of poor and rich, then the indifference toward them becomes insincerity, frivolity, cruelty. No man may doubt that these differences are not indifferent to men. From the social point of view, stoicism is either hypocrisy or unforgiveable ignorance. (*RR* 132)

It is the prophet, then, who calls us back to the moral order of the community and reminds us of the moral foundation of religion.

Monotheism reaches its pinnacle through prophetic teaching; indeed, for Cohen, one might say that religion aims at the prophet. The prophet recognizes the correlation of man and God and thus is interested in politics broadly construed—this includes not only international politics but also social politics. The suffering of the poor in one's own nation is as important as the war that might break out between two or more nations.

For the prophet, the question of good and bad morphs into a question about the differences between rich and poor. These differences, the existence of such social stratification, upsets the balance of society. What distinguishes the prophet is his ability not to fall prey to the primitive belief that such economic distinctions map neatly onto and are thus morally justified by moral distinctions—morally bad = poor; morally good = implies rich and vice versa. These social differences must be viewed on their own terms and not as correlates to good and bad. The prophet, then, is charged with the awesome responsibility of not closing his or her eyes to such moral complexity and moral corruption; he must cry out against this, as strong as the prejudice is which informs such social disparity in the first place. The concept of fellowman becomes meaningless if his goodness is simply reduced to his well-being: his woe becomes indifferent to me. And here Cohen makes this striking assertion:

> The great achievement of the prophetic teaching, and that which also shows its inner connection with true morality, consists in this: prophetic thought does not indulge in speculations about the meaning of life in the presence of the riddle of death; it puts aside the question of death and therefore also of afterlife, despite the fact that their moral significance is not hidden from it. Nonetheless prophetic thought puts aside these questions of life and afterlife in the face of the life whose meaning is in question because of the evil which is represented by *poverty. Poverty becomes the main representation of human misfortune.* (*RR* 134)

Poverty is where we see the blurring of the physical suffering and psychical suffering. Poverty, though it affects the individual who is poor, also afflicts the community, the social realm. In poverty, individual suffering becomes social suffering. Cohen asserts that whoever can explain poverty in this way, as the suffering of mankind, is the one who creates ethics. He sees the prophets as having fulfilled this task. They have the religious insight to see the magnitude of poverty as the suffering of mankind; thus for the prophets, the "the true riddle of human life is not death, but poverty" (*RR* 135). Death is a riddle that only the mystic can solve, but poverty is the riddle within reason—it is the one we can solve but have failed to. Poverty, then, is differentiated from all other ills because it rises to the level of social, psychical or spiritual suffering. It afflicts the community at the most fundamental level—it reveals those who will not respond to the suffering of the other and thus contaminate the community. Poverty is never just the poverty of the individual. As Andrea Poma observes, Cohen sees in poverty, in social suffering, not only an individual evil but also a cultural situation involving human consciousness in general (Poma 1997, 204).

If suffering then can be found throughout the history of the world, how do we reconcile God's justice with its presence? Here Cohen makes an interesting move. He compares monotheism to polytheism, the latter of which connected all of human experience to the gods. It is via the prophets that we see monotheism's departure from polytheism. In monotheism, as the prophets remind us, man, not God, is central. The concern lies with man, and the resolution of suffering lies with God. Thus, the question of theodicy, one might say, is a residue of polytheism where the gods were seen as responsible for the cause and resolution of suffering. Suffering is a social suffering, thus our attention cannot focus only on the individual for its resolution. Here Cohen rebukes Spinoza, who believes that pity arises from the same subjective source as envy and thus takes the path of stoicism.

In response, Cohen argues that Spinoza can only make such a claim if he still sees suffering as unique to the individual and does not recognize social suffering. There is a vast chasm between envy and pity that Spinoza cannot see. In contrast, Cohen argues that pity triggers our moral consciousness. Pity is not as many would say simply reflexive, originating from a negative emotion internal to the one who feels pity. Rather, pity is in response to the suffering of the fellowman. Pity is part of the discovery of the fellowman, and thus is an ethical trigger. Anticipating the work of Emmanuel Levinas in the twentieth century, Cohen asks a striking question: "[do] I myself already exist before the fellowman is discovered?" That is, might it be the case that through the problem of the fellowman which invokes pity, an ethical response, that I come into existence as such, thus grounding our relations with others as both religious and ethical? (*RR* 142). Cohen ends this section with this powerful statement:

> Suffering is to be resolved in reality and not merely in the illusory feeling of the spectator. The prophet becomes the practical morality, the politician and jurist, because he intends to end the suffering of the poor. And it is not enough for him to assume these various callings; he has to become a psychologist as well: he must make pity the primeval feeling of man; he must, as it were, discover in pity man as fellowman and *man* in general. (*RR* 143)

Atonement

Developing his views about social morality, Cohen begins this section by stating that up until Ezekiel all the prophets view morality as social morality. The individual relationship to ethics was bound up with the social. But, Cohen argues, as much as social morality is significant, the prophetic idea must move in the direction of the individual. If it is the case that suffering places man before the Other, sin places man before himself (Poma 1997, 215). Cohen believes that Ezekiel is the turning point: "*The prophecy of Ezekiel constitutes the essential stage of this progress*" (*RR* 180).

In this section, Cohen addresses the question of individual ethics—and the philosophical problem of sin. "How can man sin by himself spontaneously?" Cohen asks. What role does free will play? He replies that a misunderstanding of the Hebrew word, *yetzer*, led to the idea of *original sin*. Misinterpretations led to a view that desires of the heart are in themselves bad. But, Cohen reminds his readers, it is only the effects of the heart, the actions that arise from what we think, that can be bad, or evil. But if it is not the case that man is "born bad" or born with an "evil heart" how then do we explain the real actions, frequently bad ones, that people do commit? Put simply, "how does sin come into man?" (*RR* 182), a question that cannot be discharged simply by asserting that sin is an illusion.

According to Cohen, the social cannot account for evil, it cannot account for the individual, and so the discussion must move beyond the social prophets to Ezekiel. He differs from the social prophets insofar as he locates sin in the individual, and by so doing also locates the individual. Ezekiel moves beyond sin as something that pits person against person and argues that sin is also a transgression against God. Where the social prophets fused morality and religion, the latter receding in the background, Ezekiel draws out religion by focusing on the individual. The process of moral improvement is religious: "The discovery of humanity through sin is the source from which every religious development flows. This knowledge is conceived as self-knowledge. *Hence religion separates itself from mythology*, in which humanity is not yet the originator of his own sin but merely the heir of his ancestors and their guilt" (*RR* 20).[3] In this manner, as the individual strives to improve herself, she correlates to God. One might say, again, anticipating themes that will reappear in Levinas, that by confessing one's sins, and thus making the attempt to atone or reconcile oneself with God, one becomes singular or unique. That is, by taking responsibility for one's own moral failings and coming into relationship through this unique way, the individual identifies herself as unique.

Zionism (From *Reason and Hope*)

Cohen's understanding of Judaism necessarily commits him to an anti-Zionist position. This position led to an extended debate between Cohen and Martin Buber, a younger contemporary of Cohen's who became a renowned twentieth-century Jewish philosopher in his own right. For ease, this section will present Cohen's reply to Buber, but I will present it simply as Cohen's position on Zionism rather than as part of the debate. The section on Martin Buber will provide the larger context for this discussion.

Writing in 1916, Cohen believed that Judaism's dispersion among different nations, peoples, and geographies rather than running contrary to its purpose actually fulfills it. He acknowledges that Israel—the Jewish people—must preserve what makes it unique, but this must not, indeed cannot, be done either by creating a "state within a state" or by creating a Jewish state. Cohen recognizes this tendency, that because the Jewish people constitute what appears to be a distinct ethnic group, they form a state inside a state. Thus, while modern Jews proclaim that they do not mean to form this state within a state, their distinct religion differentiates them as a distinct ethnic group.

Judaism as a religion stands above or outside of "nation," and thus by definition Cohen believes it cannot be located in any particular place. To create a Jewish state would mean to assert the view that Israel—a place—fulfills what it means to be Jewish rather than to live by certain Jewish principles which he believes are also universal. By focusing on the prophets, Cohen is able to shift the perspective of Judaism from the land of the forefathers and mothers to the prophetic view that focused on action, which transcends nation.

Modernity presents unique problems for Judaism and those who adhere to it. How does one negotiate the demands of the state and the demands of the religion? In response, the modern Jew replies that since these tensions cannot be resolved, he or she must leave the religion for the sake of the commitment to the state. Thus, modernity's message is that state citizenship wins over religious adherence. It is the Jewish religion and religion only that sets us apart from the state and thus the nation. Cohen responds that this position is simply a cowardly expression of assimilation. Moreover, it would undermine his view that we have an ethical obligation to the state, an obligation we cannot disavow. Zionism, in Cohen's view, is an escape from this position. It disposes of those Jews who believe they can live as Jews within a non-Jewish state by indicating that these Jews are simply mistaken. Having made this claim, those who believe otherwise define Jewish reality and what it means to be Jewish. All achievements of Judaism—all cultural contributions—are viewed as "illusory," and the "ghetto mentality," rather than being seen as a problem, is viewed as the true manifestation of Judaism. To live apart is the only way that Jews can live, thus to live apart is what it means to be a real Jew. Anything else is a mythology about Judaism. Modern Judaism insofar as it is a continuation or an extension of this mythology is thus a mythology also. It is an oxymoron.

Cohen sees Judaism differently. Indeed, he sees one's participation in the state as a Jew not only possible but in fact an obligation. He sees this possibility not as a mythology or a violation of Judaism but as a constructive force for both Judaism and the nation in which the Jew resides. Cohen's fundamental view that Judaism is tied to both science (philosophy and reason) and ethics (also based on reason) motivates his notion that Judaism rather than leaving the non-Jewish state must reside in it and maintain a cultural presence, regardless of the relationship the Jew has to the state. That is, independent of how free the Jew is, whether the Jew is treated equally, for example, the Jew's obligation to be Jewish within the state, to effect change by way of Jewish ethics, remains centrally important.

Contrary to the position that modern Judaism is not authentic Judaism, Cohen sees modern Judaism as precisely the proper development of the religion. Modern Judaism expresses the universal religion that Judaism is. As such, it reminds the Jew that there is no conflict between the state and the religion. It is only when Judaism is viewed as particular and parochial, when it is viewed as not applicable to all, that the tension gains force. Indeed, recalling the affinities between Kant and Judaism, if one views Kant as the quintessential modern German thinker, then the affinity is not only between Kant and Judaism but between the German spirit and Judaism (*RH* 169). Contrary to the Zionist position that the only way to preserve Judaism is to separate it from a state that is believed to threaten its existence and house it within a Jewish state, Cohen offers a converse position. The only way to preserve Judaism is precisely to root it in the non-Jewish state, to express it universally as it is intended to be. The land of Israel is also a land of the prophets, whom Cohen views through an ethical lens. As such, the prophetic voice of Israel implores Judaism not to isolate itself for the sole purpose of "being Jewish," but rather "being Jewish" means taking on the ethical obligation of Judaism within the world: "We therefore see the entire historical world as the future abode of our religion. And it is this future alone which we acknowledge as our true home" (*RH* 170).

Hannah Arendt

Hannah Arendt was born on October 14, 1906 in Hanover, Germany. At the age of 18, she became a student at the University of Marburg, where she met Martin Heidegger, then a young faculty member in philosophy. After a year in Marburg she studied with Husserl for a semester in Freiburg. Then in 1926, she moved to Heidelberg where she studied with Karl Jaspers. She completed her dissertation on Augustine in 1929. In 1933, one year after Hitler won the election, she fled Germany. Moving to Prague, Geneva, and then Paris, she was eventually forced to leave Europe altogether. In 1941 she moved to New York where she became part of an "influential circle of writers and intellectuals." She lectured at a variety of colleges and universities, but she is most known for her faculty position as a professor of political philosophy at the New School for Social Research—sometimes referred to as the University in Exile for having provided a safe intellectual haven for a number of scholars who were forced to flee Europe during the Nazi occupation.

Arendt was a prolific writer. A complex and original thinker, she is one of the most important political theorists in the twentieth century. Among her most prominent books are, *The Origins of Totalitarianism*, *The Human Condition*, *On Revolution*, and *The Life of the Mind*. These books are considered central to political theory, yet the complexity of her ideas makes her writings difficult to classify. Her work defies the neat categories of modernity: liberalism, conservative, and socialism. As we will see below, she took pride in not seeing her views emanate from her membership in a particular group; instead, she prized thinking for herself, her independence of thought. Thus, we might say that she is difficult to classify precisely because she refuses to follow the rules of thinking. She advances a vision of the political that pulls its ideas from a variety of different sources.

Although Arendt praises the revolutionary tradition she also defends the rule of law. One common theme that runs through her work is that thought should be allowed to develop in an unfettered way. We see this most clearly not only in her work on totalitarianism but also in her lovely essay on education, which was originally part of a radio interview. While we might disagree with many of her points and even the pedagogical method she advances, there is no doubt that her aim is for the child to be allowed to develop such that she thinks for herself.

Given the strong connection between political theory and educational theory, one might then say that her political theory is constructed in order to advance this educational mission, which will in turn advance this political mission in society—where individuals are able to think for themselves, participate in a deliberative democracy, speak their minds, and vote their conscience. In that regard, as some commentators have noted, her political theory does not easily fit into a modern classification because in many ways it is more aligned with a classical tradition that most likely framed her own German education.

She gained notoriety for attending and reporting on the trial of Adolf Eichmann in Jerusalem, 1961. She published her accounts serially in *The New Yorker*. Later, she would publish her account of the trial as a book, *Eichmann in Jerusalem: A Report on the Banality of Evil*. She indicated in an interview that she had a particular interest in the trial because she was also a survivor of Nazi Germany. Her account of the trial, which included her own perspective on events, won her the ire of most of the Jewish community in the United States, Israel, and elsewhere. About this negative perception, Arendt believes it stemmed less from a disagreement with her views and more from a misunderstanding in the first place. Regardless of the response to this book and her other philosophical works, Arendt's work remains tremendously influential and her original ideas still require us to think longer and harder about the political theories that continue to inform how we construct our institutions and our personal comportment in relationship to those institutions. She died in 1975.

In his Introduction to *The Jewish Writings: Hannah Arendt*, Ron Feldman recalls that Arendt divided those who have outsider status into two types: the *conscious pariah*, that is the one who was aware of this, and the *parvenu*, the one who tries to ape the gentile world but who can never escape his/her Jewish roots. The essays collected in this volume, Feldman asserts, reveal Arendt's choice to be the "conscious pariah." She elevates the conscious pariah to a revered status, arguing that it is the conscious pariah who "does more for the spiritual dignity of her people."[4] Using Bernard Lazare as her example, Arendt observes that in "contrast to his unemancipated brethren who accept their pariah status automatically and unconsciously, the emancipated Jew must awake to an awareness of his position and, conscious of it, become a rebel against it—the champion of an oppressed people (JP 108).

Similar to the view that Emmanuel Levinas offered, Lazare also believes that assimilation was folly and duped the Jews into believing that they could leave their Jewishness behind and become like the nation in which they lived. Instead, they simply shed those characteristics that made them unique as not only individuals but also moral beings. Retaining the outward mark of the flesh—namely circumcision—they instead simply reminded others of their existence but with nothing of interest to offer, they inspired the hatred of their neighbors. What was the solution? Lazare argues that one needed to arouse the Jewish pariah in order to fight against the Jewish parvenu. Not to do this would lead to the destruction of the Jews. Lazare's observation, similar to Jost's characterization of "double-slavery," was to note the double dependence: "upon the hostile elements of his environment and also his own 'highly placed brethren' who are somehow in league with them" (JP 108). Lazare notes the connection between these two elements (a connection and a framework that could be used to explain many phenomena of oppressed groups: the few people of color or women who "make it" but who then aspire to be like the very people who constructed society such that only a few outside the dominant group can get through). The enemy who is in control enjoys the work of those who willingly join in as lackeys, being rewarded with special privileges in exchange for helping to oppress members of their group.

Lazare recommends politics, which allows the Jew as pariah to rebel openly, and acknowledge and embrace his role as outsider, and thus as pariah. He argues that every Jew should do this, "since it is the duty of every human being to resist oppression" (JP 109). To use the vernacular of existentialism, Lazare wanted the Jew to take ownership of his place, to take responsibility for it, and then to rebel against it—not by becoming rich and being duped into joining another station, but rather to be a Jew. In the end however, Lazare realized that the greatest obstacle to his political plan was not the parvenu but rather the pariah who does not rebel. That is, the person who can easily be the revolutionary for others but does not. As such, it is as if one has relinquished power to the parvenu.[5]

"The Enlightenment and the Jewish Question"[6]

Arendt opens her 1932 essay with the following statement: "The modern Jewish question dates from the Enlightenment; it was the Enlightenment—that is, the non-Jewish world—that posed it. Its formulations and its answers have defined the behavior and the assimilation of Jews" (EJQ 3). Arendt points to Lessing as the propagator of the arguments for tolerance and humanness, but more importantly, she credits Lessing with drawing the distinction between "truths of reason and those [truths] of history" (EJQ 3). Arendt emphasizes that this distinction serves to legitimate "each accidental instance of assimilation" such that we see these occurrences as an ongoing insight into truth rather than simply the mere adaptation of a culture to a particular surrounding culture. Her essay turns to Lessing for whom reason is the one trait that all humans share— and as such provides the "foundation of humanity." It is this connection—reason as bound to humanness—that produces the idea of tolerance. If at the end of the day, in spite of whatever differences we project, we are all fundamentally the same because we all possess reason, then at bottom, we are all the same human being (EJQ 3).

Arendt observes however that this view of the human does not derive solely from "the general validity of reason as a pure formal quality; rather, the idea of tolerance is intimately connected with Lessing's concept of truth, which for its part can be understood only within the context of his theological thought and his philosophy of history" (EJQ 3–4). Lessing notes that truth—indeed the search for it—was exchanged for reason. Thus, an individual or a group might have value dependent on how one determined truth—and thus, the zero-sum game meant some had it and some did not—reason as the defining trait enlarges the tent. Thus, instead of religion qua a particular religion defining the human, instead with reason as an underlying trait, all religions simply become "different names for the same man" (EJQ 4).

The beauty of this exchange—reason for truth—lies in the fallibility of truth to begin with. Truth is simply an accident of history and they are only true to the extent that they confirm the truths of reason. That is, insofar as they rely on evidence, they are contingent on reason. Thus it is reason that lies at the root. History, which is the vehicle for reason, is humanity's educator (EJQ 4). The argument concludes that revealed history is identical to reason, all of this pointing to the end of history, to what is absolutely necessary rather than historically accidental (EJQ 5). All of this points to uncovering of reason. Reason is the new religion (EJQ 5).

Although resembling Pietism at first glance, Arendt's reminder of the Enlightenment's distrust of the Bible is instructive. Because the Bible cannot withstand scrutiny that demands objectivity, the last effort to save religion comes at the expense of the Bible. If religion is separated from the Bible, there is actually some hope for religion's future. Thus recalling the old Euthyphro question that invokes a chicken—egg problem of which comes first, Lessing says, "Religion is not true because the evangelists and apostles taught it, rather they taught it because it is true" (EJQ 5). This statement establishes an order—religion precedes the Bible. Arendt establishes the two heterogeneous senses of history that Lessing's analysis details. The first is history as the search for eternal truth, which establishes a starting point—man's coming of age—but then points forward in an unbounded way.

The second is history as the educator of the human race, which becomes superfluous with man's coming of age—reason. In other words, the first begins with the man's reason, and Arendt notes that it is this history that energizes Mendelssohn's reception of Lessing's thought. Yet, Arendt also notes that it is the second sense of history that differs structurally from the one Lessing presented in his book, *The Education of the Human Race*. Indeed, she argues, it cannot be viewed as a secularization of Christianity since the focus of this history is on the human. Only God can know the truth and the search for truth simply distracts or turns man away from what should be the proper focus: the human (EJQ 6).

In contrast to this view of the Enlightenment, Mendelssohn's acceptance of the Enlightenment was not simply aligned with Judaism but dependent on it. For Mendelssohn, "thinking for oneself" and all that is reasonable is synonymous with Judaism. In making a distinction between the truths of Jewish history and eternal truths, Mendelssohn says about the latter that they hold independently of history. Additionally, he argues, there is nothing in the "Old Testament" that violates reason, thus these eternal truths are binding on everyone while only Jews are bound to those obligations that run contrary to reason. Eternal truths, then, because they bind everyone, "are the foundation of tolerance" (EJQ 7). The reason then that Jews follow strict adherence to Jewish law is that this provides the Jews their path to these eternal truths by way of a system of signs that captivate the imagination.[7] So we find an interesting impasse in the views that Lessing and Mendelssohn took, even though Lessing's motivation was precisely a defense of Mendelssohn. Where Lessing used the distinction between history and reason precisely to end religion as dogma (EJQ 8), Mendelssohn deploys it precisely to argue for the eternal truths that ground Judaism and are yet independent of any historical verification (EJQ 8). Mendelssohn's move however undoes itself. In separating reason from history, the seeker of truth is also removed. In this instance, the Jew, who as Arendt observes is "closely bound up with [her] factual position in the world" (EJQ 8). By making this separation, reality, which for the Jew is bound to this faculty position, lacks legitimation.

The eighteenth-century political thinker, Christian Dohm provides an alternative view of this relationship. Jews are just like everyone else, but their very place as historical beings is what has ruined them. It is how they have been mistreated by others, by religious prejudice, that is the cause of their undoing. Thus, we must treat them in a different way from this point forward. Dohm's view then firmly grounds the Jew in history and thus the Jew must be liberated from this past that was so harmful. To accomplish this task is part of what it means both to liberate and integrate the Jew (EJQ 8).

Not much later, Johann Gottfried Herder reverses this relationship making reason subject to history. As a result, the question of where Judaism stands reemerges, but in a different form. By making this claim, Herder is also making a claim about the "fundamental sameness of men," with which he disagrees. With history as the fundamental driver of humanity, "the deeper life is seized by history, the more differentiated it becomes" (EJQ 12). Judaism's age thus makes its differences not only more pronounced but separates it from all other people. Difference is not about ability or talent, but the effects of history on the group and the impossibility to undo both the events and those effects. The past cannot be undone (EJQ 13). Herder's revised view casts the Jew and the Jewish people in a different light with regard to assimilation. What would this mean? For Herder, the diaspora was simply the precondition for the Jewish people to have an impact on the rest of the world. The change in view for Herder is the move from religious tolerance to politics. How does the Jew, or in general any group of people, live as a nation in Germany? What does it mean for this to happen? The question is, how can this happen?

Returning to Mendelssohn, Arendt observes that his "defense of the Jewish religion and his attempt to salvage some 'eternal content' was not entirely pointless" (EJQ 15). When Herder loosened the tie binding obligations had to historical content, he also undid the uniqueness of Judaism itself. Mendelssohn's view thus preserves Judaism. But what Arendt notes is that this entire question nonetheless sees the Jew and the relationship to history as unique. Thus insofar as the Jew relates to history it is as a Jew with a particular history. This view then maintains Jewish exceptionality even as it attempts to undo it by arguing for a kind of sameness. The Jew then becomes "a people without history within history" (EJQ 16). And so Arendt concludes, "out of the alienness of history, history emerges as a special and legitimate concern of the Jews" (EJQ 16).

One year after publishing this essay on the Enlightenment, Arendt writes "Original Assimilation," in which she observes that although the Enlightenment promised the Jews emancipation, rights, and citizenship and although most Jews became Enlightenment advocates (EJQ 22), "the *problem* of Jewish assimilation began only *after* the Enlightenment, first in the generation that followed Mendelssohn." Writing just as Hitler is rising to power, one year after the election, Arendt can see that this brand of anti-Semitism renders assimilation a failure. The first round of assimilation after Mendelssohn included baptism, which is simply a means to escape, or attempt to escape, one's Judaism. But this new anti-Semitism will not allow such an escape. The fate of assimilation, Arendt notes, is more urgent than ever before and those most affected by its fate— assimilated Jews (EJQ 22).

3

Jewish Existentialism

Shestov, Buber, and Rosenzweig

Existentialism

Although the term "existentialism" is used to describe a particular approach to philosophy, and although it includes philosophers from the nineteenth century—most notably, Kierkegaard, Nietzsche, Dostoyevsky—the twentieth-century French philosopher, Jean-Paul Sartre claimed the term to describe his own philosophy. Among other twentieth century philosophers included in this kind of thinking, we find Albert Camus, Simone de Beauvoir, Maurice Merleau-Ponty, Martin Heidegger, Karl Jaspers, Gabriel Marcel, and Jean Wahl. The majority of the philosophers identified themselves as atheists, with only a few notable exceptions: Kierkegaard and Marcel. Yet, these two thinkers also identified as Christian thinkers. Typically neglected from the list of existential thinkers are the Jewish thinkers, which we will discuss in this chapter. But before turning to them, it might be helpful to have a brief summary of what existentialism is as a school of philosophy. The term has entered our common vernacular in such a way that its technical roots have been lost and thus appears less rigorous as a philosophical discipline than other schools of philosophical thought. That said, it is also helpful to see how philosophical themes have been appropriated by popular culture: films by Ingmar Bergman, plays by Isak Ibsen, literary works by Franz Kafka. And although written for comedic effect, Woody Allen's films largely deal with existential themes.

What is existentialism then? For the most part, the philosophers who we identify with this kind of method are responding to the objectivity and certainty of thought generated by the thinkers of the modern period—a period that also coincided with a rise in science and scientific explanations. From the existentialists' points of view, this increasing focus on science as the fount of answers to all questions has had the effect of pushing the human experience and the human condition further away from philosophy. That is, insofar as natural science—and more recently the social sciences—can tell us what it means to be human, other experiences of the human and that define us as human have been set aside, deemed not worthy of attention. Existential philosophy has two connected tasks—to put the human experience back into the realm of philosophical inquiry and to undo the kind of thinking that emphasizes rational objectivity. To that end, existentialism uses terms like *authenticity, dread, despair, alienation, freedom, being,* and so forth. Most recently, existential philosophers have taken up more diverse themes such as love, emotions, and ethics.

Next to Nietzsche, Sartre is probably among the most famous of existential philosophers, a name that is often heard in popular culture. Although much of Sartre's admitted inspiration came from the German philosopher, Martin Heidegger, the latter rejected not only the term but also claimed that Sartre's work bore little resemblance to his own. Nonetheless, one of the most famous of Sartre's pieces, "Existentialism is a Humanism," outlines the basic themes of this philosophical position. For Sartre, one of the most important existentialist claims "existence before essence" means that we are born and then we make ourselves through our choices. In his earliest writings, Sartre believed in a radical freedom, not recognizing social, legal, and physical obstacles that might hinder not only the choices that are presented to us but also the ones we can actually make. While these choices might reflect our commitments and our values, they also inform our commitments and values. We come to understand what those are through a variety of themes and experiences that the existentialists believe are uniquely human. In Heidegger's analysis of human being (what he called *Dasein*), he explored anxiety, death, and nihilism. By using these experiences, Heidegger was able to uncover characteristics of human experience that had been covered over by other ways that science has taught us to talk about ourselves. This scientific approach has left our analysis of human experience—as well as, some might say, the human experience, itself—impoverished. Regardless of whether Sartre's thought is in fact similar to Heidegger's, what remains in common is a desire to call into question philosophy's past and its unhealthy collaboration with science such that science reduced the description of the human to a set of mechanistic functions with no regard for any conception of the human that might stand outside of objective thought.

Resisting the trends in philosophy that cohered with the development of science, existentialism did not develop set theories in social and political philosophy, ethics, aesthetics, or any other part of philosophy related to value. Instead, existentialism developed a new approach to these categories. Existentialism does not provide a theory that tells us what to do, like Kant's categorical imperative. Rather, it reminds us what it means to be authentic, to choose authentically, to be human such that being human also means being in relationship with others (or intersubjective). So, existentialism might require us to ask the following question: "What do the political circumstances in which I find myself ask of me and who am I if I choose to act in this way rather than that way?" And existentialism might insist that it is part of what it means to be human to ask this question.

One last note on the existentialists—as I mentioned above, most would have identified themselves as atheists, and indeed Sartre had trouble reconciling what he perceived to be a contradiction in terms: to believe in a creator and to believe that one is not "anything" before one begins choosing for oneself. How can one be wholly free to choose oneself if there had been a creator who had an idea of what the creation would be and then created it? That question is not for us to answer here. But it is nonetheless interesting to note that Sartre only focused on Christian existentialists, not mentioning Buber for example. It is also interesting to note that although existentialism is not generally accepted in the wider philosophical discipline, the kinds of questions existentialism requires us to ask and the themes with which it has traditionally concerned itself have made their way into the mainstream philosophy. Finally, although Rosenzweig is less known among philosophers who do not specialize in Jewish philosophy, Buber's work, in particular *I and Thou*, is widely known and widely taught and in fact is quoted prominently in Martin Luther King's famous "Letter from a Birmingham Jail."

The Russian Existentialist: Lev Shestov

Lev Shestov was born on January 31, 1866 in Kiev, Russia under the name Lev Schwarzmann. Although he has not gained the stature of Sartre or Camus within French philosophy circles nor did he attain the popularity of those like Buber or Rosenzweig in Jewish philosophy circles, his influence on and connection with these thinkers makes his work worth exploring here. He was born into a family that was culturally active. His father was known for being a free thinker in addition to having a pronounced knowledge of Hebrew and the Jewish tradition. The latter had an impact on Shestov whose later work reflects the tension between Judaism and Christianity. He studied in both Kiev and Moscow and eventually begins the study of law at the University of Moscow, though he finishes those studies at the University of Kiev. He writes a doctoral thesis on the working class legislation in Russia, which is deemed revolutionary and thus rejected. The university accepts his thesis, though he decides not to continue in a career in law. He begins writing philosophical works while also trying to manage his family's textiles business. The stress of doing both leads to a nervous breakdown. He eventually turned the managing of the business over to his two brothers and resumed his writing.

He was a prolific writer who engaged a variety of themes and thinkers. Two of his earliest manuscripts were *Shakespeare and His Critic Brandes* (1898) and *Good in the Teaching of Tolstoy and Nietzsche: Philosophy and Preaching* (1900). In 1921, while in Paris, he wrote an essay on Dostoyevsky that caught the attention of many in the French literary, philosophical, and intellectual circles. He added to that several more essays, which he published as a book. On the strength of this work, he was invited to contribute to the *Revue Philosophique*, edited by Lucien Levy-Bruhl.[1] His essays and books continued to attract positive attention and he had a profound influence on such notable thinkers as Georges Bataille, Albert Camus, and Isaiah Berlin. Yet he remains widely unknown in the contemporary philosophical world. Shestov's work on Nietzsche and Kierkegaard place his thought centrally in the existentialist tradition even if his work resists any classification at all.[2] Yet, of his book on Kierkegaard, Emmanuel Levinas writes of Shestov, he is a Jewish philosopher but he is not a philosopher of Judaism.[3] Thus, we return again to that pesky question—what is Jewish philosophy? Who counts as a Jewish philosopher and is this question different from asking who is a philosopher of Judaism? Given the themes on which Shestov chose to focus his attention, I thought it important to include him and introduce him to readers, letting them decide for themselves what label might be attached to him, if any at all.

Shestov's Philosophy

Although Shestov is considered unique in his approach to existential philosophy such that he studied most of the history of philosophy, the majority of his writings focus primarily on Nietzsche and Dostoyevsky, two of the nineteenth century's central existential thinkers. His own positive thinking is viewed to be closest to that of Søren Kierkegaard, the nineteenth-century Danish philosopher. Just as Kierkegaard positioned himself against Hegel's reason, Shestov positioned himself against the rationality advanced by the German philosopher, Edmund Husserl. Although all the existentialists might be different from each other in their focus, the common thread was their shared attack on reason that is emblematic of modernity, even if also found in the ancients. Shestov traces the problem back to its root—the tree of knowledge in the biblical story of Genesis. His concern is the way that reason has been conceived, in particular viewed as that which has power over both God and humans, conceiving nature as delivering immutable laws that govern nature. This force of reason, Shestov worries, hides the limit of reason, that there are some things reason cannot answer or address. As we will see in the Chapter 6, we often find ourselves in predicaments that cannot be solved or resolved by reason, and yet we defer to reason as if it is the solution to all things. Yet, our very limit as humans, the human condition, if you will, is precisely such that it defies reason. Of more concern to Shestov is the way in which the epistemological rationalism merged with ethical rationalism. And we will see this point raised again the chapters that focus on Emmanuel Levinas.

In his 1937 book, *Athens and Jerusalem,* Shestov locates this merger in Socrates's philosophy as expressed by Plato.[4] Philosophy's hubris lies in its desire to see "the rule of necessity an unconditional, universal, and necessary truth."[5] Shestov's philosophy is then two-pronged. On the one hand, he wishes to criticize this view of reason and on the other hand he advances in its place an irrational theory of freedom, which is not unsurprisingly connected to his views of religion.

He begins by forcing philosophy into two possible categories: philosophy of despair, or rather a philosophy that takes despair as its starting point, and philosophy as beginning in wonder or reason. He links the former to Abraham, Job, and the prophets while the latter he links to Socrates (though really this is Aristotle). If we take the route of existential philosophy—the philosophy of despair—we will be led back to revelation and sacred scripture. Shestov's insight is to recognize not only that rationality or reason cannot lead us out of a despair that is a function of the human condition—some predicaments simply cannot be solved in this manner—but also that despair is the actual result of the structure of what it means to be human. He also recognized that in those moments thought itself is transformed. That is, we change how we think when we find ourselves in a situation that cannot be fixed by thinking. It is not that Job thinks badly; rather he needs to think differently. By focusing on objectivity, a philosophy that focuses on rationality loses sight of the way we are subjectively interested in our world.

Franz Rosenzweig

Franz Rosenzweig was born in 1886 into an intellectually vibrant Jewish home in Cassel, Germany. Although he had initially intended to study medicine, he moved to Freiburg where he studied history and philosophy and ultimately decided to write a dissertation on Hegel—*Hegel and the State*—under his teacher, Friedrich Meinecke. Resisting the influence of German Idealism, Rosenzweig turned away from a view of the human that remains abstract. Among his early intellectual influences, he notes his cousin, Hans Ehrenberg, influenced by neo-Hegelianism, as particularly important. In 1916, after moving to Leipzig, he developed a friendship with Eugen Rosenstock.

Questions that perplexed him from early on, primarily questions about the relationship between self and world, continued to occupy him and appeared again in *The Star of Redemption* and the philosophical essays that relate to those themes. On July 7, 1913, in the midst of a conversation with Rosenstock and Rosenzweig's cousin, Rudolf Ehrenberg, Rosenstock made a pronouncement about Christianity that shook Rosenzweig to his core. Almost 150 years after Mendelssohn wrote *Jerusalem*, in which he defended how one can remain a Jew, that is, why being Jewish is still viable in the Christian Enlightenment, Rosenstock proclaimed that the only real path to reconciling self and world—a reconciliation that Rosenzweig sought—could be found through Christianity. Though not an observant Jew, Rosenzweig was convinced by Rosenstock's claims, and now believed that he must convert to Christianity. Three months later, however, Rosenzweig changed his mind and not only decided to remain Jewish, but also became committed to Judaism. Rosenzweig's biographer, Nahum Glatzer, contends that Rosenzweig's decision not to convert occurred during a Yom Kippur service he attended.

Regardless of his motivation or the circumstances that led to his decision, of significance is that Rosenzweig came to believe, in contrast to Rosenstock's claim, that not only was Judaism a path to the reconciliation of self and world, but also that Judaism offered this path more naturally, that is, more organically than did Christianity. In Rosenzweig's words, "that 'connection of the innermost heart with God' which the heathen can only reach through Jesus is something the Jew already possesses [...] he possesses it by nature, through having been born of one of the Chosen People."[6] Soon after, Rosenzweig began his return to Judaism (*teshuvah*) and one can see the evidence of this return expressed in his philosophical essays. Additionally, his newfound commitment to Judaism enabled him to see the need to reform Jewish instruction, and he founded the Freies Jüdisches Lehrhaus—the Jewish House of Learning. His major works include *The Star of Redemption,* which he began in 1918 and finished in 1919, *Understanding the Sick and the Healthy* (1921), and several central essays, including his 1925 "The New Thinking," an exchange of letters between Rosenzweig and his friend Eugen Rosenstock-Heussy, published as *Judaism Despite Christianity*, and *God, Man, and the World: Lectures and Essays*, the publication of his lecture course on the New Thinking at the Lehrhaus. Rosenzweig suffered from ALS, the muscular disease known by its modern name, Lou Gehrig's disease. He died in Frankfurt, on December 10, 1929.

Reviving Jewish Education

In his address "Upon opening the Jüdisches Lehrhaus," Franz Rosenzweig remarks, "It is to a book, the Book, that we owe our survival—that Book, which we use, not by accident, in the very form in which it has existed for millennia: it is the only book of antiquity that is still in living use as a scroll." A few lines later he laments that with the Emancipation Jewish studying and learning was threatened. Jews could not keep pace with the "rapid extension," and although there is freedom in not being confined to the Jewish ghetto, the Jew now finds "his spiritual and intellectual home outside the Jewish world." As we will see in the next chapter, the French-Jewish philosopher Emmanuel Levinas shared similar concerns regarding Jewish education and assimilation, which he communicated in the essays collected in his book *Difficult Freedom*.[7]

The connection between Levinas and Rosenzweig has been well documented. However, this scholarship focuses primarily on the role Rosenzweig's *Star of Redemption* played as an inspiration for the themes that guide Levinas's analyses in *Totality and Infinity*.[8] Similar to the general neglect that philosophers pay to philosophy of education, there is little scholarship documenting the connection between their thoughts on Jewish education. My aim in this part of the discussion of Jewish philosophy is not to suggest that Rosenzweig's essays influenced Levinas in this same area. Rather, my aim is to signal to readers the nonetheless striking parallel between Rosenzweig's concerns, expressed well before World War II and Nazi Germany, and those expressed by Levinas. Their conclusions, however, are very different, and it is difficult not to consider the time periods and the political events each experienced at the time they wrote. This part of the chapter will focus on Rosenzweig's essays collected in *On Jewish Learning*. These essays include a letter Rosenzweig penned to Martin Buber in 1923 in addition to an exchange between the two philosophers. We might then find it productive to read in tandem their respective views on Jewish philosophy of education.

In his 1917 letter to Hermann Cohen, titled "It is Time: Concerning the Study of Judaism," Rosenzweig explains that the problem with Jewish education is religious schooling as it is manifested in the "largest and most influential sections of our intelligentsia" (*OJL* 28).[9] They have received "their religious instruction from a few years of 'religious classes,' and some High Holiday sermons," thus indicating that Judaism—and its corresponding education—has been reduced to a series of tasks rather than being practiced as an organic part of one's life. We see this concern most clearly when Rosenzweig contrasts the difficulty of developing Jewish religious instruction from that of developing Christian religious instruction. He points out that

> we are not concerned with creating an emotional center of this world to which the student is introduced by other school subjects, but with this introduction into the 'Jewish sphere' which is independent from, and even opposed to, his non-Jewish surroundings. Those Jews with whom we are dealing have abandoned the Jewish character of the home some time during the past three generations, and therefore for them that 'Jewish sphere' exists only in the synagogue. Consequently, the task of Jewish religious instruction is to re-create that emotional tie between the institutions of public worship and the individual, that is, the very tie which he has lost. (*OJL* 28)

In this discussion, Rosenzweig articulates the unique problem facing the Jews. No matter how much the Jews "possess" their own world, this world will always be within another world. It will be a Jewish world within a non-Jewish world.

The problem with assimilation, as Rosenzweig notes, is that in order to become part of the larger world, one must leave the world he or she inhabits. As a result of assimilation, the Jewish world has been reduced to a set of literary documents and rabbinic writings. Yet, while these writings are "a signpost for historical Judaism," Rosenzweig tells us that it is the Jew who still turns to the prayer book who understands what the essence of Judaism is (*OJL* 29). That is, the prayer book is a sign of living Judaism, not simply studying it. Because Judaism must be lived, the Jewish world is not to be viewed as a step on the way to acquiring, or better acquiring, the surrounding world. Significantly, Rosenzweig anticipates Levinas's assertion that although the German can read the Bible in the

German language—like Herder or Luther—"the Jew can understand it only in Hebrew" (*OJL* 30).[10] He focuses on Hebrew with an eye toward what this means in a classroom. He believes that insofar as Jews participate in Hebrew prayer and Hebrew worship they will be part of the continuation of Judaism and will make possible a Jewish world (*OJL* 30).

In the ensuing pages, Rosenzweig lays out his curricular plan for Jewish education, recognizing full well the difficulties he will face implementing it, especially within the context of the German state. The entire structuring of the content and the calendar will be against the backdrop of the Jewish sacred year. The week will be organized by Shabbat, and the year will be organized by the Jewish festivals and holy days. Out of this structure, students will learn Jewish history, scripture, and legends. The topics for learning will emerge organically. Through this method, Rosenzweig believes that the student will learn the Hebrew language not as a dead language but as a living tongue. Language and meaning are co-related; thus it is worse, as Rosenzweig sees it, to learn basic phrases of Hebrew but learn them only in translation. It is like not having learned them at all. His hope is that the schools will restructure their schedule so that instruction in the Christian religion is held on Saturdays, thus releasing the Jewish students to attend the synagogue on those mornings.

Finally, Rosenzweig broaches the topic of the Talmud. He believes it is "improper" that Jewish students are not exposed to this book, which he sees as the unifying book of the Jewish people. The study of this book, in Hebrew and Aramaic, should lead to a talmudic way of thinking; that is, the mind will be cultivated to think in a particular kind of way that corresponds to the complexity of the book itself. After laying the complex plan for a curriculum in Jewish studies, Rosenzweig indicates that the last year of study can be devoted to Jewish philosophy. The hope is that a student who has been exposed to this curriculum will engage with Judaism as something more than just his or her own religion, "but also a spiritual power to be guarded as such in his own life" (*OJL* 41).

Although Rosenzweig recognizes the problems with introducing the content, arranging for students to go to Shabbat services, and so forth, the real problem for Rosenzweig is finding teachers who are trained with a university education. These teachers must be trained in both theology and the science of Judaism. That is, they will be teacher-scholars, on equal footing with the rabbis because of their theological training, yet will also have additional education. These teachers are currently not available. There is no corresponding intellectual in the religious sphere that one finds in Jewish secular life. We can see remnants of this view now where religious thinking is contrasted with scientific thinking, and to be religious carries a pejorative connotation. Contrary to the view that Rosenzweig holds—to engage in this curriculum is precisely to be learned—the religious mind is one that is viewed as decidedly not learned.

Indeed, Rosenzweig astutely observes that all the Jewish literary societies will themselves not succeed unless the basis for reading the accompanying periodicals (e.g., Jewish magazines)—the school—is supported. Without the continuation of a Jewish education that those with education now take for granted, Jewish literary culture has no future. The science of Judaism will be displaced by non-Jewish thinkers, and biblical interpretation that does not rely on knowledge of Hebrew will suffer as a result. All of this knowledge will in turn be applied to a Jewish text that will be watered down such that any Jewish elements will not be readily seen. A Jewish reading of the text will be unknown. The Protestant reading will become dominant in such a way that without Judaism's voice, the dominant reading will appear also to be the "neutral" reading. Additionally, this lack of knowledge about Judaism and Jewish reading renders Judaism vulnerable to internal attacks and criticism that are unwarranted. Rosenzweig advocates for the teacher-scholar who is not burdened by the everyday administrative duties of a rabbi. These teachers should not be discriminated against based on political affiliation. Political affiliation should not become an obstacle to teaching. Rosenzweig notes, however, that what remains the biggest hindrance to the sustaining of Jewish education is still the state, in spite of whatever friendly or supportive words it has offered. Nonetheless at the end of the letter, he professes his hope that the spirit of Judaism will emerge organically from a community committed to this kind of educational curriculum. Citing the title to the letter, the time for this education has come.

If Rosenzweig's letter to Cohen lays out the curriculum necessary for Jewish learning, his 1920 letter to Eduard Strauss, titled "Towards a Renaissance of Jewish Learning," reveals the philosophy that underlies this plan. Rosenzweig begins by stating that it is not more Jewish books or books on Judaism that we need, but more Jewish human beings (*OJL* 55). In the wake of Jewish assimilation, Rosenzweig asks after what it means to be a Jew. To be a Jew does not preclude one from being German, in the way that being German precludes one from being French. Rather, to be Jewish is not to be Christian, not to be heathen. Judaism, as Rosenzweig describes it, is a way of being human, a way that one breathes, a "something that courses through the arteries of our life, strongly or weakly, but at any rate to our very finger tips [...] [it is] a greater or lesser force flooding one's whole being" (*OJL* 56–57). Judaism is not grasped in religious literature, it is not entered as a creed on a civil document (e.g., marriage license), it is not something undergone. For Rosenzweig, Judaism is lived—it is part of one's very being, it is the way that someone comports oneself. One *is* Jewish (*OJL* 58).

Yet Rosenzweig insightfully notes that Judaism is more than simply a way of being. It is also something that stands outside the individual—it existed before the individual and will continue to exist long afterward. It is because of this existence that we have Jewish literature—the body of writings that Judaism comprises. And it is because of this body of writing that Jewish education is at issue. If Judaism were simply a matter of being comported in a certain way, one could be anything; but part of what it means to be Jewish is also to be versed in this literature. He notes that Hebrew does not have a word for reading that does not also include learning (*OJL* 58). To live in the moment is not to read—it is simply to live. It is because we develop into something, that we are projected toward something, that we have books—that we need to learn. The child wants to learn—and she asks; as does the child that is in us, the child that needs to be awakened and developed into a living thing.

Rosenzweig recognizes that Judaism is both lived experience and the experience of learning, of reading, that allows us to develop that lived experience. The child might "practice" an observance of the Sabbath, but it is not enough simply to light candles and say blessings. The child must eventually live life in a certain way and know something about the life that she is living. Life, Rosenzweig tells us, stands between two points, between the past and future. It is the flame of the day that burns toward the future and illuminates the past. The worry for Rosenzweig is that Jewish study and learning are dying among the Jews, and his greater concern is that these things are dying because we have no teaching profession—no scholars and no learning. He laments, "Teaching and study have both deteriorated because we lack that which gives animation to both science and education—life itself" (*OJL* 60).

The emancipation of the Jews and Jewish assimilation created a void between the past and present. Jews no longer live a Jewish life; they no longer live in the present. The gap between those who keep Jewish law and those who do not grows wider and accentuates the difference between Jew and Jew more than between Jew and Gentile (*OJL* 61). More significantly, he notes that the three ways that Judaism was lived have changed radically. The law, the home, and the synagogue in the time of emancipation are no longer the sites of an organic Jewish life. The vast majority of Jews do not adhere to Jewish law, the home is no longer the life force of Judaism, and our occupations are no longer natural extensions of Jewish law and home. Though many will visit the synagogue—for a memorial service or marriage—the synagogue does not "wash over and around" us. Jews have come together in their common struggle for civil rights and in so doing have become apologists for rather than celebrants of Judaism. He thus offers a new model of Jewish education, which he describes as follows:

desires are the messengers of confidence [...] For who knows whether
desires such as these—real, spontaneous desires, not artificially
nurtured by some scheme of education—can be satisfied? But those
who know how to listen to real wishes may also know perhaps how
to point out the desired way [...] For the teacher able to satisfy such
spontaneous desires cannot be a teacher according to a plan; he must
be much more and much less, a master and at the same time a pupil.
It will not be enough that he himself knows or that he himself can
teach. He must be capable of something quite different—he must
be able to "desire." He who can desire must be the teacher here.
The teachers will be discovered in the same discussion room and the
same discussion period as the students. And in the same discussion
hour the same person may be heard as both master and student. In
fact, only when this happens will it become certain that a person is
qualified to teach. (*OJL* 69)[11]

In this description, education transforms those engaged in the
experience, and "real" education occurs in those fleeting moments
in a classroom where listening to others and discussion with others
takes place. For Rosenzweig, it is less important that the desire be
satisfied than that we can meet at the seminar table and that we can
desire in common with others (*OJL* 70).[12]

In his essay "What Does it Mean to Receive Tradition," Martin
Kavka explains that "desires," as Rosenzweig deploys the term
here, refers to the desire to possess something whole, to become
whole, and that confidence, as Rosenzweig states, is the position of
readiness, to be prepared for the future without having a map of
that future. Kavka concludes that for Rosenzweig, confidence means
"this faith that desire can bear fruits, that a link to the past is really
possible."[13] Although Rosenzweig's interest focused on adult Jewish
education, and thus the text at the seminar table is a Jewish text,
it is not out of bounds to argue that the goal of both K–12 and
higher education is similar to what I find in Rosenzweig's view of
education—education in a profound way aims to enflame and free
the mind.

Younger contemporaries of Hermann Cohen, Franz Rosenzweig (also a student of Cohen) and Martin Buber exchanged a series of letters on this topic. It is worth looking at their exchange, which exemplifies the fundamental importance of Jewish education not only to the development of a sophisticated mind, as we see argued in Rosenzweig's essays, but also to the development of a Jewish humanism as we see in Buber's. Emmanuel Levinas blends the two and comes to see that given the complexity of morality and politics, one cannot have Jewish humanism without also having the sophisticated mind to respond to the multitude of human crises. In his essay on Rosenzweig's Lehrhaus, Glatzer notes that "Rosenzweig aimed at more than imparting information on Jewish topics; the audience, accustomed at best to a passive enjoyment of lectures, should be taught to participate actively, to feel personally challenged by the texts before it."[14] One such course was related to his "New Thinking."

Four years after publishing *The Star of Redemption*, Rosenzweig wrote an essay called "The New Thinking," in which he attempted to clarify themes published in the dense book.[15] It is not clear that the explanatory essay succeeds where the book initially did not, and indeed as he stated, he did not intend the essay to be read in lieu of the book. It was not meant as a shortcut. In between the publication of these two texts, Rosenzweig offered a lecture course in the Freies Jüdisches Lehrhaus in which he would try to explain the themes found in the *Star* but without the technical or philosophical language characteristic of that work. As commentator Barbara Galli notes, there is a striking parallel between the three parts of the lecture course and the *Star*.[16] For the purposes of this book, we will focus on the description of the themes found in the lecture course, which are more easily summarized than a reading of the *Star* would allow.[17]

The lecture course was presented in three parts: "Science of God"; "Science of Man"; "Science of the World." "Does God exist?" is the question that occupies the first lecture course. Rosenzweig opens this discussion with a mother and child each answering the question differently. The mother represents a strict empirical view that leads to atheism—she cannot see God, and thus, God must not exist. The child on the other hand represents faith; he responds to her, but yes there is one (NT 37). Rosenzweig indicates that they are both correct: "If we don't succeed in making her *see* God, then we may not affirm that 'but' of the child" (NT 37). Thus, Rosenzweig's task to make God as "visible" to his students as what they "*experience* of life" (NT 40).

The question that occupies the second lecture is not does man exist—that is a given. Rather, the question pertains to the essence of man existentially: Is man free or bound? "Do I have a choice? Am I responsible for my actions?" (NT 64). In other words, what is the human like? Here, Rosenzweig considers one of the most perplexing philosophical questions. What does it mean to have being and to be responsible for that being such that freedom and the responsibility for the choices that one makes, makes sense? To explain the problem, he recounts the paradox: My actions flow out of my Being precisely when they are my actions. Am I responsible for my Being? We could easily wind up in an infinite regress that raises questions about creation, the beginning, identity, and responsibility. Rosenzweig answers the question by asserting that this freedom is not my freedom per se but the freedom of God operative in me.

What does this mean? For Rosenzweig, and we will see resonances of this kind of phrasing in both Buber and in Levinas, there is a fundamental intersubjectivity that defines the I. I am I because I say I to a you. Indeed the I only makes sense because I address you. My "I will," which reveals pure presence, becomes "I must." The move Rosenzweig makes in this course is to demonstrate how God, man, and world—initially thought of as isolated and unrelated—are in fact fundamentally related. The human being is free but in a particular kind of way—in his choice to be alone with God.

In the final course, Rosenzweig indicates to his students that the question with which they are now concerned is "What is the world like?" Is the world really as it appears to us? We can ask if the world goes away when I close my eyes. Is there nothing? Or something? If the latter, what is that if I do not perceive it? What remains when I am not perceiving the world? At its most basic level, Rosenzweig is asking after the question of reality.

Martin Buber

Martin Buber was born in Vienna, Austria, in 1878. His mother left the family when Buber was three years old, leaving him to be raised by his grandparents until he was fourteen when he returned to live with his father and his father's new wife. While living with his grandparents, Buber was surrounded by two people in whom he recognized a love of words and the word. He lived a comfortable life and enjoyed a childhood where his grandparents were respected in both the Jewish and non-Jewish communities in which they interacted. He was educated mostly at home where he learned French, Latin, and Hebrew. Later he enrolled in a gymnasium populated mostly by Poles. Although Buber points out that he was shown no intolerance by the non-Jewish students, he does indicate that the morning prayer and "signing of the cross" had such an impact on him that he developed a staunch aversion to missionary endeavors (*IT* 1923, 3). At age 14, with an intellect in the process of development, he immersed himself in the study of philosophy, in particular, the ideas of time in Nietzsche and Kant. He enrolled in the University of Vienna and studied widely. From there he went to Leipzig where he encountered Zionism. In 1938, five years after Hitler came to power, Buber immigrated to Israel after receiving a faculty position at the Hebrew University in Jerusalem. He died on June 13, 1965.[18]

Buber's *I and Thou*

In 1963, writing to his fellow clergymen from a Birmingham prison where he was confined for civil disobedience for protesting racial segregation, Martin Luther King, Jr., penned these words:

Segregation, to use the terminology of the Jewish philosopher Martin Buber, substitutes an 'I it' relationship for an 'I thou' relationship and ends up relegating persons to the status of things. Hence segregation is not only politically, economically and sociologically unsound, it is morally wrong and sinful.

King wrote these words forty years after Martin Buber's *I and Thou* first appeared in Germany, and they aptly describe the dehumanizing effects of racial segregation that King spent much of his adult life protesting.

Nearly fifty years after King wrote his letter, Buber's *I and Thou* remains a classic text not only in Jewish philosophy but in philosophy classes more generally. Although not necessarily Buber's aim, the book is frequently appropriated to describe the human life in existential terms. This text is one of the few texts central to Jewish philosophy that has not only ecumenical appeal, but also secular appeal. Excerpts from this book are frequently anthologized in edited collections of philosophy readings and with a widely intended audience, ranging from first year college students to graduate students.

Divided into three parts and fewer than 130 pages, *I and Thou* leads readers through Buber's original and persuasive description of the multiple ways a subject, an I, can be in relationship. The discussion in *I and Thou* turns on two distinct word pairings: "I-It" (*Ich-Es*) and "I-Thou" (*Ich-Du*). The word combinations signify that we always stand in relation. What remains in question is how we are in relation and to what. More significantly, Buber is also interested in what the I is like when it is involved in these different kinds of relations. That is, it is not only that the "it" in the relation is perceived as an "it" and thus treated accordingly, but also that the "I" changes depending on how the other part of the relation is identified. Referring back to his emphasis on dialogue, the whole of the relationship is categorized differently depending on the I-Thou/I-It pairing. The I-Thou is dialogical while the I-It is characterized by monologue. The first part of the book describes how these two relationships take shape. In an I-It relationship, the I defines the It.

The I treats the It as an object that can be manipulated, defined, controlled, managed. "It" exists for me. More importantly is how the I is understood in this kind of relation. In the I-It relation, the I sees the It as existing only for the I and the I's experiences. In contrast, the I-Thou relation is dialogical and thus the I sees the thou as boundless, uncontainable, not defined by the I, but rather in a relation such that the center lies between the two, as fundamentally part of the two. The center of experience arises because of the relation between the I and thou, and more importantly, this relation is recognized by the I. Thus, here, Buber emphasizes the reciprocity that is fundamental to the I-Thou relation. The relationship not only affects the thou, but also the thou affects the I.

Our relations exist in three different spheres: our life with nature, our life with other human beings, our life with spiritual beings (*IT* 1923, 6). Buber begins with the example of a tree and the different ways in which an I can experience a tree: I can look at it like it is a picture; I can perceive it as producing wind; I can classify it as a species to be studied; I can subdue it. In all these ways, I still see the tree as an object. It is also possible, however that when I consider the tree I become bound up in it, not seeing it as something separate, something to be studied, but something with which I am in relation. Does it have consciousness, Buber asks? He is not to know. But this is not the salient question. The encounter the I has with the tree is of a different order than the experience one has when one studies it. We will see later that this view of the tree is not much different from how Levinas understands the problems posed by the social sciences. The study of the tree led to the study of the human such that the human is broken down and stripped of all that is in fact human. It is possible that Buber is getting at a similar point. Insofar as one can be in relation with a tree as an I-Thou, he seems to indicate that there is the possibility of encountering the tree as a tree and to do this is not to study it or subdue it; it is not to stand apart from it. To truly enter into a relationship with a natural object, e.g., a tree, or a non-human animal, e.g., a cat, would mean not to see it as a scientist sees it—as simply a collection of attributes and parts—but as a singular being.

Two points need to be made before continuing with the summary. The first point is that the I-Thou relation is momentary in its purity. Just as an I can enter an I-Thou relationship with a non-human object, so too can the I's relationship with a thou slide away into a relationship with an it. As Zachary Braiterman observes, the tree is "not fixed and frozen, but precisely the opposite [and] subject to the flow of time and place."[19] The only relationship that is always only I-Thou is the relationship with spirit. It is the only relationship in which the thou can never become an it. What does Buber mean by spirit? This is not an easy question to answer, although the most common and probably the most compelling way to answer this question is that spirit refers to God, or the divine. Additionally, Buber tells us that the relation can lead to meeting (*Begegnung*, sometimes translated as "encounter"). But Buber tells us, this meeting happens through grace. It cannot be forced or planned. This meeting is not something that I direct. Rather it happens because a thou enters into a direct relation with another thou, and thus each part of the relation is simultaneously I and thou: "I become through my relation to the *Thou*; as I become *I*, I say *Thou* […] All real living is meeting" (*IT* 1923, 11).

Insofar as this kind of encounter and indeed relation is considered reciprocal, one can easily raise questions about the possibility of the I-Thou relation as it applies to the human and nature. Is it possible to engage in a reciprocal relation with a tree? A rock? A cup? The case for relations with animals can be made more easily insofar as a relation with an animal has an effect on the I. What cannot be said is if an animal can be an I—can an animal be in relation with a Thou? The third realm is often the most difficult to grasp. It is not clear if Buber means God or something else. Yet, what seems clear is that the I becomes an I through the relation with thou. That is, God or spirit is found in the relation, in the in between as it were. Buber emphasizes that not only is God found in the in between, but the in between, which requires two parts who meet, is the fundamental goal. In contrast to the Eastern view of the self, which is a self turned inward to find spiritual life, Buber emphatically declares that it is only in the relationship with another that we find the divine

(*IT* 1923, 89). The divine is neither outside of us nor inside of us but in the meeting. Moreover, reality is determined by action (*IT* 1923, 90). Just as the Western philosophers of modernity lived under the illusion of the I as solitary and independent, Buddhism rests on a similar mistake regarding the individual.

> All doctrine of absorption is based on the colossal illusion of the human spirit that is bent back on itself, that spirit exists in man. Actually spirit exists with man as a starting point—between man and that which is not man. In renouncing this its meaning, its meaning as relation, the spirit that is bent back on itself is compelled to drag into man that which is not man, it is compelled to make the world and God into functions of the soul. This is the spirit's illusion about the soul. (*IT* 1923, 93)

Buber's discussion that follows this passage indicates the profound way in which he sees the I bound up with the thou. There is no turning back on itself that then reveals reality or spirit. Rather, all this turning back serves is an illusion that one can be removed from the world rather than the recognition that one is bound up with the other in the world. There is no world or life that is separated from man or God (*IT* 1923, 95): "He who truly goes out to meet the world goes out to God" (*IT* 1923, 95). A few pages later, Buber refers to God's revelation on Mt. Sinai, when God speaks with Moses in reference to himself. The standard translation of Exodus 3:14 and the one used in Buber's earlier version of *I and Thou* is "I am that I am." But between 1923 and 1926 Buber worked with Rosenzweig on a new translation of the Hebrew Bible into German. Together they concluded that this phrase meant something more, and the previous translators had not captured what this more was in their now common phrasing. Buber and Rosenzweig believed instead that God announcing itself implied presence, and that a better translation was "I will be there such as I will be there." As one commentator notes, this small yet crucial change in translation also changes how one is in relationship to or with God.

Important for our summary, however, is that for Buber the meeting with God is not about God. The goal of this meeting is not so that man might or will concern himself with God. Rather, it is to confirm that there is meaning in the world (*IT* 1923, 115). To take this one step further, it is so that man will concern himself with the world (*IT* 1923, 115). One way to think about Buber's point is to consider how one understands the narratives in the Hebrew Bible—are they about God or the people? A Jewish reading might require us to focus less on God and more on the characters—Who are they? What do they do? What should they do? What can we learn from them?

Resembling the existential philosophers who were writing at the same time, Buber's discussion of the human subject is described in terms of development. The I is an ongoing process or achievement, one that must be cultivated and one that is determined or influenced by the relations that one has. The self can become either more whole, more unified, or it can become more fragmented. The former happens through the I-Thou relation, through an emphasis on the intersubjective, the dialogical. Through this kind of relationship, one develops as a whole person. Buber's discussion emphasizes the importance of the I-Thou relation and privileges it.

Recalling the philosophical influences on his thinking, readers can see an unsurprising similarity that Buber's approach to ethics has with that of the eighteenth-century German philosopher, Immanuel Kant. In Kant's *Groundwork to the Metaphysics of Morals*, the kingdom of ends describes a society in which all are treated as ends in themselves. We ought not, Kant says, treat others solely as a means to an end. He recognized, as did Buber, that it is impossible not to treat others occasionally as a means to an end—a waiter brings you a meal, a taxi driver drives you to a destination, a construction worker builds you a house. Yet the emphasis is on "solely." We ought to treat others also as an end in themselves, recognizing the dignity and worth of the other person.

As similar as these two philosophies sound, however, Buber's starting point differentiates his ethical stand from Kant's in crucial ways. First, Kant's emphasis was on the "ought." How ought we act given the intrinsic worth of the other person? Buber's, more similar to Levinas's writings, emphasizes the ontological structure of humanity as one that is actualized through the relation to the other person. It is not that I treat the other as a thou because my own rationality indicates my dignity and thus the dignity of other rational creatures. Rather, who I am, what I hope to be, is bound up with the kind of relation I am in with the other person.

To get a clearer sense of what Buber means by "dialogue" we can turn to his 1932 essay of the same name. In this essay, he provides an example that helps illustrate this term. He asks us to imagine two men sitting next to one another. They do not speak or look at each other. They know little about each other, though they have gotten to know each other somewhat on their travels that morning. One man's disposition indicates that he is really there, that he is ready to listen. The other holds himself in reserve. But then something happens and his reserve is lifted. "Communication streams from him and the silence bears it to his neighbor," and his neighbor receives it unreservedly. He knows not what happened and even though the "communication" was wordless, it is what Buber calls dialogue.[20]

Later in this same essay, Buber takes up the question of responsibility. As if responding to those who would say his I-Thou relation resembles the second formulation of Kant's categorical imperative, Buber is quick to say that the "the idea of responsibility is to be brought back from the province of specialized ethics, of an 'ought' that swings free in the air, into that of lived life. Genuine responsibility exists only where there is real responding" (*MBR* 194). As we will see, Levinas will use this phrasing, which appears in multiple places, to express his own form of responsibility, a responsibility that some have argued is simply an interruption. As we see later with Levinas's appropriation of Buber, responsibility implies a real response—yet, as Buber asks, "Responding to what?" And one can ask, responding in what way? What does it mean to respond?

In a curious passage of *I and Thou*, Buber writes, "You cannot make yourself understood with others concerning it, you are alone with it. But it teaches you to meet others, and *to hold your ground* when you meet them" (*IT* 1923, 33, emphasis added). The passage is curious because it appears to be an attempt to mark the I-Thou relationship in particular ways, to circumscribe it or limit it, to indicate that while meeting is important, while real listening and responding are important, this relationship is not one of self-denial, nor of martyring oneself. It is not self-sacrifice or an unreflective altruism. This passage returns us to the question of responsibility and response—responding to what, to whom, and how? Rather, to respond is to know to whom one is responding, what the situation demands, and what is required of a self, including the possibility that one must be responsible to oneself. Indeed, Buber uses the example of Nazi Germany to illustrate his point.

In contrast to Mahatma Gandhi's call for pacifism directed at the Jews, Buber replies that Gandhi's call indicates a profound lack of understanding regarding the Nazi plan. The resistance that was so effective for Gandhi was effective in large part because it was public, and the response to that resistance was public. The world watched and the perpetrators felt shame, or at least responded to public opinion, even if for purely pragmatic reasons. This was not the case with Nazi violence against Jews, which took place largely out of the line of sight of the world. There were no witnesses, who were not also victims, to speak out against the Nazis; to do as Gandhi suggests and succumb to the Nazi violence willingly, would not have garnered sympathy from the world; it would have simply made the Nazi's job that much easier.

In a letter to Mahatma Gandhi, dated February 24, 1939, Buber parses the difference between the oppression of Indians that led to Gandhi's response and the violence directed at Jews and Judaism under the Nazi regime.[21] In this letter, Buber indicates that while many of the incidents appear to be similar, if only in larger quantity in Nazi Germany, they are in fact different. The violence directed at Jews was also directed at Judaism—the burning of synagogues and sacred scrolls. Buber responds to Gandhi's negative reaction to the Jewish call for a state by asking Gandhi if he would feel the same about India, should India experience the same kind of diaspora which in turn involved the sharing of India with another nation. Buber asks if Gandhi is not in bad faith when he goes to South Africa to speak to the Indian population living there with the reality of India and the 200 million people that inhabited it at the time. In other words, Buber is asking if Gandhi is really listening, if he really understands what it means to be a Jew persecuted in Nazi Germany and if his application of passive resistance is too quick and easy a solution that did not require him to imagine in any sophisticated way how these situations might be different from each other. In closing that letter, Buber writes, "we should be able even to fight for justice—but to fight lovingly."

Like many Jewish thinkers writing in the wake of Nazi Germany, several of Buber's writings reflect the simultaneous despair for the situation and the hope for the future. Buber, like we will see with Levinas, deposits his hope in the future generations even as he knows that the future generations have their own precarious relationship to Judaism. He is led then to reexamine this relationship and what the Jewish community might do to encourage its youth to become stronger, more active members of the religion. In his 1941 essay "Hebrew Humanism," Buber admits that he had written his 1933 essay "Biblical Humanism" in response to Nazi Germany and as a call to strengthen the spirituality of the Jewish youth (*MBR* 158–66).

Education

As if anticipating those who would ask, "Why *Hebrew* humanism?," Buber replies that he wishes for this emphasis to encompass something more than the intellect, though the intellect is not excluded. He wishes for the whole of humanity to be included, for a movement that "will encompass all of life's reality" (*MBR* 159). He recognizes those who would ask if a human pattern developed under one set of conditions in a particular period of time can be applied to or could be appropriate to patterns of life in another time. It is no different from asking if parts of the Hebrew or Christian Bibles are still relevant today. Buber replies that they are, but he is clear that although the Bible may have many features to offer—literary, historical, and so forth—of interest to him is the normative value of the human pattern that is exhibited through the Hebrew Bible. For Buber, it is a matter of discerning those features of the Hebrew Bible that are constrained by time and place from those that transcend it. The normative value transcends the Hebrew Bible.

Buber opens "Biblical Humanism" by recalling that twenty years earlier he had convened a group of Jews who were interested in Jewish education. Their task was to consider how one would fashion a human being with new Jewish dignity (*MBR* 46). This humanism, this new Jewish dignity, returns him to the Hebrew Bible for the source of those values. It is in this essay that Buber distinguishes between a Hebrew man and a biblical man. The Hebrew man is the one who lets "himself be addressed by the voice that speaks to him in the Hebrew Bible and who responds to it with his life" (*MBR* 47). A biblical humanistic education, then, means the fulfillment of not only the Hebrew language but also Hebrew being. If humanistic education aims at transforming individuals through language, biblical humanistic education aims at the same thing but through a difference of kind with regard to the manner in which speaking is enacted. If Western humanistic education aims to transcend the time and the problems in which it is learned, biblical humanistic education seeks to return the individual precisely to those problems, to become attentive to them, "to stand fast in them [...] Thus would biblical humanism declare a rebirth of the normative primal forces of Israel" (*MBR* 50).

Buber opens his 1939 essay "The Education of Character" with the statement that "education worthy of its name is essentially education of character."[22] His statement reflects a theme that runs throughout his writings—that of the overall person, of unity, of wholeness. Thus, this statement reflects that when one educates, one is teaching and educating a whole person. And yet as Buber makes this claim, he also realizes that there are limits to what an educator can do in this capacity. Aiming at the development of character is of a different order than for example explaining algebra, which Buber suggests is something that can be explained even to children who seem least able to grasp it. But aiming at the development of character is fundamentally problematic. It is not a matter simply of explaining, as it is with algebra, which students can grasp even if only in a rudimentary way. Even if students *understand* that lying can destroy one's life, that bullying the weak is mean and wrong, that envy is an ugly expression toward another, this understanding will not necessarily form or transform character. It will not necessarily lead to the development of a person who has a well-formed character and thus acts rightly.

As Buber points out, the difficulty in this kind of education lies at a deeper level. When he tells his students of his aim to teach them something like algebra, eager eyes await his instruction. There is no need to hide what the aim of the instruction is. However, when it is apparent to the students that he aims to alter or cultivate their character, the shields are engaged, resistance immediately sets in. Yet unlike the tutor we find in Rousseau's educational treatise, *Emile*, Buber warns against being deceptive. Not only will it not be effective simply to hide this intention, but education itself would be undermined by this kind of duplicity. While not sufficient, what is fundamentally necessary is the relation between teacher and student and how this relation is established. The most important dimension is the confidence that the pupil has in the teacher, and by this, Buber also means a kind of trust that the pupil, needing guidance on the right thing to do, can approach the teacher with a question. It is at this point, when the pupil approaches the teacher, that the teacher is opened to the possibility of educating character.

This education is not formed by argument. And in one sweeping moment, Buber dismisses Kant and those whose education of character derive from Kant's philosophy as a useless endeavor for the education of character. Education of character can be neither a system of maxims nor a system of habits. Rather, one must act with the whole of one's substance. Although there are all sorts of similarities and differences that allow one to generalize or draw from maxims and habits that one has learned, it is that which makes each situation unique that cannot be captured by rules or past practice: "It demands nothing of what is past. It demands presence, responsibility; it demands you" (*MBR* 114). And in what one might call the most eloquent formulation of education, Buber writes:

> I call a great character one who by his actions and attitudes satisfies the claim of situations out of deep readiness to respond with his whole life, and in such a way that the sum of his actions and attitudes expresses at the same time the unity of his being in its willingness to accept responsibility [...] And one might perhaps say that for him there arises a unity out of the situations he has responded to in responsibility, the indefinable unity of a moral destiny. (*MBR* 114)

For Buber the education of character implies that one recognizes that responsibility calls each of us individually. Where maxims are abstract and command a third person who is yet unidentified, responsibility is for each of us individually in the situations in which we continually find ourselves being addressed by another person. And education begins with the possibility of cultivating the person so that she is filled with this responsibility rather than becoming one with a sterile soul. Returning us to Buber's discussion in *I and Thou*, Buber ends this essay with the following statement: "The educator who helps to bring man back to his own unity will help to bring him again face to face with God" (*MBR* 117).

In his 1951 essay "Society and the State," Buber makes explicit the connection between the development of the state and the educational process that brings citizens into that state.[23] The essay, a condensed whirlwind tour of the history of political philosophy from Plato's *Republic* to Hegel's *Philosophy of Right*, argues that the problem common to political philosophy is its inability to distinguish between social and political principles. Buber points to Plato's *Republic* as the classic example illustrated by the conflation of a division of labor with a categorization of those who rule and those are ruled. That is, the economic—or social—conditions of the polis determined by a division of labor are then converted into a justification, or rather are confused with a system of governance—who rules, who is ruled. It is not simply that there is the guardian group that rules over the others, this group is separated from both private property and private marriage, raised above the general community into a separate society (*PW* 162).

The concern that Buber expresses throughout this essay is the confusion between political principles and social principles. The first outlines the role that both the rulers and the ruled play, while the second outlines the social organization of the people. Although they are virtually inseparable, they are not the same, and Buber believes much confusion in discussions about the state stem from this originary conflation of principles. By confusing the two principles, individuals ruled over by others is a situation confused with social cohesion and community. In essence, Buber's point can be framed in the following way. Society comprises a variety of different groups united for different reasons: habit, custom, way of thinking, and so forth. Yet, as the different societies come into conflict with each other, there is a need for the state to enter and "keep the peace" as it were. The state, then, resembles a unifying force, but this is misleading. If societies were able to keep the peace among themselves, there would be no need for the state: A permanent state of true, positive, and creative peace between the peoples would greatly diminish the supremacy of the political principle over the social. Thus, because so much of the state's energy is exerted to keep up this illusion of unity and because the different social groups have been subsumed under the state's power, the political principle has given the illusion of this supremacy. Buber wants to reverse this thinking such that the real communal dimension of society emerges as most significant. What would happen, his essay asks, if there were real cooperation among groups, among nations, among peoples? His essay concludes with the following:

Will Society ever revolt against the 'political surplus' and the accumulation of power? If such a thing were ever possible, only a society which had itself overcome its own internal conflicts would ever venture to embark upon such a revolution; and that is hardly to be expected so long as Society is what it is. But there is a way for Society—meaning at the moment the men who appreciate the incomparable value of the social principle—to prepare the ground for improving the relations between itself and the political principle. That way is Education, the education of a generation with a truly social outlook and a truly social will [...] social education is the exact reverse of political propaganda [...] True education for citizenship in a State is education for the effectuation of Society. (*PW* 175–76)

Buber's own interest in communal living and his belief that such a community has not yet been manifested, leads him to advance a view of education that promotes the social self. He believes that such a society is not simply an ideal—not simply utopian—but possible. It is something toward which we can and should work, but we cannot do this without transforming the way we understand the relationship of the social to the political and then changing the way we educate in light of that understanding. Where the previous philosophers focused on the nation-state and the educational process that brings someone into the polis, Buber separates the social from the political and then inverts the significance of the two by emphasizing the social and pulling the curtain back from the political—the power of the political lies only in our need for it to govern over the social groups that live inside and outside its boundaries.

The Gendered Subject

In her essay "Dependency and Vulnerability: Jewish and Feminist Existentialist Constructions of the Human," Leora Batnitzky offers an interesting analysis of the way in which both Buber and Rosenzweig offer an account of the human that is not only dependent and vulnerable but also described in gendered terms.[24] I am going to present Batnitzky's argument briefly. Batnizky observes that Rosenzwieg's reliance on gender is most blatant in Book 2 of Part 2 of *The Star of Redemption*. Here, Rosenzweig offers a reading of the Song of Songs that moves between both an abstract account of the feminine and also a reference to real women. She notes the contradiction that arises from comments that Rosenzweig makes between the beginning of this section and remarks he makes further on. Early in the section, Rosenzweig's references to the lovers suggest that he is referring to actual men and women. However, later observations suggest that the roles of masculine and feminine lover are not confined to real men and women. Contrary to how he frames the passage from the Song of Songs early in this section of the *Star*, Rosenzweig suggests that male and female are being used metaphorically. Batnitzky maintains that the argument Rosenzweig makes with regard to real women is "intimately connected to the argument that [he] makes in Part Three, about the reality of the Jewish people. Real women, who are not reducible to a metaphorical 'feminine,' function for Rosenzweig in this text as a foil for real Jews" (Batnitzky 2000, 138–40). Batnitzky continues, a woman is always already prepared for eternity "just as the Jewish people are a priori eternal" (140). She notes that although Rosenzweig does explicitly reference maternity, as Levinas after him does, he expresses his understanding of Judaism through a reference to pregnancy, tying it not only to women but also to nature and blood (140–41). Here Batnitzky reminds her readers that the reference to the blood community is made in explicit contrast to Judaism as a community of land. Finally, the role of the feminine here also serves as a way to contrast Judaism and Christianity. Where Judaism is defined in terms of the feminine, Christianity is masculine, birthed by Judaism. Yet because of the tie Christianity must maintain to Judaism, Judaism forces Christianity to become evermore feminine, Jewish, and ethical (141–42).

Following her analysis, Batnitzky notes the concerns that arise from such a gendered notion of Judaism. First, this kind of account does not allow for differences that are in fact different. She notes that while the use of a dependent and vulnerable subject is philosophically important to recasting a view of ethics, this view is undermined when it is gendered, and more specifically when it is defined in terms of the feminine. In spite of this potential problem, however, Batnitzky does offer that feminist philosophers might benefit from looking at Jewish philosophers and in particular how and why they utilized a gendered account of the subject that is in deep contrast to the one typically offered through modern Western philosophy. Here Batnitzky points out how that subject has typically been white, male, and Protestant—the last part of which is typically overlooked, even by feminist philosophers, thereby overlooking the way that religion has also figured the subject in the history of philosophy. Yet, even if we wish to take issue with the idea that the subject is feminine, even if positively portrayed, the examination of this subject might be put in productive tension with the subject as normally envisaged in Western philosophy.

At the end of her essay, Batnitzky redirects her readers to Hermann Cohen's philosophy and argues that his ethical Socialism might provide a more useful model than the one offered by Buber, Rosenzweig, and Levinas (an account we will get to in the next chapter). Batnitzky points out that in spite of Cohen's deep reliance on a neo-Kantian framework that emphasizes consciousness, and which is rejected by the existentialist thinkers, he would nonetheless be a useful resource for feminist thinkers. But she believes that returning to his conception of compassion, which in fact serves as the basis for the thought of these three philosophers, might be a way to deliver an ethical project that is not reliant on the gendered conception of the subject, one that emphasizes problematically, even if positively, a view of the feminine that essentializes women.

It nonetheless makes sense that Batnitzky would focus her attention initially on Rosenzweig, Buber, and Levinas, whose philosophical position, which more closely resembles existentialism and in that sense provides a critique of modern philosophy, offers a more fruitful engagement with themes that have become central in feminist philosophy. Buber's I-Thou relation—which fundamentally implies intersubjectivity—undercuts a modern view of the self that is often viewed as autonomous and self-sufficient. Similarly, Rosenzweig also presents an account of the self that is in conversation. Both point to a view of the human that is vulnerable and dependent. Even if these are terms that feminist theorists wish to contest as defining features of the feminine, they nonetheless point to a view of the human subject that is in relationship with others. Additionally, the many other themes that we see both Buber and Rosenzweig encounter, in particular, education, Zionism, and violence, also point to dimensions of our lives that are more commonly found among the existential theorists of the time—the need for philosophy to engage concerns that are central to human existence and human subjectivity.

4

Emmanuel Levinas
and Abraham Joshua Heschel

Response to Modernity

Levinas was born on January 12, 1906, in Kovno, Lithuania, a country where, as he explains, "Jewish culture was intellectually prized and fostered and where the interpretation of biblical texts was cultivated to a high degree" (interview with Richard Kearney).[1] In 1915 the Jews of Lithuania were expelled by government decree, and his family moved to the Ukraine, returning to Lithuania in 1920 where Levinas finished his early schooling. In 1923 he left for France and enrolled at the University of Strasbourg, studying under a number of professors, including Charles Blondel and Maurice Halbwachs. It was here that he met Maurice Blanchot, who would not only become his life-long friend but also a person instrumental in saving his family during the Nazi war years. Intending to study with the German phenomenologist, Edmund Husserl, Levinas left Strasbourg for Freiburg (1928–29) but he discovered Martin Heidegger while he was there.

In 1930 Levinas returned to France where he became a naturalized citizen.[2] He later credited his French citizenship with saving his life, believing this is why he was sent to a labor camp instead of an extermination camp. In that same year, upon returning to France, Levinas immediately went to work for the *Alliance Israélite Universelle*, an organization founded in 1860 by Adolphe

Crémieux, in response to several recent anti-Jewish incidents in Europe. Its primary aim was to share Jewish education with Jews in the countries of the Mediterranean, primarily in North Africa, e.g., Morocco and Tunis. In 1932 Levinas married his childhood friend Raissa Levy, and together they had two children: Simone, who was born in 1936 before World War II, and Michael, born in 1948, several years after France's liberation.

In 1934 Levinas published "Reflections on the Philosophy of Hitlerism," in the French Personalist journal *Esprit*. It was the first of seven essays to be published in *Esprit* and that together would be classified by the philosopher Howard Caygill as Levinas's political essays. In 1935, just after publishing his essay on the philosophy of Hitlerism, Levinas published a short follow-up essay translated as "On Escape." Then, in 1940, when he was fighting on the side of the French in World War II by serving as an interpreter of Russian and German, his unit was captured. He spent the years between 1940 and 1945 in a labor camp in Germany—Fallingbostel, near Hanover—for Jewish POWs, where he wrote the bulk of *Existence and Existents*. It is said later that he would never set foot in Germany again, taking long detours when he traveled in order to avoid the country.

As soon as he was released from the camps, he returned to France and immediately returned to the AIU. In 1945, he was appointed as a teacher at the *École Normale Israèlite Orientale*, the school that trained the male teachers for the Alliance. In 1946, the same year that he became the director of the school, he gave a series of lectures at Jean Wahl's invitation, which would be published in 1947 as *Time and the Other*. In this same year, he published *Existence and Existents*.

From 1947 to 1951 Levinas studied Talmud with the mysterious Mordechai Chouchani, whom Levinas refers to as "prestigious and merciless." Chouchani also taught Elie Wiesel at the same time. During the 1950s Levinas wrote a series of essays to be published under the title *Difficult Freedom: Essays on Judaism*. The majority of these essays are meditations on themes that correspond to themes in his philosophical work, though with a particular focus on Judaism and Jewish identity. In these essays, we find Levinas struggling with the political issues of assimilation, universalism, parochialism, secularity, Christian supersession, humanism, and Zionism. In 1960 he gave his first talmudic lecture to the Colloquium of French Jewish Intellectuals and gave another almost every year for nearly thirty years. In 1961 he published his first major philosophical book, *Totality and Infinity*, and he accepted his first university position at the University of Poitiers. In 1967 he accepted a position at the University of Nanterre, and then in 1973 he was appointed to a position at the Sorbonne. In 1974 he published his landmark book *Otherwise than Being*. He died on December 25, 1995.

Levinas Contra Paganism[3]

In "Reflections on the Philosophy of Hitlerism,"[4] Levinas reveals the two poles of thinking that provide the context for the tension between immanence and transcendence when both are traditionally understood.[5] His own words indicate that he also saw the dangerous ethical implications of Hitlerism, even if he could not imagine the real horrors it was still to produce. Although he was not to employ the word "ethics" until the 1950s, it is clear from how he frames his concern, that even in this early essay the problem of ethics motivated Levinas from the beginning. He ends this 1934 essay issuing a warning to his readers, even if he has not yet named the problem and even if he is not yet aware of its remedy. This essay also reveals that as early as 1934 Levinas had glimpsed the fundamental difference between Judaism and other modes of religion—the former's emphasis on a relationship to others and the latter's emphasis on self-sufficiency (paganism) or the saving of individual souls (Christianity). If Levinas's concern emerges from his view that the pagan is "sufficient unto himself," then it should not surprise us that his ethical model, which emerges directly out of his reading of Judaism, not only assumes but also privileges a dependent relationship.

Beginning with the ancient Hebrews and the split between the respective abilities of both Judaism and Christianity to deal with atonement and the refashioning of the self, Levinas takes us on a lightning tour of the history of philosophy ending with the dangers of a view of the self that is rooted in blood kinship. For Judaism, there can be forgiveness of past "sins," but the self remains. When Christianity entered, it allowed for a total rebirth such that the history of and the potential impact on philosophical thinking was profound. With noble intentions to establish total equality by determining the self through the soul—there is no race, no sex, and so forth—the materiality that tethered us to this world was also abolished. Yet the self within Christianity still had a past, hence the need for the Eucharist. Set in contrast to the destiny of fate we see in the Greeks, for example, the curse over the house of Atreus, the Eucharist nonetheless made freedom possible and allowed the individual to remake him or herself. Exchanging the mystical drama with reason, and moving the self from a religious to a secular register, the liberalism that emerged from the Enlightenment period offered this freedom to everyone.

Levinas's discussion of liberalism, which offered the sovereign freedom of reason ("Hitlerism," 66), emphasizes how this exchange altered the terms of the game. One can now participate in this equality without having to accept a particular set of metaphysical beliefs, *viz.* the virgin birth, resurrection, or the trinity. Political liberalism promotes a self that is unencumbered by history and seemingly unencumbered by particular characteristics. Its secular alternative to what Christianity promised provides a useful antidote to the religious view of the soul. Yet, in spite of the simplicity of this exchange, the exchange is not complete. Unlike Judaism or Christianity, liberalism claims freedom from one's history and therefore opens up possibilities for choosing one's destiny: logical choices are presented and a dispassionate subject makes those choices ("Hitlerism," 66).

Levinas then turns to Marxism's critique of liberalism, which he claims places limits on the human spirit. Contrary to what was previously thought, the human spirit, which is prey to material needs, does not enjoy pure freedom. Rather than suggest the human spirit transcend these material needs, Marx presents a reversal in the relationship. Marxism attempts to contradict both Christianity and political liberalism but cannot part with the latter insofar as it upholds the principles of 1789 and the Declaration of the Rights of Man. That is, it upholds the basic principles of freedom and equality. But Levinas's analysis reveals that this kind of freedom is a myth and any view of society or a social structure that allows for emancipation with respect to the body is viewed as a betrayal. Any view that promotes this emancipation is viewed as false and deceitful.

Levinas concludes that to confront the power of reason to change the past and create a new destiny, we must have a new view of European man. This task can be accomplished only if the situation to which the European subject was bound was not added to him but formed at the very *foundation of his being*. That is, in Levinas's view, it is not a matter of the liberal subject rethinking itself. Rather, this subject needs to be refashioned. This means a return to a self that negotiates the body without reducing the self to it.

One of Levinas's most interesting observations in this quick tour of intellectual history, lies in his concern about the dangers of skepticism, which emerge ironically from a particular emphasis on reason itself. In his return to liberalism and the view of reason that it produces, Levinas reminds us that in liberalism the freedom of spirit is characterized by the distance reason has from its material needs, from the body and the world in which it lives. It is distant and passionless; it can choose anything. The individual is also free not to make a choice, thus making skepticism possible. That is, the responsibility to make a choice, to act, that accompanied both Judaism and Christianity is absent from liberalism. One can reside in a state of perpetually not choosing. Regardless, even when one does choose, freedom is retained and thus the choice can be undone, the choice can be unmade. Within the choice resides its own negation. One might argue that philosophical existentialism was a way of responding to this danger—a secular way of imposing responsibility on a subject who might see himself as being able to refuse responsibility.

For Levinas, however this inability or refusal to choose makes thought into a game ("Hitlerism," 69). He believes that it is in this inability to choose, this lack of responsibility, that we find the roots of Hitlerism, a philosophy that allows society to be based on blood kinship.

Levinas's critique of both immanence and transcendence reflect his own struggle to maintain some aspect of each. He wants to avoid a view of transcendence that looks to another place and time and thus allows us to ignore the ills that plague humanity on a daily basis. If pure transcendence takes us away from this world, away from the banal, and quite simply, denies the reality that we are riveted to our bodies, that our bodies suffer, and that this suffering demands attention, the turn to materiality does not "fix" the problem. Instead, it simply adds to it. Materiality, though it acknowledges our connection to daily life and to our material needs and therefore the material needs of others, leads to a view of the body that enchains us to it without any hope for escape from it. Thus, it leads to a dangerous view of humanity that is defined by blood and kinship.

This enchainment in turn precludes "man" from seeing his own ability to escape himself. In other words, to believe that we are enchained simply leads to self-deception regarding the choices that we do make, but more importantly, that we can make. What follows from this kind of thinking is a view of the body that becomes a universality that then gives way to expansion. As Levinas remarks, "the expansion of a force presents a structure that is completely different from the propagation of an idea" and this is how universality gives rise to, or allows for, racism ("Hitlerism," 70). The very way in which this power is wielded allows some to be part of it while others are necessarily excluded. This power yields the world of masters and slaves determined by blood and body, in short, the world of Nazi Germany. Levinas's task henceforth is to reconcile a view of transcendence with a view of being chained to one's body. How can we give an account of transcendence that does not dispense with this world, the world of suffering? How can we give an account of the body that does not leave us enchained?[6] Levinas's aim in this essay is to demonstrate how a certain kind of intellectual thinking yields a view that believes society is or should be based on blood kinship. It is not hard then to see how we come full circle from Moses Mendelssohn and the promise of assimilation. Two hundred years later in Nazi Germany this possibility is absent. The limits of the Enlightenment emerge and a fissure in the ethics reason produced cannot be repaired.

Nearly forty years later, in his 1971 essay "Hegel and the Jews," Levinas defends the Jews against Hegel's attack.[7] As is familiar to most of us, neither Christianity nor Judaism is the end of the Hegelian system; they are both steps along the way, being superseded by something else. Levinas observes, however, that while it is true that both are superseded, each is represented quite differently from the other. Christianity, though not necessarily recognizable to some Christians, is also not represented in such a way as to be offensive to them. In contrast to the representation of Christianity, Hegel's critical discourse surrounding Judaism, Levinas notes, has "nurtured anti-Semitism."[8] The most common charge against Judaism, one that is easily found within Hegel's reading, is the view that Judaism is "particular" as opposed to "universal."

The Hegelian rendering of Judaism sets the stage for Judaism to be viewed as particular, while Christianity is viewed as universal, able to accommodate or include anyone. "Hegel and the Jews" was published in 1971, but as we can see from the above discussion, Levinas had already begun to counter these simplistic critiques of both Judaism and materiality in the mid-1930s. Yet what is at stake for Levinas at this point is not simply the critique of Hegel's view of Judaism but his own interest in advancing a positive position that argues for a universal dimension of Judaism. Indeed, Levinas's interest in returning to and promoting a Jewish humanism rests on his view, contrary to Hegel's reading, that fundamental elements of Judaism are in fact universal.[9]

Levinas's most immediate charge that the pagan is "sufficient unto himself" appears to be his central concern and this philosophical and ethical problem occupies his attention for much of the rest of his career. We can see then how his announcement that "there is no one more self-sufficient than Rousseau," at the beginning of his 1935 essay *On Escape,* not only accurately and succinctly characterizes Rousseau, especially if we recall the eighteenth-century French philosopher's thoughts on education,[10] but also continues the discussion he began the previous year. Where Rousseau's philosophy is often emblematic of a kind of mythological freedom to which Levinas's project responds, Levinas also reveals in these early writings the way that our bodies have been overlooked in the development of this mythological freedom.

Yet, one can also see that Levinas would be drawn to Rousseau, whose writings are considered influential to the French Revolution and the development of the French Republic, in part because out of Rousseau's writings emerged a radical polity that granted civil rights to Jews, though admittedly the history of France in the Enlightenment period (and certainly previously) is a history that continues to raise the "Jewish question"—in this case, should the Jews receive full emancipation? Should the Jews receive full civil rights? Regardless, that the Jews were indeed emancipated in law is a fact of history that is not lost on Levinas—indeed he embraces it even as he also expresses his ambivalence about this kind of universalism. Yet, just as Levinas is drawn to Rousseau's influence, he is also able to see what is fundamentally flawed in Rousseau's political project. Wittingly or not, Levinas is able to counter this flaw precisely by turning away from a Western conception of subjectivity and looking to Jewish sources for his answer.[11]

Levinas's writings follow the trajectory that begins with these early essays. In striking contrast to Rousseau's philosophical position, they advance the view that we are essentially dependent on others and this dependence is part of what it means to be human. As we see in his later philosophical writings, especially *Totality and Infinity* and then *Otherwise than Being*, subjectivity is defined by one's ethical response to the other, not by one's freedom or ability to make autonomous decisions. Interestingly, this thread entwines with another, that of his treatment of the feminine. In his early formulation of the ethical relation, the feminine inaugurated the experience of alterity and then developed into a transcendental condition for the possibility of the ethical, i.e., it provided the means for the subject to transcend to the level of the ethical, while not participating directly in the relation.[12]

Levinas ultimately names the feminine, defined as the maternal body, as the paradigm for the ethical relationship itself.[13] However, he does not expect that it is only women who either are or should be capable of ethical response. His use of the maternal as a simile—"the psyche is *like* the maternal body"—assures us of that.[14] Rather, it is the feminine, in this case, the maternal body, that provides him with the best description of that which he cannot otherwise describe—an unwilled, irrecusable responsibility. He uses the feminine to define the ethical, but it is the ethical that defines us, all of us—men and women—as human. Again, in contrast to Rousseau, Levinas's view of subjectivity simultaneously endorses and rejects a rigid emphasis on sexual difference. His philosophical project exploits this originary dependency, revealed by our own primary needs and our original relationship to the maternal body. In contrast to Rousseau's aversion to dependence, dependence forms the ground for Levinas's radical subjectivity and the ethical project based on that subjectivity.

The New Humanism

Levinas introduces his 1968 essay, "Humanism and An-archy," with the following epigraph taken from Nietzsche's *Thus Spoke Zarathustra*: "I love him whose soul is overfull so that he forgets himself, and all things are in him: thus all things become his downfall."[15] In this aphorism, which is part of his teaching, Zarathustra proclaims the need for overcoming the self but also laments the failure to accomplish this task. Levinas uses this epigraph to introduce an essay that opens with this claim: "The crisis of humanism in our times undoubtedly originates in an experience of human inefficacy accentuated by the very abundance of our means of action and the scope of our ambitions" (*HO* 45). How should we understand Levinas's use of the epigraph? Does he agree with it or does he cite it for irony? What is the connection between the epigraph and the "crisis of humanism" that he announces at the beginning of this essay?

Rather than argue that Levinas is taking an opportunity for a gratuitous jab at Nietzsche, I would offer instead that Levinas is nodding at Nietzsche's own awareness of the failure of his project. Or, instead, that like the eighteenth-century philosopher, Jean-Jacques Rousseau before him, Nietzsche displays the ability to identify a problem accurately but the constraints of his own thinking lead him to the natural, even if untenable solution. That is, both Nietzsche and Rousseau offer solutions to problems that on the surface seem correct and even compelling; but they in turn create even more problems. Additionally, Levinas's "Humanism and An-archy" connects a critique of Heidegger's humanism to Zarathustra's self-awareness regarding the ineffectiveness of his own teaching.

Although all three essays collected in *Humanism of the Other* are directed at Heidegger's philosophy, and indeed, the third essay has a section devoted to Heidegger by name, this second essay, "Humanism and An-archy," offers the most pointed critique. Returning to the first sentence of the essay, Levinas announces that the crisis of humanism in our times originates in a belief that we have a certain element of control over our lives, and he links this belief to a view of technology that encourages it. We believe we have control over our lives, that as *rational animals* we are accorded a privileged position in the cosmos. Yet the unburied dead of wars and the death camps betray that view of ourselves and indeed even create an ambivalence, a tragicomic response to the care of ourselves. We cannot control how or when we might die. We *must* care for ourselves and yet our life and death are beyond our control.

In the concluding section of this essay, we find his most compelling statement:

the Ego brought down to Self, responsible in spite of itself, abrogates the egoism of the *conatus* and introduces sense into being. There can be no sense in being except for sense that is not measured by being. Death renders senseless all care the Ego would like to have for its existence and destiny [...] Nothing is more comical than the care for itself taken by a being doomed to destruction, which is just as absurd as questioning, in view of action, the stars whose verdict cannot be appealed. Nothing is more comical or nothing more tragic [...] But the pre-original responsibility for the other is not measured by being, is not preceded by a decision, and cannot be reduced to absurdity by death [...] No one, not even the promisers of religion, is hypocritical enough to claim that he took away death's sting; but we may have responsibilities for which we must consent to death. The Other concerns me despite myself. (*HO* 56–57)

In the above citation, Levinas draws on themes that were first explored almost ten years prior in *Totality and Infinity*. He contrasts the responsibility for others with the temptation of eros. He then describes the temptation as a temptation to play, to enjoy the freedom in being "not my brother's keeper" (*HO* 55). Yet, while he contrasts the two, he also claims that responsibility needs this temptation. He concludes this essay by stating, "Modern anti-humanism may be wrong in not finding for man, lost in history and in order, the trace of this pre-historic an-archic saying" (*HO* 57). One cannot help but think that in addition to responding to Heidegger he is also speaking directly to Rousseau and Nietzsche.

Levinas's humanism as he describes it in these essays is not the anti-humanism of Heidegger, where the human loses its central place. Rather, the central focus here is not on one human but two—one becomes a subject not by virtue of being a free ego, required to make choices. Rather, one becomes a subject in the face of the Other, in response to the ethical claim of the Other. This turn, to put the Other first, needs to become the *guiding condition* of our lives. He describes ethics as not simply that the Other is our concern; rather, we must give up the sovereignty of the ego and the self-certainty of introspection and reflection and turn toward the Other.

We see the connection to Heidegger most clearly in, "No Identity," the third essay in this collection, when he concludes with the view that Heidegger "led the triumph of mathematical intelligibility, sending the subject back into ideology, or else rooting man in being, making him its messenger and poet" (*HO* 61). Yet, if Heidegger is indeed a target in this essay, the social sciences are more so. Continuing the discussion he began in "Humanism and An-archy," Levinas argues that the social sciences have stripped the human of all that is human. Indeed what he wants to say here is that the social sciences, in spite of their own objective, are incapable of measuring or observing the very thing that makes the human: the opening of vulnerability where opening is represented by the stripping of the skin so that it is exposed, the uncovering or the passivity that he mentioned in the previous essay. And we should note that he uses an interesting biblical expression found in Lamentations to make his point about the human as that which is vulnerable: "turning the cheek to the one who slaps him" (*HO* 63). For Levinas, to turn the cheek again, as we find in Matthew, is to make a choice, to deliberately seek suffering or humiliation. But receiving the initial slap reveals the fundamental vulnerability, the primary possibility of suffering, and the "impotence or humility 'to suffer' that is beneath the passivity of submission" (*HO* 64). It is without choice and it defines all of us.

If Levinas's 1934 essay on Hitlerism was prescient, it was so not only because of the violence and inhumanities that came to pass during World War II but also because it signaled a failure of modernity's ethics in its reliance on reason to save us. Levinas concludes that essay with the claim that the very humanity of man is at stake. One could argue that the very definition of the human and how intellectual thought would be influenced for most of the twentieth century were at stake in the 1929 Davos debate between Cassirer and Heidegger, where Levinas initially sided with Heidegger. The question of how these two ideas are related is precisely what Levinas seems to work out in his essays on Jewish education—the humanity of man is contingent on that very definition of man and where and how "man" is positioned in the world.

As novel and interesting, and indeed influential, as Heidegger's thinking is, it would be not only too easy to blame all of the problems of the twentieth century on him, but also inaccurate to do so. It would attribute way too much power to a thinker than is probably warranted. The danger lies not necessarily in the thinker but in the appeal a thinker has to sentiments that may have already emerged and gained traction. And yet, in spite of that influence of Heidegger's thought, Levinas views Heideggerian philosophy as fundamentally hostile to the message of the Hebrew Bible, thus allowing us to posit that his critique of Heidegger is also a critique of that which runs counter to this biblical message (*DF* 281). That is, if Levinas's philosophy is viewed as a critique of Heidegger's philosophy, and certainly this is a prominent scholarly tack, then by Levinas's own account, indeed even his own words, his own positive philosophy is a formulation of Jewish ideas that are not only fundamentally amenable to the biblical message but also advance that biblical message.

Levinas closes this third essay with a section entitled "Youth." Here he offers a passing commentary on the student protests of 1968 and he observes that what appeared to be a revolt against conformity did not take long to lapse into that very conformity. In spite of—and in the midst of—the pressure to conform, there emerged the youth who were defined by sincerity. That is, these youth were defined not by a brutality of the violence of the act, but rather by an approach to others and a taking charge of one's fellow man that comes from human vulnerability: "Youth that could find responsibilities under the thick layer of literature that releases from responsibility, youth—that can no longer be chided with if youth only knew—stopped being the age of transition and passage and showed itself as the humanity of man" (*HO* 69). Here Levinas notices an authenticity that for the moment lacks cynicism. The youth's protests were motivated by beliefs—an approach toward the Other. Similar to Buber's expression of humanism cited in the previous chapter, Levinas appreciates that realizing the humanity of man depends on how we educate our youth and thus he turns to Jewish education for his solution to the crisis. What the youth of 1968 had was not found in "secular" literature.

Returning to the epigraph, if Zarathustra is successful in teaching the Overman, the Overman will be he whose soul is so full that he is open to all others, that self-preservation is no longer his highest priority. This capacity to open himself to the world is both superlative and self-destructive. He allows all influences to touch him—thus, he lets everything come into him. This view, like Levinas's, runs counter to the prevailing themes promoted by the social Darwinists, who believed that self-preservation is the highest priority.

From Ethics to Politics

In 1961 Levinas published *Totality and Infinity: An Essay on Exteriority*, which was the most developed account of his ethical project. The status of this book as a work of Jewish philosophy remains in question. Yet, insofar as his writings as a whole describe a similar ethical subject, we should examine the overarching themes that inform this important book. In a famous 1982 interview, which we will examine more closely later in this chapter, Shlomo Malka refers to Levinas as the "philosopher of the other." In light of the subordinate position that otherness holds in most of Western philosophy, Levinas's philosophical project runs contrary to that history. Additionally, his project is not always easily understood. Most notably, Levinas transforms the Other from a subordinate position to a privileged position, one in which the Other is my master, has power over me, teaches me. The Other is the one for whom I am responsible. Additionally, he transforms ethics from that which emerges from knowledge and power—I can only be held responsible for things about which I have knowledge and things about which I can control—to that which precedes knowledge and that which claims me before I have a choice. I cannot recuse myself from responsibility. Additionally, the ethical relationship is identified most uniquely by asymmetry. Levinas refers to the ethical subject in the first person—I am infinitely responsible for the Other—yet he makes no reference to the Other's reciprocal responsibility.

In his 1946 lectures *Time and the Other*, Levinas addresses specific themes in the history of philosophy, and in particular, several that have culminated in Heidegger's philosophy of being, in order to raise questions about their adequacy. In this book, Levinas does not name the ethical relation as such, though he does make reference to responsibility. This set of lectures addresses standard philosophical themes: reason, light, death, solitude, transcendence, and so forth. Levinas opens the lectures with the following description of his purpose: "The aim of these lectures is to show that time is not the achievement of an isolated and lone subject, but that it is the very relationship of the subject with the Other" (*TO* 39). His interest is in an ontological exploration, not one that is either sociological or anthropological. In the same way that Heidegger addressed Being—as an ontological structure—so too does Levinas explore the question of time as a relationship to the Other that is structurally fundamental. Levinas positions his analysis as a correction to Heidegger's discussion of *Mitsein*, or Being-with. Although it is true that Heidegger does take seriously Dasein's relationship to the Other, that relationship does not play a significant role in the drama of Being. In the end, it is the solitary nature of Dasein that is privileged. Levinas's aim is to go beyond Mitsein as the reciprocal relationship that typically identifies it. "Mit" implies side by side. It overlooks or does not consider the radical asymmetry that will become the signature feature of Levinas's ethical relationship, identified early in this book as the "face-to-face."

Recalling his work from the 1930s, Levinas returns to a discussion of "existents" and expands his analysis of the *il y a*, or the "there is." In his interview with Philippe Nemo, Levinas refers to the *il y a* as the "silence before creation." It is a difficult term to understand. How does one explain a sense of the nothing or the not? It is a feeling of anonymity where identification has not happened. If one recalls the story of creation in Genesis, it is a bit like the time before naming, before separation and individuation occurred. For example, before land was separated from water, sky from earth, and so forth. Prior to that separation, there was no identity. It is not that things did not exist in some kind of metaphysical sense; rather they did not exist in a way that was meaningful. He calls it a rumbling, and he compares it to the sound one hears when one puts a seashell up to one's ear—you hear something but nothing that can be identified. Just a murmur. Levinas ultimately refers to the *il y a* as a "vigilance without possible recourse to sleep."

Following his discussion of the *il y a*, Levinas introduces the *hypostasis*—the rupture of the anonymous vigilance of the *il y a*. He cannot explain why it takes place; his task is to show its significance. The hypostasis is where existent contracts existence. This leads the existent to believe it has mastery over its existence, a return to the discussion of this mythology from his writings in the 1930s. Recalling his glib comment from 1934 that there is no one more self-sufficient than Rousseau, we see the importance of Levinas reiterating the paradox of freedom in this book: "a free being is already no longer free, because it is responsible for itself." The subject is encumbered by itself. The fundamental materiality of the subject cannot be ignored. That is, a certain view of solitude is deceptive, and Levinas's aim is to undermine that view. This move is a radical change in how the subject is viewed, as fundamentally in relationship to others, not as a means to escape from the Other in order to understand truly what Being is, but rather to see that at bottom, our subjectivity is defined first and foremost by responsibility, thus limiting the radical freedom through which the modern subject had been defined.

Ultimately, still concerned with the problem of transcendence that occupied him in his work in the 1930s, Levinas turns to the feminine as the Other in the second half of this book. The lectures close with a discussion of fecundity as the possibility of transcendence. Levinas states emphatically that it is only through paternity that the ego can become other to itself. When the child appears, a relationship like no other is formed: "paternity is the relationship with a stranger, who entirely while being Other, is myself, the relationship of the ego with a self who is nonetheless a stranger to me" (*TO* 91). The son is neither my work, the way I might produce a book, a play, or a song, but neither is he my property. And yet he is still me: "I am in some way my child," but the "I am" is more than a simple reference to being. As we will see later, for Levinas, the child symbolizes a disruption, or an interruption.

Levinas returns to these themes in fuller form in *Totality and Infinity*, published fifteen years after *Time and the Other*. The feminine, which still provides a mechanism for fecundity at the end of the book, has a more prominent role at the beginning. Levinas expands the role of the feminine to include what he calls "habitation" or "dwelling." The latter term looks suspiciously Heideggerian but the dwelling for Levinas is not simply the place where Dasein inhabits; it is a home, a site of domestic tranquility, a site away from the call to responsibility by the Other. Yet the feminine provides the space from which the male, the subject, must emerge and go out into the world. Here, he is interrupted by the face of the Other to which he must respond. In this book in particular, Levinas often refers to the biblical phrasing, "the stranger, the widow, and the orphan," in order to exemplify or portray the extreme vulnerability of and our infinite responsibility to the Other.

In the final section of the book, titled "Beyond the Face," we find a series of discussions that together comprise what looks like a romantic narrative—there is the erotic moment, the caress, the birth of the child and the unfolding of the family into the community and the larger world around them. These sub-sections appear as though they were written first even though they come at the end of the book. That is, they appear to expand the discussion that Levinas provides at the end of *Time and the Other*. If understood as written first, they help explain the genesis of ethical subjectivity as that which takes place within the framework of a family—that is, as part of a developmental process. Without that ordering, we are left wondering how the subject becomes an ethical subject.

EMMANUEL LEVINAS AND ABRAHAM JOSHUA HESCHEL   129

Running through all of Levinas's philosophical writings is the continuous reference or use of the feminine. Although the feminine takes on different roles as his ethical project develops, the feminine nonetheless plays an important role at each stage. In *Time and the Other*, the feminine is cast as alterity, as the Other. In *Totality and Infinity*, the feminine is cast in the role of hospitality, the one who created the safe space, which made the male subject's ethical responsibility possible. At the end of the book, the feminine is cast as eros, which made fecundity possible. The significant change from *Time and the Other* to *Totality and Infinity* is the move from the feminine as Other to the feminine as that which made the relation with the Other possible. In his last major work, *Otherwise than Being*, published in 1974, the feminine named as such disappears, though Levinas does introduce the concept of maternity as a renaming of the ethical relation. Some have argued that Levinas responded to the early criticisms launched against *Totality and Infinity*, in particular those of Jacques Derrida, by reformulating his project in *Otherwise than Being*. In short, maternity exemplifies the ethical relation because it describes most effectively the seeming oxymoron of "passive responsibility." By this, Levinas means the way in which I am claimed (in the passive sense) by a responsibility from which I cannot recuse myself. I do not have a choice in this responsibility and I cannot opt out of it.

Response to the Feminine

In a footnote to her 1949 landmark book *The Second Sex*, Simone de Beauvoir took Levinas to task for recycling a dangerous view of woman as Other in *Time and the Other*. In her footnote, Beauvoir refers to Levinas's 1947 book and says this:

Is there not a case which otherness, alterity [*altérité*], unquestionably marks the nature of a being, as its essence, an instance of otherness not consisting purely and simply in the opposition of two species of the same genus? [...] Otherness reaches its full flowering in the feminine, a term of the same rank as consciousness but of opposite meaning.

She then responds to him by asking if he has forgotten that woman too is also aware of her own consciousness. Further, she takes him to task for deliberately taking a man's point of view, disregarding that subject and object can exchange places. Thus, when he refers to woman as a mystery, he necessarily means "as a mystery for man." While he intends to be objective, she argues, his position does nothing more than assert old-fashioned masculine privilege.

Beauvoir's response to Levinas makes sense if we recall that the only work she had available to her was this set of lectures and that she brought to her interpretation of Levinas's use of the Other her own project, which is a sustained argument against the way women have been subordinated as the Other, where the Other has fundamentally held a subordinate position to the male subject. Thus the conclusion that Beauvoir draws is a natural one. However, while her conclusion might be the natural one, it is not necessarily fully correct. Beauvoir fails to see how Levinas has privileged the Other, even in this early set of writings. Although *Time and the Other* reads like a standard manifesto that links woman to otherness and to death, this early project is a draft blueprint for the larger project he delivers in 1961. The Other for Levinas is not subordinate; rather, it sets the activity in motion. It inaugurates the relationship through interruption. In a more troubling move, the feminine, though it still does work as that which sets things in motion, nonetheless drops out as the Other. Indeed, this move becomes cause for another round of criticisms whereby Levinas is accused of confining the feminine to a life of domesticity and insofar as she cannot leave the house, she is also excluded from playing a role in the ethical relation. That is, in this round of criticisms, the concern is precisely that the woman cannot be the Other.

Even when the privileged position of the Other is known, Levinas has not been immune to the feminist critique of work. Writing forty years after Beauvoir, the French feminist theorist Luce Irigaray also took him to task, though her concern was much different. Her concern is not so much that woman is Other but rather that woman is not Other enough. Why cannot woman be an Other like the son who renders the return to the self incomplete, thus making ethics possible? For Irigaray, the concern is one of sexual difference and the role that this does or does not play in Levinas's project. Irigaray's critique focuses specifically on the way that the feminine is equated with eros, and she worries that his conception of the erotic is strictly utilitarian—the role of the woman as lover is simply to facilitate the birth of the son. In Irigaray's view, Levinas characterizes voluptuosity such that it can be redeemed only in the marriage-bed, and with the intent to produce a child. And yet, Irigaray also calls into question this assumed relation, or unification, by recalling that when the erotic relation comes to an end, or rather, is fulfilled temporarily, the lover is "left to his solitary call to his God," while "the beloved woman is relegated to an inwardness that is not one because it is abyssal, animal, infantile, prenuptial."

The son blocks the return to the self, the return to the same. The birth of the son causes this return to be incomplete, but only for the man. The beloved woman, through eros, maternity, and birth, makes the son possible, but it is the man who reaps this benefit, as "the seduction of the beloved woman serves as a bridge between Father and son." Through her, "the beloved, who is only an aspect of himself, the male lover goes beyond love and pleasure toward the ethical." Thus, here again, the woman provides the conditions that enable the man's entry into the ethical world. According to Irigaray, moreover, the entry is purchased at the expense of the woman. She is left without subjectivity, without access to the ethical, and outside any relation to God. For the man to engage in voluptuosity and bring about the birth of a son, he, the lover, must tarry on the wrong side of transcendence; he must risk the "loss of self in the wrong infinity." Interestingly, Irigaray's criticism falls short, and what she seems unable to realize is that her criticism is actually directed at him from her own religious standpoint, which is decidedly Christian.

She seems unwilling to read his text in the places where the erotic is for itself and that the birth of the child results from an overflowing, from a need for the lovers to make themselves permanent as a couple. The child represents them in the future. Levinas's reading and use of the feminine seems clearly rooted in Jewish texts, and his view of love and the erotic also appears to have a Jewish orientation, even if one allows that there is no such thing as one Jewish orientation but multiple views. My point rather is that Levinas was criticized for taking the position of the male, yet what other position could he take? But Irigaray's criticism is more worrisome than a simple reading of Levinas's work as sexist or an accusation of him ignoring sexual difference, and it is important for all the criticisms of him that follow, especially those that raise questions about his political standpoint.

Irigaray attacks the very structure of the erotic relation as Levinas conceives it. She criticizes his project on the grounds that, according to his account, the erotic relation cannot provide the means for transcendence. She also questions the way in which he posits the child as that which enables the erotic relationship to transcend a return to the same. Irigaray is right insofar as she conceives the erotic relationship differently. Her criticisms, furthermore, reveal the limitations of Levinas's project—namely, that it excludes other characterizations of eros. Her critique is both complex and compelling. However, her criticisms also reveal two problems with her reading of Levinas: first, she conflates the erotic and the ethical in a manner that, when followed to its conclusion, may not actually be desirable, if one recalls how Levinas defines each; second, her reading reveals her own biased perspective, which neglects to acknowledge the Jewish dimension of Levinas's project.

Although Levinas resists the use of the feminine in his last major work, the feminist critiques persisted. His use of maternity implies the feminine—what other body becomes pregnant? Yet, in this last book, the feminine is sanitized of the eros that preceded the pregnant body. Thus, the criticism that Levinas had used the erotic relation as a means to arrive at fecundity is now replaced with the criticism that the fecundity—or maternity—is now sanitized of eros. At the very least, Levinas's use of the feminine is provocative. It asks us to consider how women, and the feminine, have been portrayed historically in the philosophical canon. In what ways has Levinas, in spite of his insistence to offer a new view of subjectivity, reinscribed a traditional view of women in the service of that project? In other words, by conflating ethics and eros and arguing that the woman *in the position of the erotic* should also occupy the ethical position, Irigaray reveals that she does not understand the ethical relationship as Levinas describes it. The ethical is asymmetrical and not reciprocal. Certainly, that is not how we would want to cast our erotic relationships. This is not to say that Irigaray is somehow subject without recourse to the violence Levinas might direct at her. Rather, his point is that we should be very careful about distinguishing between these different kinds of relationships with others. And we see a similar conflation again with regard to his very distinct ways of describing ethics and politics.

Levinas's Political Judgment

In his essay, "Levinas's Political Judgment: The *Esprit* articles 1934–1983," Howard Caygill writes, "The critical neglect of the political dimension in Levinas's thought is surprising given its centrality to his life and work."[16] Caygill alludes to Levinas's personal stake in the political—he lived through a number of extraordinary and violent political events: the October Revolution in Lithuania; the Nazi occupation of Europe; he taught students from North Africa and the Middle East; he watched Israel become an independent state; he witnessed the student unrest in Paris in the 1960s. This essay provides an excellent summary of the seven essays Levinas published in *Esprit*, the French Personalist journal. Although Caygill's analysis does not encapsulate everything Levinas had to say on the political or on political events, Caygill's survey does, however, provide an interesting perspective into the development of Levinas's thought on the political in addition to discussing Levinas's view on very specific political events.

As Caygill notes at the beginning of his article, Levinas's own reference to and use of the political is "inconspicuously ubiquitous" in his work. And yet with few exceptions, the focus on Levinas as a political thinker remains largely absent. Although Levinas is often chastised for not offering a conception of the political—and one could argue that he never intended to pursue such a project philosophically—Caygill's essay collects Levinas's writings on very particular political events in order to make the opposite case. He does not argue that Levinas intended to offer a robust political theory, and indeed Levinas does not offer such an account of the political. Rather, Caygill establishes that the political is indeed a natural extension of his work and one that is tied to the ethical project he pursued.

Ethics and Politics: The Infamous Interview

At the same time that Levinas's commentators often accuse him of negligence for not offering a robust politics, they also scold him for the political opinions he did offer. The reprimand often takes the form of a philosophical claim that Levinas's political opinion violates the very ethical project he claims to promote. The most notable of these is his 1982 radio interview with Shlomo Malka and Alain Finkielkraut less than two weeks after the September 1982 massacres in the Sabra and Shatila Palestinian refugee camps in Beirut, Lebanon.

In the wake of these events, Finkielkraut and Levinas were invited by Malka to discuss in particular the theme of Israel and Jewish ethics. That is, Levinas was asked to comment on the theme of Israel and Jewish ethics within the frame of a horrific massacre motivated by politics. In the middle of this interview, Malka turns to Levinas and says, "Emmanuel Levinas, you are the philosopher of the 'other.' Isn't history, isn't politics the very site of the encounter with the 'other,' and for the Israeli, isn't the 'other' above all the Palestinian?" (*LR* 294). Levinas replies, "My definition of the other is completely different. The other is the neighbor, who is not necessarily kin, but who can be [...] But if your neighbor attacks another neighbor or treats him unjustly, what can you do? Then alterity takes on another character" (*LR* 294). This comment, taken out of context of both the interview and the violent events that motivated the interview in the first place, have led many of Levinas's critics to call him a hypocrite. When his ethical project confronts an actual event—the political—the ethics not only do not stand up, but also his own political judgment reveals that he is not concerned with the other. To understand then how Levinas's ethics and politics coincide, let us put his comment back into the larger context of the interview and the political events.

The massacres, which began on September 15 and continued until the morning of September 18, were committed by Christian Phalangists in response to the assassination of Bachir Gemayel, the elected president of Lebanon. At the time of the radio interview, the assassination was originally thought to be the work of Palestinian terrorists and this view did not change until early October when it was discovered that Habib Shartouni, a member of a Lebanese leftist group, had planted the bomb that killed Gemayel. That is, if one reads the accounts of the events surrounding Lebanon, Syria, Israel, and the PLO at that time, it initially looks like Palestinian terrorists assassinated the recently elected president of Lebanon who had just allowed Israeli forces to enter Lebanon in order to clean out the PLO. To Israelis, it seemed that Lebanon's new president could be a friend, and peace between the two countries might soon become a reality.

The violent attacks on the men, women, and children of Shatila and Sabra—who were also found not to be members of the group who assassinated the president, nor were they harboring such members—were horrific. Prime Minister Begin's initial response upon hearing of Gemayel's assassination, that Israel needed to enter the camps in order to establish a presence in the event that the PLO were trying to set up a new leader after the ouster of Yasir Arafat, puts Begin and Israel in a difficult position in light of what actually happened. Rather than Israel entering the camps to establish a peace-keeping presence, Begin instead allowed the Phalangist militia to enter with the understanding that they intended to weed out any PLO terrorists. But that is not what happened, and the Phalangists went in swinging and shooting at everyone, asking no questions and making no distinctions. And Israel appeared to play a role in allowing the massacres to occur and then did not stop them earlier than they did. Although what happened in these two camps is now well documented, what Levinas knew at the time of the interview is unclear. Even the most thorough news accounts did not report what happened until at least a week after the events (Friedman, *NYT*, 1982).

Malka opens the interview by posing this question to Levinas: "[is Israel] innocent or responsible for what happened at Sabra and Chatila" (*LR* 290). And Levinas replies, "Despite the lack of guilt here—and probably there too—what gripped us right away was the honour of responsibility [...] Prior to any act, I am concerned with the Other, and I can never be absolved from this responsibility [...] I would insist on this responsibility, even if I am not speaking of direct guilt." Before concluding this response, he adds, "I have always thought of Jewish consciousness as an attentiveness which is kept alert by centuries of inhumanity and pays particular attention to what occasionally is human in man: the feeling that you personally are implicated each time that somewhere—especially when it's somewhere close to you—humanity is guilty" (*LR* 290).

Finkielkraut adds that what disturbed him was the response by the deputy mayor of Jerusalem who said, "Nobody can teach us anything about morals," as if to imply that having been victims of the Holocaust there was nothing left to learn. Levinas agrees though he adds that the Holocaust will always be part of the fabric of Judaism. But to have survived such horror does not give one a free pass to close one's ears to the cries of the Other. Evoking the Holocaust as if to say that the victims of this atrocity are always and everywhere right is "as odious as the words 'Gott mit uns' written on the belts of the [German] executioners" (*LR* 291). Levinas unequivocally asserts that *my* responsibility cannot be mitigated. But what is one to do when an Other attacks another? Is there not a place to say they have no right to attack, that within this feeling of unbounded responsibility there is also a place for defense? "There is certainly a place for a defence, for it is not always a question of 'me' but of those close to me, who are also my neighbours. I'd call such a defence a politics, but a politics that is ethically necessary. Alongside *ethics*, there is a place for *politics*" (*LR* 292). Finkielkraut replies to Levinas that this relationship itself needs to be contested and the demonstrators who lined the streets of Tel Aviv precisely to protest not only the massacres but also the Israeli response were asking to have this relationship rethought. Political necessities cannot always be used to justify a violent response. Finkielkraut, speaking in Levinasian terms, asks Levinas if there might have been some slippage, if ethical imperatives had been forgotten or covered over in the name of political necessity, precisely the kind of slippage Levinas's entire ethical project tries to counter. Finkielkraut read this demonstration as revealing the contradiction in the relationship between ethics and politics—that they are not in fact compatible.

Levinas replies that there is a direct contradiction if the two are each taken to their respective extremes. In Levinas's view, politics comes with its own justification. The essence of Zionism for Levinas is that it comes with an army and arms, which function both as a deterrent and, if needed, the means necessary for defense. Most importantly, it allows for the defense of its neighbors, what Levinas sees as the oldest responsibility. Yet he also recognizes that while defending one's neighbor is an ethical responsibility, there is an ethical limit to this responsibility. And indeed those events at Shatila and Sabra might reveal that place where ethics and politics come into confrontation and as a result the place where their limits are revealed. Yet, for Levinas, these limits are not abstractions that can be thought about, much less resolved in some thought experiment. They are real limitations that are found only through the lived experience and confrontations we make daily with real situations, real choices. Thus, for Levinas, the question of the relationship between ethics and politics is not one that can be decided outside the very events which brought that relationship into question. Rather, it is in those events that this relationship is being decided. Levinas continues that in these events at Shatila and Sabra everyone is responsible including, maybe even especially, those who are innocent—no one can turn away; no one can say, it happened over there and thus does not concern me. Additionally, this means that those who are directly engaged, those who are in Israel, cannot say, "you are in Europe; you have no right to judge."

It is just after this response that Malka asks the question with which I began this discussion: "Levinas, you are the philosopher of the 'other.' Isn't history, isn't politics the very site of the encounter with the 'other', and for the Israeli, isn't the 'other' above all the Palestinian?" If one puts Levinas's reply back into the larger discussion, his answer—that he thinks of the Other differently and that one's neighbor might need to be defended against an attack by another neighbor—makes more sense. At the time of the interview, it was believed that the attackers were Christian Phalangists responding to the assassination of their president, whom they thought was killed by Palestinian terrorists. Writing just a week after the attack, *New York Times* war correspondent Thomas Friedman writes this: "The full truth may never be known. Too many people have already fled the scene. Too many people were killed on the spot. Too many people are now under pressure to hide their deeds."[17] It was only several weeks later that the identity of Gemayel's assassin became known. This point is not to justify the massacre. Rather, my point is to place Levinas's comments in context. At the time of the interview little was known, and he believed the Palestinian terrorists had assassinated a leader who might be able to bring peace between Israel and Lebanon. The national relationships in this part of the world are complicated to say the least, but it is clear that to Levinas, one might have to attack or defend a neighbor against the attack by another. He is quick to condemn the massacre. The violence was unjustifiable. Even in alterity, one can find an enemy, and if this enemy attacks another neighbor, what should one do? How do we decide especially when in some instances, "there are people who are wrong" (*LR* 294)?

In response to Malka raising a concern that mysticism may turn into politics, Finkielkraut responds that he is concerned with the opposite: politics turning into mysticism. After the 1967 war, a victory which was fast and broad, something entered into the Israeli psyche. It was as if they could not help seeing this victory as a messianic moment. Levinas counters with a view that Israel is less in danger of this possibility than other places. He believes that ethics will never be the "good conscience of corrupt politics" and that the protests by Israelis demanding an accounting of what happened demonstrate that point. Yet for Levinas these events are not only about ethics and politics, but in a sense about the truth of Judaism, about the books that inform Judaism. At the end of the day, "a person is more holy than a land, even a holy land, since, faced with an affront made to a person, this holy land appears in its nakedness to be but stone and wood" (*LR* 297).

Levinas's critics, in particular those who trot out this interview with the hope of disclosing Levinas's personal hypocrisy and thus also revealing the failure of his philosophical project, frequently fail to remember two related points that are fundamental to how he defines ethics and, in turn, to his conception of the political. The first is ethics before ontology. That is, my responsibility for the Other comes prior to any idea of who that Other is. Once the Other is named, e.g., Palestinian, the relationship is no longer self and Other, but an Israeli (or a Frenchman, or any other nationality) and a Palestinian. Second, and this is related to the first, the ethical description of the face-to-face implies two people. When a third enters, a judgment must be made. Levinas is clear about this point in *Totality and Infinity* (1961) among other writings. He is also clear that one must not stand idly by while evil happens. Thus action is called for in particular instances, though he does not prescribe which instances those are. How could he?

Levinas's commentators often fall into two opposing camps taking sides on a question that turns on pacifism and the possibility of war. Levinas's opening remarks in *Totality and Infinity* lead one to believe that the question of whether we are duped by morality is a question about the truth of nihilism. Yet a closer examination reveals that the question might in fact be a reference to war. Is war the opposite of ethics? It is possible to read Levinas as if his answer to this question is "yes." Levinas's ethical subjectivity advocates a turn from egoism, from an ego that is centered on itself in terms of a responsibility that emerges out of freedom, which would be a responsibility I can choose to respond to or reject. He sees egoism as the root cause of war. Insofar as I am concerned with myself and see myself as having an unquestioned right to be, then what would ever motivate me to give up that right in the face of another who asserts a similar right. Once we begin from this position, war is inevitable. Thus, Levinas's ethics turn away from the ethical subjectivity as a decision-making ego. He instead sees ethical subjectivity as an infinite responsibility from which I cannot recuse myself.

Returning to the discussion of the massacres at Sabra and Shatila, we might say that Levinas's response would need to be very complex. On the one hand, he might need to condemn the actions of the Lebanese Phalangists who in retrospect simply invaded these camps in order to exact revenge for the assassination of their president simply because these acts were violent. On the other, he is asked what he thinks of what happened between two others, and state violence, violence enacted between two others might be too complex for any easy or pat answers. He is not defending his own actions, nor was he part of a group that was defending itself. Rather, he is put in the position to make a judgment about what happened between two other groups. There is no other quintessential definition of the political for Levinas than this particular moment. While we may or may not agree with his view that action was called for in the events that led to the Sabra and Shatila massacre, and while Levinas might even, and in fact does, condemn the violence that took place there, that he calls for a defense of a third party is not inconsistent with his ethics. Indeed, it is perfectly in line with how he outlines both the ethical relationship and the political that he differentiates from it. Whether we agree with his judgment becomes irrelevant. His judgment is consistent with his philosophical project.

Assimilation, Jewish Education, Israel

Though not mentioned in Caygill's essay, Levinas's own relationship to the idea of a secular state and what it means to be a particular, in his case, a Jew, within that nation-state is important to examine in relation to his philosophy. It is not only that he was a witness to these events, but he was also personally touched by them.

Levinas's essays on Jewish education reflect similar concerns to those of Franz Rosenzweig, who was writing his essays on Jewish education nearly thirty years before World War II. The tone of Levinas's essays reflects an urgency that is absent from Rosenzweig's essays. Levinas's biography is significant in this regard. For Levinas, Jewish education is intimately tied to the cultivation of an ethical subject. Although the history of philosophy reflects a significant connection between educational and political theory, the connection was severed in the way philosophy was approached in the twentieth century. Yet we can see in the emphasis that both Rosenzweig and Levinas place on the role of Jewish education in the formation of Jewish identity that this issue was of particular importance for both thinkers processing what this identity means for the Jew living as a Jew in the non-Jewish nation-state.

Many of Levinas's essays on Jewish education were published in *Difficult Freedom*. The original publication venue of these essays varies—a few were published in journals specifically devoted to teacher education; a few others were published in the *Les Cahiers d'Alliance*. Still others were published in journals directed more generally at French Jewish intellectuals. The purpose of these essays in total was to convince their audience of the need to return to a traditional model of Jewish education, specifically, a model that includes instruction in the Hebrew language and literature and while also reassuring this audience that "returning" to Jewish education did not mean turning away from French culture and modern life. That is, Levinas was careful to reassure his audience that his goals would not take the school too far from the original mandate of the *Alliance*.

Levinas's essays on Jewish education, written after World War II, expand on themes he introduced in his writings of the 1930s—specifically in his essays "Reflections on the Philosophy of Hitlerism" (1934) and "On Escape" (1935). Insightfully examined by Howard Caygill, these two essays demonstrate Levinas's initial attention to the question of human subjectivity. Though he does not mention ethics, the last line of the 1934 essays indicates that he believes the future of humanity is at stake. As we saw previously, the early essay is a whirlwind tour through major moments in the history of philosophy, with an emphasis on the transitions in thinking that focused on a philosophy of immanence versus a philosophy of transcendence.

In both essays, we see Levinas struggling with the problems of both views, recognizing at the same time that he cannot jettison either. He must find a way to blend both accounts of our relationship to the world without letting enter the flaws that undermine them. Levinas revisits the themes in these two essays, which were written before he was taken into captivity, when he returns to philosophy in the late 1940s. Once again we see him struggle with the problem of transcendence, recognizing that absolute immanence would not address his concerns. Although his ethical project comes to fruition in his 1961 book *Totality and Infinity*, he refers to ethics and ethical subjectivity in his essays on Jewish education in the 1950s. These essays demonstrate that he is clearly concerned with how the Jewish population can and must respond to the atrocities that have been unleashed in the world in the first half of the twentieth century. Levinas's biography, though intimately tied to the Holocaust, personally ties him to other significant horrors: Stalinism, pogroms, nuclear weapons and so forth.

This section will explore several of Levinas's primary essays on Jewish education in order to draw out two themes. The first is the connection that these essays have to his larger philosophical project on ethical subjectivity. The second is to reveal the underlying political questions that these essays explore. By tracing the roots of the problem back to 1789, Levinas links the problems of Jewish assimilation, Jewish humanism, and Jewish education to the development of the French republic. These essays on Jewish education, written during his thirty years as director of the *École Normale Israélite Orientale*, mirror themes in his philosophical project, *which he was developing at the same time*. Although Levinas gestures toward the problem of liberalism as early as 1934, he does not yet identify liberalism as an issue confronting Jewish identity. Levinas's most explicit accounts of the "crisis in humanism" are in his essays on Jewish education written after World War II.

Although he outlines philosophical factors in this crisis, ultimately, Levinas views the crisis as a crisis in religion. Recognizing that the intended audience for these essays included teachers and staff at the *Alliance*, as well as secular Jewish intellectuals in France, is crucial to understanding the significance of these essays. They are his gentle attempt to persuade his readers to replace the secular mandate of the *Alliance* with one that is more religious—indeed, more Jewish. As a result, his educational writings implore the Jews to become more Jewish (i.e., particular). Levinas distinguishes Jewish education from other forms of education, for example, *les belles-lettres*, or an education in the classical humanities, in that Jewish education contains within it not simply a few geniuses whose work we try to repeat, but also the breadth of experience amassed over thousands of years; it calls us to return to its wisdom—the Word, when elevated, is the Word of God (*DF* 282). It calls for a new (or old) relationship to the law and moral obligation.

Although Levinas published several essays in the 1940s which reflect his concerns about being Jewish in a secularized society, "Reflections on Jewish Education" (1951), published only five years after he assumes the directorship of the ENIO and six years after he is released from the POW camp, shares his earliest reflections specifically on Jewish education. Similar to an argument that Mendelssohn made two hundred years earlier, Levinas insists that the religious instruction suitable for Catholics and Protestants is insufficient for Jewish education. Jewish education is not about teaching a catechism; rather it is about the development of a subject devoted to humanism. The source of this teaching is found in the Jewish sacred texts and specifically in the hermeneutic dimension of the Hebrew language that is found in the interpretations of these texts. In this essay he makes an oblique reference to what he sees as the failure of assimilation and the luck that allowed Judaism to survive in light of one hundred and fifty years of assimilation.

In "Assimilation Today" (1954), published just ten years after the end of the war, Levinas explicitly ties the Dreyfus Affair, a black mark of anti-Semitism in modern French history, to the years of National Socialism. Because of France's collaboration with the Nazi's during the war years, these two events raise doubts about the promise of the principles of 1789 for French Jews. For Levinas, these bookend events signify the failure of assimilation. His essay recounts not only the details that show how it did fail but also why it failed. Although Jews might have thought that assimilation would bring an end to anti-Semitism, it did not. In fact, in Levinas's view, assimilation might have fanned the flames. Even Jews who assimilated remained Jews. That is, Judaism, in spite of assimilation, did not go away. Assimilation was not complete. It simply renounced particular dimensions of Jewish practice, in particular public practice. At the same time that this essay calls into question the problem of assimilation, Levinas also calls out the hypocrisy of a so-called church-state separation. Although juridical lines might be in place that prevent a state-sanctioned religion, the ways in which religious life often inform the everyday are harder to see and to resist. It is only when a Jew resists that he or she can see how infused Christianity, in its secularized form, is in the everyday. The state of Israel—that is, Israel's actual existence—presents an opportunity to Jews that up to this point had not been available. Jews now have an opportunity to breathe Judaism, to live a life where conscience is not in contradiction with life in the state.

Yet, Israel's presence and the opportunity that it presents also make more noticeable the impossibility of living life as an assimilated Jew. Israel's existence, then, presses the Jew to make a choice. For Levinas, the choice is not between assimilation and immigrating to Israel. In fact what makes Levinas's analysis so interesting is that he does not call for Jews to pack up their belongings, renounce their current state, and move to Israel. He is more interested in what the productive tension might be to live as a Jew in a nation-state that believes itself to be secular. Jews need to ask if they still want to be Jews, and if the answer is yes, they must respond accordingly. For Levinas, if Jews are to be leaders rather than followers of the homogeneity that the state requires, if they are to resist simply being an echo of the larger culture in which they live, they must live as Jews in France. This involves reviving Judaism—returning to Hebrew, studying Talmud, providing a robust Jewish education, cultivating in the next generation a subjectivity that is ethical and responsive. To do this, Levinas argues, is not to turn away from the Principles of 1789, it is to live up to them, to fulfill them. What then is the connection between Levinas's critique of assimilation and the Jewish humanism he promotes?

In "For a Jewish Humanism" (1956), the tone Levinas takes is one of reassurance. Recalling the original secular mandate of the Alliance, Levinas recognizes that he could easily alienate both the Alliance and the larger French-Jewish audience if his views are thought to lead the Alliance too far afield from its roots. He claims that the Jewish school in its new format will not betray the ideals of the secular school. He tells his audience that by supporting "Jewish humanism the Jewish school actually becomes relevant in the modern world" (*DF* 273). He argues, then, that the aim of the Jewish school is twofold: to provide Jewish education in order to sustain Judaism itself and to reinforce the Jewish humanism found in and promoted by the Jewish sources. The latter aim connects his essays on Jewish education and his belief about what Jewish education can accomplish to his larger project in ethics.

The political dimension of this essay is revealed when Levinas identifies as a primary problem Jewish assimilation and the desire to be homogenous with the population with which the Jewish people live. In this move, the Jews lost that which made them unique (*DF* 275). Part of this uniqueness is the self-reference that frames Judaism—a fundamental part of Judaism is not simply that Jews read but that within the religious tradition is the command to read and "to teach these things to your children." That is, Judaism holds as one of its most important values the knowledge of its own sources (*DF* 276). Embedded in this teaching, Levinas believes, is the promotion of Jewish humanism. Thus, rather than seeing Judaism as parochial, which is how it is portrayed throughout the Western philosophical canon, culminating in Hegel, Levinas sees the Jewish tradition as binding Jews to others through their ethical responsibility to them—a responsibility that is cultivated through Judaism.

"Antihumanism and Education" (1973), published approximately twenty years after "For a Jewish Humanism," is the most developed of Levinas's essays on Jewish education. This essay was originally published in *Hamoré*, a journal devoted to teachers engaged in Jewish education (*DF* 277–88). It should also be noted that this essay is published just one year before Levinas publishes his last major philosophical work, *Otherwise than Being*, which itself assumes a decidedly religious tone, certainly at the end when he makes reference to the messianic. In this essay, Levinas argues that we are in a crisis of humanism for which Jewish education is ultimately the solution. Additionally, Levinas's argument in this essay draws an explicit connection between the "principles of 1789," the result of the French Revolution and French Republicanism, and the problems Jews faced through the assimilation that was encouraged by these events.

His largest concern is that while emancipation allowed Jews to become full citizens, the price they paid was to relinquish a dimension of being Jewish—certainly a public dimension. Assimilation then led them to retain only certain elements of their Jewish life. Judaism became a series of actions or events and not an organic part of how Jews lived. To retain a Jewish life was to remain parochial, unsophisticated, and separated from the larger cosmopolitan community. Thus, whatever wisdom Judaism had remained buried in its texts (*DF* 280). Most importantly, but not unsurprisingly, Judaism became separated from the very humanism that informed it in the first place (*DF* 280).

The violence the world unleashed in the first half of the twentieth century raised questions for Jews about the choices they had made to exchange being overtly religious with having the rights of French citizenship. Admittedly, it is not clear that such a choice is a real choice. Indeed, one can ask the philosophical question if assimilation has embedded within it a manipulation—who would not want the right to vote, the right to live freely among one's other citizens? But if that right can only come with giving up a large portion of who one is, to the extent that one risks losing this identity altogether, is this a choice?

Levinas indicates that this violence might have been enough for Jews to reconsider the promise of liberalism. His list of inhumanities include: World War I, the Russian Revolution refuting itself in Stalinism, fascism, and Hitlerism, the 1939–45 War, atomic bombings, genocide, and most certainly the philosophical discourse of Heidegger, which subordinates the human to the anonymous gains of Being (*DF* 280). But Levinas is clear that whatever humanism the Jews promote, it must be humanism that does not allow them to become the persecutors. Significantly, he believes this humanism must include the religious dimension, which he believes had been cleansed of the flawed humanism modernity provided (*DF* 280–86).

It is through this humanism that Jews must become the leaders rather than allowing themselves to be carried along by the secular communities in which they have made their homes. Instead of assimilating to the surrounding civilization, Levinas implores French

Jews to take the lead. Instead of repressing Judaism's ethical impulse, Judaism must embrace it. The crisis of humanism that Levinas identifies is a crisis of Judaism that is resolved by a robust return to Judaism, but more specifically a return to Jewish education. By making this return, Judaism revives its signature style of reading, which includes midrash or rabbinic exegesis. This style of reading has a performative dimension. By exposing contradictions, drawing out muted voices, allowing different interpretations to stay in tension, Judaism privileges the Other, the marginal, the otherwise silent. By embracing rabbinic interpretation, Judaism responds to the hermeneutic methods of the West that had disqualified this mode of reading and in doing so had abandoned the Hebrew roots of humanism that otherwise are said to inform Western thought. The crises of the twentieth century revealed to the Jew the fragility of humanism, and the failure of Western humanism propped up by philosophical reason. It was a failure of Western ethics. Levinas concludes that Western humanism failed because it is fundamentally flawed—and the flaws entered when Judaism was abandoned. Western humanism cannot capture all of what makes us human, the most significant part of what makes us human: our responsibility for the Other. Levinas wants to remind his readers that literature is not the same as revolution. The humanities are not the same as being human. If we do not actively cultivate an ethical subject, we have only ourselves to blame when we are confronted with a world filled with violence.

Religion, Education, and the Prophets

In the introduction to Abraham Joshua Heschel's book, *Moral Grandeur and Spiritual Audacity*, his daughter, Susannah Heschel, quotes her father from the 1960s: "To speak about God and remain silent on Vietnam is blasphemous" (1997, viii). Heschel's comment is directed toward his fellow clergy who will not speak out about the war in Vietnam. In light of the many comparisons made now between the Vietnam War and the invasion of Iraq, it makes sense to recall Heschel's statement in light of our current situation. For Heschel, speaking out against the war was not only a moral responsibility; it was also a religious obligation. If one is going to invoke God's name, then it is incumbent upon that person to think about what is going on around us—who is dying and for what reasons. But for Heschel, the distinctions that define the boundaries of podium, pulpit, and lectern are not always so clearly demarcated. More significantly, this split, similar to the public-private division, has realms that could collide in unforeseeable ways. In his explanation for why he embarked on a study of the prophets, he confided that he thought philosophy had become an isolated, self-subsisting, self-indulgent entity, encouraging suspicion instead of love of wisdom (Introduction to *The Prophets*). Heschel took his role as an academic and an educator seriously, and his actions teach us that insofar as one does take these two roles seriously, they cannot be successfully kept separate from the political. This debate over the podium and the pulpit is not new and we see it in the current attacks on academic freedom. Although one can question the status of Abraham Joshua Heschel as a philosopher, his work covers themes that we find clearly in the realm of Jewish philosophy. For that reason, I include a section on his thought in this chapter.

In his 1962 book, *The Prophets,* Abraham Joshua Heschel explains that he turned to the prophets because philosophy had become too detached from the concerns most pressing to him.[18] Why the Jewish prophets? At the time of the book's publication Heschel had been teaching at the Jewish Theological Seminary in New York, the seminary for the Conservative branch of Judaism. He explains that his work within the academic environment began to feel isolating and self-indulgent. It had lost contact with the "real" world, the world that demands from us our attention. More importantly, he believed that the work of the academy led to a life of "suspended sensitivity in the face of stupendous challenge, indifferent to a situation in which good and evil became irrelevant, in which man became increasingly callous to catastrophe and ready to suspend the principle of truth."[19] The prophets, according to Heschel, are "some of the most disturbing people who have ever lived," for their intense anguish about even the most banal of life's unjust events is relentless.[20]

Heschel's reading of the prophets asks us not to think as much about the truth or the validity of the prophets' claims. Instead, he asks us to think about who the prophets were. What distinguishes them as prophets? What did they feel? He tells us that before we can even begin to address the question of what the prophets mean to us, we must understand what they mean to God: "Prophecy is a sham unless it is experienced as a word of God swooping down on man and converting him into a prophet."[21] He further explains that although he does not wish to discount the method of "impartial phenomenology" this kind of impartiality has no place in his investigation. He confesses that he has long become weary, even suspicious of such impartiality, which indicates either that the situation has no relevance to us or it does, in which case the impartiality is simply a pretense. Reflection is not separate from the prophet's conviction.[22]

Heschel is not discounting the power or necessity of pure reflection. He is simply indicating its limits. If we wish to clarify what the prophet asserts, then we call in pure reflection; if we wish to know what it is like to be a prophet, i.e., his existential character, then pure reflection will not be sufficient. As Susannah Heschel observes,

Rather than debate theological interpretations, the prophets denounce hypocrisy and insist on justice as the tool of God and the manifestation of God. Neither religious ritual nor belief holds meaning for the prophets as ends in themselves; what God wants, Amos insists, is not worship but an end to war crimes and exploitation in the marketplace. For the prophets, justice is the means of redemption, including our redemption of God from the constraints of religion, human mendacity and complacency in the face of evil. They also are adamant that evil is never the climax of history.[23]

According to Abraham Joshua Heschel, "the prophet was an individual who said 'No' to his society, condemning its habits and assumptions, its complacency, waywardness, and syncretism."[24] We find a similar relevance in how both Levinas and Heschel discuss education in terms of religious language.

In his essay, "Education and Prayer," Emmanuel Levinas explores the problem with prayer, particularly Jewish prayer, in a contemporary world.[25] He begins by making two assertions: he maintains that prayer is central to Judaism, but, knowing this, he wishes to accord it a secondary position. In his discussion of Jewish prayer, in particular, the Sh'ma, he affirms that the centrality of community, which while still indispensable for its meaning, has nonetheless been lost from prayer itself. In Levinas's view, essential to the Sh'ma is not only the connection between God and Israel but also the one among the people of Israel themselves. That is, what Levinas "hears" in the Sh'ma is a call to humanity that is both united and unique.

Although prayer is often thought in terms of the individual, for Levinas prayer transcends the individual. It is what makes Judaism religious—that is, it tethers us to our history and ties us to the community. According to Levinas, it is prayer that paved the way for Jewish nationalists. That is, it is in prayer that we are bound to Israel as a people and then as a nation. Although he does not want to renounce the role of prayer, he asks after the role of prayer in the modern world. He asks us to consider what the call of the modern world is and if there is a way for Judaism to respond to this call. He recognizes that many who have left the fold of Judaism are among the brightest and most active of humanity in part because they believe that religion cannot provide salvation as long as "reason and justice are left unsatisfied" (271). Old-fashioned Judaism, as Levinas refers to it, is dying off. Thus, he calls for a return to Jewish wisdom but it must be a Jewish wisdom revitalized by emphasizing the Jew of the Talmud rather than the Jew of the psalms. Reason, he asserts, must take precedence over prayer. In order to avoid "a Judaism without Jews" (271), Judaism must respond to the modern world by recognizing the role of reason that is already a fundamental part of Judaism's identity.

In a later essay, "On Religious Language and the Fear of God" (1994), dedicated to Paul Ricoeur on the occasion of Ricoeur's 80th birthday, Levinas offers a reading of a passage from the Babylonian Talmud, Tractate *Berakhot* 33b.[26] In this commentary, Levinas emphasizes the role of study in our relationship to God. This essay, written late in Levinas's philosophical career, reflects many of the themes we find in his philosophical writing, though here these themes are applied to sacred texts rather than to the ethical other, per se. Early in this essay, he sets out his task. As he understands the role of the sacred texts, Torah and Talmud study are communal endeavors. Judaism calls us from outside of ourselves—so outside that we are required to engage these texts with others. We see the importance of study for Levinas when he states that study of the Word of God entails a closer contact with God than even liturgy does. Judaism calls us from outside ourselves and it teaches us to engage with the other. One cannot help but conclude that if the implication of Levinas's comment is that study is not only embedded in prayer; it is also in fact more religious than prayer.

Similar to Heschel's concerns, Levinas anticipates the accusation that prayer becomes mindless recitation. Levinas responds that such mindlessness would imply a familiarity with God—the Absolute Other—that is not warranted. Thus, Levinas argues that according to the commentary found in *Berakhot* 33 such a mindless act of prayer would be considered carelessness and thus by definition prayer cannot be simply rote or mindless. Levinas insightfully observes that prayer must assume a certain comportment of the self in order for it to be authentic.

In his essay "The Spirit of Jewish Prayer," Abraham Joshua Heschel similarly alerts us to a problem in modern Jewish life. Heschel begins this essay with the declaration that although services run smoothly, full of "pomp and precision [...] decorum, voice, and ceremony," they are devoid of life. Ironically, the place of worship is lacking soul.[27] That is, contrary to the claim that prayer by definition, as found in the commentary to *Berakhot* 33, cannot be mindless recitation, Heschel's concern is that prayer has become just that. Judaism has developed a new habit of "praying by proxy," where the congregants "let" the rabbis or cantors do the praying for the congregation.[28] In order to correct this problem Heschel explains that we must first know what prayer is, and in order to answer this question, we must first know who we are when we pray and for what we are praying. In his analysis, to pray is to expose oneself to God, to enter into that relationship with God.[29]

Contrary to common characterizations of prayer, in Heschel's characterization, this relationship with God does not remove us from this world; rather, prayer is how we "bring God back into the world."[30] And although prayer in Judaism can be either praise or petition, the former ranks foremost.[31] The danger that must be avoided is prayer becoming mere habit or mechanical performance. The solution is to approach prayer with the proper *kavanah* (disposition or mindset).[32] Citing Maimonides, he states, "Prayer without *kavanah* is no prayer at all."[33] And like, Levinas, Heschel refers to *Berakhot* to impress upon us the significance of approaching prayer properly.[34]

Both Heschel and Levinas offer descriptions of prayer as *a way in which we comport ourselves,* direct ourselves, and find ourselves in the presence of God. Levinas wants to return Jewish education to the Talmud, to the wisdom of the talmudic thinkers, since he believes it is through this text that modern Jews will be able to respond to Judaism. Heschel on the other hand thinks that without prayer, Judaism will have lost its soul—it will have lost the very thing that commits Jews to the moral life that Judaism promotes. Like prayer in general, certainly the Sh'ma has the potential to be recited with the thoughtlessness that both Heschel and Levinas note. But even as this potential exists, the very construction of the Sh'ma—as a program for education into the Jewish faith—seems to provide a further defense against a mindless relationship to it.[35]

Additionally, one of the most interesting parts of Jewish prayer is seen in the emphasis both Levinas and Heschel place on "being ready" or readying oneself. One is asked to approach a Jewish text in a certain frame of mind, to be prepared to study, to engage the Torah with all one's mind, heart, and body so to speak. Judaism's requirement to approach prayer with a particular readiness is intended to cultivate a thoughtful, critically engaged person.

Heschel sees prayer as the mechanism for not becoming indifferent. Contrary to the view that prayers are said to make one feel better or to soothe, Heschel's view is that prayer is a disruption, a "tending to" the mind only so that the mind is not distracted by other things and can therefore become alerted to what really matters—a focus on the injustice in the world so that one is able to confront that injustice. The opposite of good, according to Heschel, is not evil, but indifference, a view we also find in the commentary on Deuteronomy 22:1-3.[36] Yet, in spite of their differences, for both Heschel and Levinas, prayer is not about finding answers and becoming complacent; it is about being open to and allowing oneself to be interrupted by the Other. In this way, both advocate that we are to become like the prophet, the individual who is continually disrupted by the Other, who lives in a state of anxiety continually worried about the community and its ability to live justly.

5

The Limits of Philosophy

One of the most famous imperatives in philosophy, "Know thyself," is attributed to Socrates and his relentless questioning portrayed in Plato's dialogues. In his dialogue *Charmides*, Plato alters the dictum slightly, yet the meaning changes dramatically. In this dialogue the word "mortal" is added to the end, making the phrase, "Know thyself, mortal." The phrase now appears to command one to know one's boundaries and limitations; one ought to know who one is, and more importantly, who one is not. In this particular instance, one is to know that one approaches the Delphic Oracle not as a god, but as a mortal. Hence, hubris, the common fatal flaw for heroic mortals is not merely a display of arrogance or excessive pride but also a transgression of boundaries. It is a crime so heinous that it is frequently the common cause of one's own undoing and ultimately one's death. Is it possible for philosophy itself to be guilty of this hubris? That is, is there a view that portrays philosophy as capable of answering anything? Is it the case that truth can be in conflict with ethics, and if so, what does that mean for philosophy? Has philosophy transgressed a boundary—and if so, what is on the other side?

Fackenheim's Response

In his essay "The Holocaust and Philosophy,"[1] Emil Fackenheim opens with the claim that "philosophers have all but ignored the

Holocaust." And he asks, "Why?" He provides three related answers: the first is connected to philosophy's need to address the universal. If the Holocaust is unique, singular, how can philosophy address it? Yet he immediately counters this claim by indicating that historically philosophers have in fact dealt with particular events, for example, the French Revolution. Second, he adds, philosophers seldom consider "things Jewish" (129). Finally, he adds, where the French Revolution can be treated positively, the Nazi regime was decidedly evil, and philosophers, he says, have always had a tough time with evil. And yet Fackenheim's observation raises a peculiar question for philosophers to address—how does philosophy treat the Holocaust, and what do we say about a discipline that cannot incorporate these events into its discipline, especially when that discipline includes in its purview ethics? As we will see, especially when we approach the literature of Primo Levi, in the age of the Holocaust, philosophy's concern with wonder is now a wonder accompanied by horror, and it would be cowardly, among other things, to turn away from asking how we think about such horror in the age of Enlightenment.

Fackenheim wrote several essays asking philosophical questions of the Holocaust. It is worth looking at them in some detail. In an essay simply titled "Holocaust," he asks after the uniqueness of the Holocaust. He begins by raising a question about the name itself. Might not the word *Shoah* (catastrophe) be better? Does not Holocaust signify a burnt offering? The Nazis and their henchmen threw live babies into open fires to burn, but these were not acts of sacrifice. They were acts of murder. The term "Holocaust" might simply be inappropriate if not completely misleading.[2]

Fackenheim addresses the question about the Holocaust's uniqueness by suggesting that "unprecedented" is a preferable description of it. In spite of "Katzetnik 135683," the pen name of the novelist Yechiel Dinur, declaring Auschwitz like another planet, "uniqueness" implies that the event is somehow outside of history and thus mystifies it (121). By using the term "unprecedented" rather than unique, Fackenheim impels historians to ask if this kind of event can then become a precedent for the future. Even if unprecedented, were there causes that led to it that might lead to another? If we call it unique, it stands alone—idiosyncratic, sui generis, no causes then, no causes later. We have no reason to consider how we might prevent this kind of event in the future. Fackenheim points to the Turkish genocide of the Armenians as a precedent to the Nazi genocide of the Jews. The difference, he observes, lies in how planned, pre-meditated and calculated the Nazi genocide was. Here he indicates that the term "unique" does in fact apply. Additionally, he points out that the justification that accompanied Nazi Germany unlike other genocides was also unique. In order for the "why" to work, philosophers, theologians and historians had to rewrite history, including our understanding of what we called the human. The human could no longer be that which preceded the Aryan ideology. Theologians rewrote Christianity so that any trace of the Jewish Jesus was erased. Everyone who knew the truth had to hold their tongues, thus betraying their own calling, their own vocation. But the why of "why did this happen" remains a mystery in the largest sense. In a more immediate sense, the raw anti-Semitism was apparent—the Jew was the Devil and fighting the Jew was fighting evil. This seems to have become the sufficient condition for entry into heaven. Fackenheim thus powerfully proclaims that never before had

> a state attempted to make a whole country—indeed, as in this case, a whole continent—*rein* [free] of every member of a whole people, man, woman, and child. Never have attempts resembling the Holocaust been pursued with methods so thorough and with such unswerving goal-directedness. It is difficult to imagine and impossible to believe that, this having happened, world history can ever be the same. The Holocaust is not only an unprecedented event. It is also of an unfathomable magnitude. It is world historical. (123)

The problem here as Fackenheim identifies it is that the discussion easily devolves into simplicity. If one sees the Holocaust within history, do we see this as fascism—the logical end to capitalism? Do we see it as the trite "man's inhumanity to man, especially in war"? Will the philosopher be able to investigate more deeply, asking for a more complex explanatory thesis, and will this thesis make sense or will it also be reduced to an explanation that is historically specific? Fackenheim points out that along with everything else that Nazi Germany introduced, it also introduced a new way of living and dying. Where previously such a question was not a question, Nazi Germany introduced, via Primo Levi's reflections, the *muselmann*, the person who is technically still alive, still walking, nearly nothing but skin and bones, but who is in all other ways a walking corpse, existing between life and death. Thus, Nazi Germany introduced not only a new way of being a victim but also a new way of being a victimizer. As we will see in the analyses that follow later in the chapter, genocide was in fact the aim, but equally part of that aim was the humiliation and torture of those who survived. It exemplifies a strange paradox—to simultaneously have as a goal the total extermination of a people while also making as a primary goal the humiliation, shame and dehumanization of those who have not yet died.

Although various kinds of evil were already familiar to philosophy—sadism, evil for the sake of evil, moral weakness and so forth—until the Holocaust, Hannah Arendt's naming of the "banality of evil," was not known. There was an ordinariness of the evil practiced by regular citizens, not folks associated with the war machine. And then when the war was over, they returned to their respective ordinary respectable lives without showing any signs of moral anguish (124). Significantly, he notes, the evil is banal not because of the type of crime but because of the type of person— the person was simply an everyday person, not the image of the monster we imagine capable of committing this kind of evil. But this is a concept with which philosophy still struggles. The human condition was defined because there existed that which was outside the realm of human possibility. But the Holocaust became not only a watershed event, but also as we will see, a break or a fissure. Indeed, it cast doubt on modernity and the promise of it.

What other consequences did the Holocaust produce? Was it a fissure or a break for Christians as it was for Jews? Fackenheim notes that missionizing now takes on a whole new meaning, for it attempts to complete in a different way what Hitler could not. To convert the Jews is just another form of genocide, of making the Jews disappear. What does this mean for Judaism's future? That remains unclear.

In his essay on Claude Lanzmann's masterful film *Shoah*, Fackenheim asks his audience to consider three scenes from the film: one concerns a witness, another the bystanders, and a third the criminal—the one, Fackenheim tells us, we most wish to push back into the deepest recesses of our minds. The witness Felix Muller was a *Sonderkommando*. His job was to remove all the dead bodies, feces and all, from the gas chambers. One group, knowing what fate awaits them, becomes defiant, and they begin to sing—they sing the Czech national anthem and the Ha-tikvah. Muller is moved and in that fleeting moment reflects on his life and the meaninglessness of it. He walks into the gas chamber to die with them. Lanzmann stops him and repeats back to him: You were in the gas chamber? Yes, Muller replies. But another victim tells him he must leave; he must live and bear witness.

The bystander tells the story that has become familiar over the years: the story of Jewish blood libel, of the Jews as perpetrators of deicide. The Jews are Christ-killers and for this they must pay the price with their own lives. In this retelling, however, the bystander insists that it was a rabbi who told this to his flock, thus making more palatable both the possibility of the crime and the willingness to accept the punishment for that crime.

The final scene is the perpetrator, the criminal, the one responsible for taking the Jews to their deaths. But what Fackenheim points out is that philosophy is not equipped to talk about the Holocaust. Analytic ethics does not even come close. He refers to R. M. Hare (in his essay, Fackenheim refers to him as J. M. Hare, which I assume is a typo) as someone who believed that through the strength of philosophy the inconsistencies in the Nazi position could simply be revealed and that would be that. Hare, for example, would simply ask the Nazi: Are you an Aryan? If the answer was no, then well, the Nazi should join the others in the gas chambers. If yes, well the conversation would end, but few Nazis, Hare surmises, are actually idealistic. Fackenheim then glibly states, should Hare have encountered the Nazi and tried to ask such a question he would have been lucky to leave such a conversation unbeaten and unbruised, indeed even alive (139).

The simplicity with which philosophy has tried to address the question of such enormous evil, and evil that is at once also banal, makes a mockery of the Holocaust and reveals just how powerless philosophy is. Up to this point, philosophical language had not been able to express what Lanzmann was able to express in his film. What then is the philosopher to do? This is Fackenheim's question. How should we approach the Holocaust? The Jewish philosopher and the Christian both bear a responsibility to undo the story of deicide that has been perpetuated by Christians over the centuries. Fackenheim believes that the Holocaust could not have happened without the bystanders who were convinced that the Jews not only deserved this, but believed this about themselves. The philosopher must consider all the stories—the self-deceptions that allow anyone, but in particular philosophers, to believe that thirty years later they can still report the events of what happened as cold as a reporter stating the facts of a case. There is no remorse. What is the philosopher to say about this? How does the philosopher talk about this kind of evil? For Fackenheim, *Shoah* is itself an act of resistance, since each story resists easy acceptance. It is the struggle against forgetting, and for Fackenheim the philosopher's task has only just begun.

At the Limits of Philosophy

In his talmudic reading "The Temptation of Temptation," Levinas presents a description of both philosophy and religion, the latter becoming necessary precisely because of the limits of the first. In his biography of Levinas, Salomon Malka tells us that in Levinas's view of the two, philosophy comes to a threshold of a mystery that it cannot cross. There are some things that philosophy cannot do and cannot know—and it is precisely at this point that religion must enter. The Shoah marked such a threshold. This book is not a book about the Holocaust, though it is becoming increasingly difficult to discuss Jewish philosophy without accounting for its relationship to this catastrophe. For some philosophers, the Shoah marked the failure of Enlightenment ethics—the height of Weimar Germany, the height of reason in twentieth-century Germany delivered what was a horrific and efficient machine designed not only to exterminate groups of people, centrally the Jews, among others, but also to exterminate them with gratuitous cruelty.

The Shoah was not the result of a war machine as usual, which could be justified, even if badly, using various kinds of philosophical arguments including self-defense. Instead, the Shoah revealed a gratuitous violence that was set in contrast to the Weimar Republic which had exemplified the pinnacle of the development of culture, including the development of rationality. What the Enlightenment could not predict is the way that reason would be used precisely to justify such violence, that contrary to the glib way some people dismiss Hitler as crazy, implying there was no rationality to what he did, others could see the logic as it unfolded from the ancients through the modern period into the twentieth century. As we saw in the previous chapter, Levinas traces this lineage in his 1934 essay "Some Reflections on the Philosophy of Hitlerism." For Levinas there is a philosophical logic that runs through the history of intellectual thought culminating in Hitlerism. His point is not to say that Hitlerism is rational, as in morally justified, but rather to say its roots can be found in the history of ideas if one knows where and how to look.

In 1963, thirty years after Levinas published this essay and twenty years after the end of World War II, the political philosopher and journalist Hannah Arendt published *Eichmann in Jerusalem: A Report on the Banality of Evil* after watching the trial of Adolf Eichmann, the bureaucrat who made sure the execution machine ran smoothly. Writing from the perspective of both the journalist and also a trained philosopher, she cannot help but notice that modernity has witnessed something new and horrific. In addition to the obvious cruelty unleashed by the Nazis, there was a new kind of evil, which Arendt named the banality of evil. It is the evil perpetrated by Eichmann, who, in his own words, quotes Immanuel Kant, and offers as his defense that he was only doing his duty. The banality referred not so much to the evil but to the man who participated in it. How does one argue with this?

What we learn from Eichmann, and what becomes fodder in most introductory ethics classes, is precisely this example—the failure of the categorical imperative, the failure of an ethics based on a rationality secured in every direction. What does one do when the Nazi comes to your door and asks if you are hiding a Jew in your attic? Do you lie? If we answer, yes, we lie, then what mechanism in the ethics based solely on rationality justifies this response? It does not matter if we say Kant could not imagine such horror that would raise questions about the uncategorical wrongness of lying. Arendt's analysis reveals the fissure of ethics based solely on reason. What follows from Arendt's analysis is the post-modern response to ethics, which includes Levinas's new ethical subjectivity described in the previous chapter. What we also learn is the limit of philosophy, its total inability to produce an adequate response. For this, we might need to turn to literature—not to justify what happened but rather to help us see the implications of what happened. In this chapter, we will focus on three texts: Elie Wiesel's *Night* and Primo Levi's *The Drowned and the Saved*, and *Survival in Auschwitz*. I focus on these texts, and in particular, *Night*, because this is a text that is often read by middle-school-aged students, and they rarely return to it. What does it mean to ask kids, who are barely able to understand their own extraordinary and rapid development, to grapple intellectually and emotionally with a text that retells unspeakable cruelty and moral choices that we cannot imagine ourselves facing. This chapter is an opportunity for students to return to these books. At the end of the chapter, I turn briefly to Levinas's "Toward the Other," which recounts a talmudic passage on Yom Kippur and the possibility of forgiveness, but is deployed for the specific reason of asking if the Germans can be forgiven. What is evil? And are there acts so evil that they cannot be forgiven? And if so, what options for justice do we have that will not simply reproduce the violence that begat the need for justice in the first place? Before turning to these texts, it is worth looking briefly at the controversy that erupted over Arendt's reporting of the Eichmann trial.

The Eichmann Controversy

In her 1952 essay, "The History of a Great Crime,"[3] which is her review of Léon Poliakov's *Bréviaire de la haine:* Le IIIe Reich et les juifs [Breviary of Hate: The Third Reich and the Jews], Arendt commends Poliakov for resisting the temptation to provide easy answers to the question, "Why?" The significance of Arendt's analysis of Poliakov's book lies in how she arranges Poliakov's unearthing of the "facts" or the chronology of the events to demonstrate that much of what took place early on simply had to do with Hitler and the Nazi regime calculating how best to proceed with their vast plan.

Hitler's first target was the "feebleminded," which resulted in "mercy killings." Arendt tracks the move to kill the families of these victims when the families of these victims protested. Yet, the "reason" Hitler supplied was again the purity of the nation—families of feebleminded also needed to be eliminated, lest they lead to more contamination. It is clear from early documents, and documents were abundant—Hitler's megalomania leading to his concern that he be forgotten by history led to an extraordinary accounting of every act, every victim, every murder—that Hitler had planned to liquidate all "racially unfit" people regardless of nationality (*JW* 456). The Madagascar "solution" to the Jewish problem was rejected because it was no longer enough for the Jews simply to be removed—as might happen with Zionism; rather, the Jews, likened to a disease, had to be extirpated; not simply moved, but exterminated.

Arendt's fascination with Poliakov's book lies in his observation that Hitler was shrewd, capitalizing on events that coincided with his own plans, even, for example, capitalizing on the growing pacifism movement in Germany. For the pacifists, all killing, including those in war, were slaughter. By focusing attention on the war that was killing so many able bodied and healthy Germans, Hitler was able to draw attention away from "mercy-killings" at home. Poliakov, and Arendt concurs, makes a case that this is the reason for why the "mercy killings" did not begin until the actual outbreak of war (*JW* 457).

After recounting the details of events provided by Poliakov, Arendt astutely observes that

> there is a mystery about the Nazi regime, but it has nothing to do with secrets. It resides solely in a response, humanly unavoidable, that makes us go on asking, Why—but why? long after all the facts are reported, all stages of the process known, all conceivable motives considered [...] Only if the reader continues, after everything about the exterminations has been made tangible and plausible, to feel his first reaction of outraged disbelief, only then will he be in the position to being able to understand that totalitarianism, unlike all other known modes of tyranny and oppression, has brought into the world a *radical* evil characterized by its divorce from all humanly comprehensible motives of wickedness. (*JW* 460)

In 1961, nearly ten years after publishing this review, Arendt covered the trial of Eichmann in Israel for *The New Yorker*. Eichmann was convicted in May 1962. Her reporting of the trial, subsequently published in 1963 as the book, *Eichmann in Jerusalem: A Report on the Banality of Evil*, unleashed extraordinary fury against her, most notably for her criticisms of the Jewish Councils (*Judenräte*) that from one perspective looked like they had aided the Nazis. Yet, Arendt's analysis is not so simple. In the review of Poliakov's book,

Arendt also makes this point, yet she does so precisely as a means to illustrate the complexity of the Nazi regime. How had they managed to get both Germans and Jews to be tools in a vast machine? Indeed, she comments explicitly about the "terrible dilemma" of the *Judenräte*, "their despair as well as their confusion, their complicity and their sometimes pathetically ludicrous ambitions" (*JW* 459).

Arendt was trained as a philosopher. Thus, her reporting could not help but be influenced by philosophical questions that concerned her. When she was accused of using her opportunity to report to advance ulterior motives such as discussing the nature of totalitarianism, it is not necessarily clear how this functions as a criticism. If her book is about the question of justice, then as a philosopher, she has no choice but to consider the different ways in which justice and injustice manifest itself, even if not obviously so to the community at large. In Arendt's portrayal of Eichmann, he appears as a dolt, a conformist, someone who simply does his job. He is a civil servant following orders and appears even to lack political conviction. In Arendt's analysis it is not clear that Eichmann is either an anti-Semite or motivated by anti-Semitism.[4]

Arendt's book took on a life of its own and is a staple in philosophy classes that treat the question of evil, justice, ethics, the Shoah, and so forth. Her phrase "the banality of evil," requires us to rethink what evil means. And although she was deeply critical of the Israeli courts for allowing survivor testimonies, the act of doing so altered how we consider what it means for justice to be served. Is it simply about what the perpetrator did or can what the perpetrator did ever be separated from the victims who suffered that violence? Although Arendt questions this act as a distraction from the question at hand, this act of allowing survivor testimony has influenced war criminal trials and the views of human rights activists since.

Arendt's book prompted the response of the Jewish philosopher of mysticism, Gershom Scholem, captured in an exchange of letters between them. Scholem wrote to Arendt shortly after her book appeared in print. In his letter to her, he questions her "love of the Jewish people" and her right and her ability to judge events for which she was not present. Both of these criticisms raise philosophical questions—what does it mean to love a people and what does it mean to say that we are not in a position to judge if we were not there to appreciate the events that led to such actions? Arendt responds to Scholem's letter addressing these points. Beginning with the first, she tells Scholem that while she has always identified as a Jew and cannot imagine doing otherwise, she does not know what it would mean to love a people; she only loves individual persons. She distinguishes between "belonging" to a people and loving them.

In her response to the role played by the Jewish functionaries, she agrees that while there was some resistance—and she lauds those instances—resistance was itself futile. She does not blame the Jews for not resisting. She blames them instead for *not* doing nothing. That is, she argues that while there might not have been a space to resist, one could have done nothing rather than made lists and helped the Nazis in their cause. She further distinguishes between two time periods—before 1941 when it was less clear what was happening, and after 1941 where being part of the "Final Solution" makes their actions all the more problematic (*JW* 468). Using the frame of totalitarianism, Arendt argues that there is always room for some other kind of decision even if minor. The SS officers could have asked to be relieved of their "murderous assignments" with no consequence—we need to remember that before we excuse them. Similarly, Arendt argues that these functionaries could have said no. Looking back, with the benefit of hindsight, I do not know that Arendt is correct.

Her last response to Scholem concerns her point of view and for whom she speaks. She argues that she speaks for no one but herself. Recalling Lessing, Arendt declares that it is important that she think for herself and that she speak for no one else. She is independent—not speaking for a group and thus not being influenced by an ideology that might define that group. She ties this point to her view of Zionism. Although she never eschews her relationship to Judaism, she refuses to accept that to be a Jew is also to be an uncritical Zionist. To be a Jew is precisely to be the pariah.

Finally, she argues that she stands by her position that the execution of Eichmann was not only correct from a juridical standpoint, but also a necessary action. Stating this point in strong words, she says, "it would have been utterly impossible not to have carried out the sentence" (*JW* 470). The only other alternative was to hand Eichmann over to the UN, which no one wanted to do nor did Arendt think that was feasible. Mercy or pardon was also not possible. Mercy, Arendt says, indicates that the person is somehow more than the crimes that he or she committed. This, she says, is simply not true of Eichmann—there was nothing more to him than the mass murders for which he was responsible.

At the closing of the letter, she explains her term, "the banality of evil," arguing that it is not a slogan—she is the first to use this phrase. Rather, she means to indicate that there is no depth to evil; rather it defies thought. When one tries to penetrate evil, there is nothing. Only the good, she says, has depth.

Briefly returning to her concern about one's ability to think for one's self, Arendt responds to an interviewer's question about the Jewish response to her book that she is not concerned with public opinion, and indeed public opinion has a way of stifling individual opinions. She recalls the Founding Fathers who equated rules based on public opinion with tyranny, and indeed we see a similar view advanced by the nineteenth-century British philosopher, John Stuart Mill who argued in *On Liberty* that we needed to guard against the tyranny of the majority. Indeed, her need to defend herself against the Jewish community that vehemently criticized her for voicing her analysis speaks to this point.

Later in the interview she responds to the criticism of her term "banality of evil," by again stating that she means evil, and those who commit it, have no depth. They are thought-less. She suggests "we resist evil by not being swept away by the surface of things, by stopping ourselves and beginning to think—that is, by reaching another dimension than the horizon of everyday life" (*JW* 479). The more superficial someone is—and by this Arendt means, the less someone thinks for himself—the more likely he is to commit evil, or to be co-opted by a machinery that is evil. She points to Eichmann precisely because at each turn he would say "Who am I to judge [...] if all around me think it right to murder innocent people?" For Arendt, this statement becomes the example par excellence of the unthinking, the superficial, the banality of evil. How can one utter those words and not see the problem with that sentence? Indeed this sentence points to the inverted world that prompts a literary response to these events.

An Inverted World

In William Styron's novel *Sophie's Choice*, we find Sophie depressed and alcoholic, unable to move beyond the tragic choice she made upon entering Auschwitz. The book is structured in such a way that we do not know Sophie's secret until the very end. But I am less concerned here with the literary structure than I am with the significance of the story itself. In one scene, we find Sophie attempting to persuade Rudolf Hess to allow her son to leave the camp and join the Lebensborn program. It is only later that we find out what happened to Sophie's daughter, and herein lies the key to understanding Sophie as we come to know her through the story. Upon entering the camp, a Nazi doctor forces her to choose one of her children to be sent to the gas chamber. If she does not choose, they will both be killed. She chose her son to be spared. Her daughter, Eva, was sent to a crematorium. How does one reconcile oneself with such a choice? No matter how many times one might tell oneself it is not my fault, the weight of responsibility would nonetheless be unbearable and unshakeable. Such is the existentialist position that even in a situation where we do not choose, we nonetheless feel responsible. This kind of choice reveals the inverted world of Nazi Germany. Was this a choice? Was Sophie responsible? No matter what answer we give to this question, her anguish cannot be assuaged. And, yet, had Sophie not chosen, both children would have been sent to the crematorium.

Jean Amery's struggle with his experience in Nazi Germany published as *At the Mind's Limits: Contemplations by a Survivor on Auschwitz and its Realities*, led him to suggest that torture was the essence of Nazi Germany. That is, if we consider Sophie's choice, it was not the child's death per se, but the trauma of the choice carved into the survivor that defines the Nazi. Tracing Amery's point through some of the testimonial literature written by survivors, we cannot help but see this claim everywhere. The world became inverted when the Nazi's entered. We see this theme over and over, in *Night* and in the works by Primo Levi.

Two thirds into Wiesel's *Night*, the author's testimony of the horrors he witnessed and experienced in the Auschwitz and Buchenwald Nazi death camps, he recounts this particular scene:

> I witnessed other hangings. I never saw a single one of the victims weep [...] Except once.[5] [The Oberkapo] had a young boy under him [...] The Oberkapo had been arrested for stocking arms but his young servant had been left behind, also tortured though he would not speak, he would not offer other names. The SS sentenced him to death along with two others [...] Three victims in chains—and one of them, the little servant, the sad-eyed child [...] This time the Lagerkapo refused to act as executioner. Three SS replaced him. The three victims mounted together on the chairs. The three necks were placed at the same moment within the nooses. "Long live liberty!" cried the two adults. But the child was silent. "Where is God? Where is He?" Someone behind me asked [...] The two adults were no longer alive [...] But the third rope was still moving; being so light, the child was still alive. For more than half an hour he stayed there, struggling between life and death, dying in slow agony under our eyes. And we had to look him full in the face. He was still alive when I passed in front of him. His tongue was still red, his eyes were not yet glazed. Behind me, I heard the same man asking: "Where is God now?" And I heard a voice within me answer him: "Where is He? Here He is—He is hanging here on this gallows." (*Night* 61–62)

Theodicy, otherwise known as the problem of evil, has long perplexed philosophers and theologians: how does one reconcile a good and loving, all-powerful God with the presence of evil? Certainly, the presence of any evil would need to be justified, but the presence of such enormous evil, the gratuitous cruelty expressed under the Nazi regime, requires an even stronger call for such a justification. Although the horror that Wiesel recounts, one piece of which I quoted above, certainly speaks to the theme of theodicy, Wiesel, along with other survivors, resists the temptation to find the "good" in such evil, for to do so would justify the evil that the Nazis unleashed.

Following the theme of inversion, Elie Wiesel's *Night* gradually shows the shift between father and son. The father, becoming increasingly helpless, needs the son who in turn sees the father's weakness as threatening his own survival, a feeling that will weigh on Wiesel long after the camp is liberated. When the Jews are in the cattle car being transported to the camps, a woman in the car screams that she can see the flames, and she screams until she is beaten into silence by the other passengers. The moments of cruelty that creep into the camps themselves, committed not by the Nazis but by those who in their quest to survive had become like those in charge, are wrenching. For it is in these moments that we see the fragility of humanity, the easy way that good becomes evil.

Once in Auschwitz, Elie silently lies on the top bunk while his father is beaten in the bunk below his. The next morning he finds another man in his father's bunk, the Kapos having removed his father during the night. And this happened after his father, sick with dysentery and unable to leave the bunk to relieve himself was beaten by those in his bunk: a Frenchman and a Pole. Soon after, the head of the block lectures Elie not to give his ration of food to his father. He tells Elie that there are no brothers, fathers, or sons—it is everyone for himself. In other words, there are no family relations; we are islands unto ourselves. This event immediately follows from Elie initially searching for his father, even as he secretly wished not to find him, the dead weight of his father's sick body holding him back—from what, we do not really know, but maybe from hope that he might escape. Like Sophie's choice, these thoughts—that he might not find his father, that his father might die—tied to a secret hope for these things, haunt him long after he leaves the camp. What we see in this event is the undoing of Elie's moral self. We recall that twenty pages earlier when the rabbi was searching for his own son, Elie remembers that the son had sped ahead of the father to escape being tied to him so that he might have a better chance to escape the camp. And in spite of himself, Elie finds himself praying to the very God he has renounced to give him the strength "never to do what Rabbi Eliahou's son has done" (*Night* 87). And in spite of himself he has become exactly what he wished he would never become—the son who would renounce his father in order to save himself. Just before we read about his father's final hours, Elie is searching for him, yet secretly hoping he does not find him, and he says about himself, he felt ashamed, ashamed forever (*Night* 101). His father's last words the night before Elie wakes to find his father not in the bunk anymore was Elie's name: Eliezer. How could this not haunt him forever? A few weeks later Auschwitz is liberated by the Soviets, and the Americans are approaching Buchenwald. With the order of liquidation, it looked like the Jews were once again in danger of not being liberated. On April 11, 1945, the Jewish resistance attacked, the SS fled, and the resistance took charge of running the camp. At 6pm that evening, the first Americans approached. Elie was free.

The recounting of these events such as we find in *Night* is not about finding a justification or a reason for it all; rather, it is about sharing with the world the eyewitness testimony so that we would know not only what happened—in some kind of factual way—but also what such evil does to people, both in terms of inspiring courageous behavior as well as bringing otherwise good people to the limits of their darkest tendencies. The abstract and frequently hypothetical question, "what would you do if..." is presented here as quite frankly a lesson in accepting that we simply do not know what we would do. We would all like to believe about ourselves that we would do the right thing, whatever that is, but events during the Nazi regime reveal to us that we simply cannot count on what we believe about ourselves. Indeed, *Night* tells a story that what we believe about ourselves, what we hope we will do, is simply not to be trusted.

Wiesel's book struggles with his faith in God, theodicy, responsibility, choice, shame, evil, and, in some sense, the very core of Judaism. While reciting the Kaddish, the prayer for the dead, early in his arrival at the camps, he wonders if the Kaddish had ever been recited for oneself. The idea that the self is separated from the self, or more specifically, dead while alive, comes through most clearly in Primo Levi's two books: *Survival in Auschwitz* (originally published in 1947 under the title *If This is a Man*), chronicles Levi's capture as a member of the Italian resistance and his ultimate stay and survival in Auschwitz. *The Drowned and the Saved*, published forty years later, is a series of essays that raises questions about memory, the complexity of morality, shame and responsibility. His motivation for this set of essays is the worry that the Holocaust will come to be seen as one of many events in history, and the enormity of evil and cruelty that defines it will be forgotten.

Although arrested in 1943, Levi was not deported to Auschwitz until 1944, which he considers lucky. With the shortage of labor, Levi believes that the timing of his entry into this camp might have saved his life. The poem, written by Levi, that precedes the first chapter of *Survival in Auschwitz* addresses the readers in the form of a command:

You who live safe
In your warm houses,
You who find, returning in the evening,
Hot food and friendly faces:
    Consider if this is a man
    Who works in the mud
    Who does not know peace

Who fights for a scrap of bread
Who dies because of a yes or a no.
Consider if this is a woman,
Without hair and without name
With no more strength to remember,
Her eyes empty and her womb cold
Like a frog in winter.

Employing the style of the *V'Ahavta*, the prayer that follows the *Sh'ma*, one of the central prayers in Jewish liturgy, Levi concludes his poem:[6]

Meditate that this came about:
I command these words to you,
Carve them in your hearts,
At home, in the street,
Going to bed, rising;
Repeat them to your children,
   Or may your house fall apart,
   May illness impede you,
   May your children turn their faces from you.

The poem captures the central theme of the book: what does it mean to say this is a man—the one treated with such inhumanity, the one degraded, the one called subhuman. How does one retain one's humanity when on the verge of (having become?) so inhuman? Indeed, Levi recalls the term *Muselmann* "used by the old ones of the camp to describe the weak, the inept, those doomed to selection [for the gas chamber]" (*DS* 88), those who in a sense are already dead.[7] This reference appears in a chapter also titled "The Drowned and the Saved." Here Levi describes those who are on the bottom, who have given up, who are alive but dead.

The Italian philosopher, Giorgio Agamben explores this reference in his book *Remnants of Auschwitz: The Witness and the Archive*. This work, largely an examination of Levi's and Wiesel's testimonies, raises interesting philosophical questions about what it means to bear witness to such dehumanization and cruelty. What does it mean to bear witness to death when only those who have died can really tell us? Those who are so near death but who survive are unable to relate what this means for those who did not make it. In other words, testimony is its own paradox. Those who survive can bear witness to their experiences in the camp, but because they ultimately survive, they cannot bear witness to the finality of the cruelty in succumbing to death. Thus the survivors—Levi and Wiesel included—ultimately bear witness to that which is impossible to bear witness. The witness, like the *Muselmann*, sits at the border between human and inhuman, between alive and dead, and the question of testimony is put into question. As our reminder, however, the *Muselmanner*, does not survive. They have resigned themselves to death, they are dead while alive, but they do not ultimately survive the camps, thus in the end, they cannot provide the very testimony that is needed.

Returning to Levi, the philosophical issues that run throughout his work are both penetrating and troubling. In "The Gray Zone," an early chapter in *The Drowned and the Saved*, Levi explores the complexity of the hierarchy inside the camps. Those of us who never lived through the experience of Nazi Germany tend to see things in black and white—there were the Nazis and their victims. One was bad and the other good. Case closed. But Levi's book, like Wiesel's *Night*, complicates that hierarchy and exposes the way that evil infiltrates the hearts of all men. What allows this to happen? Why to some and not others? And how do we understand morality when the perpetrators and victims are not easily classified? What does it mean when the righteous are not so easily distinguished from the evil? As Levi writes,

The young above all demand clarity, a sharp cut; their experience of the world being meager, they do not like ambiguity. In any case, their expectation reproduces exactly that of the newcomers to the Lagers, whether young or not; all of them, with the exception of those who had already gone through an analogous experience, expected to find a terrible but decipherable world, in conformity with that simple model which we atavistically carry within us—"we" inside and the enemy outside, separated by a sharply defined geographic frontier. Instead, the arrival in the Lager was indeed a shock because of the surprise it entailed. The world into which one was precipitated was terrible, yes, but also indecipherable; it did not conform to any model; the enemy was all around but also inside, the "we" lost its limits, the contenders were not two, one could not discern a single frontier but rather many confused, perhaps innumerable frontiers, which stretched between each of us. (*DS* 38)

Thus, the hope that one might have had—the solidarity with the others undergoing the same suffering—was not to be found. Indeed, one's fellow prisoners were often to be feared, as we saw with Elie's father—the initial beating came from the Pole and the Frenchman with whom he shared his bunk—and with the son who ran from the father so that he might have a better chance to escape. It is not only that bonds of intimacy and familial relations are broken; it is also that those suffering turned on each other such that the victims could not be classified wholly as victims.

In this chapter, Levi explores why this happened. He recalls that the goal or aim of the Nazi camps was to break down the ability of those who were imprisoned to resist. The new arrival, coming with energy and hope, was automatically viewed as an adversary and thus must enter a situation that quickly and unambiguously changed the view of the new arrival. The new person must be broken immediately. Although the method for this introduction varied by camp in the details, the overall strategy was the same: violent punches and kicks, screams of rage, raggedy clothes, shaving of hair, nakedness and so forth. And yet upon entering the community of other prisoners, the newcomer was often envied for the newcomer still "smelled of home." The newcomer was new and thus by definition had enjoyed freedom for that much longer than those already in the camp. What the newcomer notices upon arrival is not the neatly drawn categories of enemy on the outside and comrade on the inside; instead, the newcomer notices that there is a system of hierarchy inside the camp and that there are prisoners who are privileged (in whatever way this makes sense) and those who are not. In Levi's words, this is the gray zone "where the two camps of masters and servants both diverge and converge. The gray zone possesses an incredibly complicated internal structure and contains within itself enough to confuse our need to judge" (DS 42). But Levi's astute observation continues—if the adversary betrayed one, he or she is equipped (morally and otherwise) to betray again. Thus, their "loyalty" must be secured. To this end, the task the adversary is asked to do is a task that indicates there is no going back—they have blood on their hands; they have been compromised beyond any point of return. What then impelled some prisoners to collaborate? And why might others have refused? How do we understand this? Is there anything here to understand? Does it fall in the realm of rationality? And what are the implications for morality regardless of how we answer any of these questions?

Before beginning his analysis Levi warns against hasty moral judgments. We cannot forget that the system that created this is ultimately to blame and bears the greatest weight of responsibility. He then moves to the low-level functionaries, reminding readers that the camps continued with the help of "non-violent" and less evil help, for example lice checkers. Levi confesses that he would absolve those whose guilt was minimal (DS 44). But judgment, he says, becomes more tentative, more difficult when we move to those who we call Kapos, those holding commanding positions. Although some who occupied these positions took enormous risks with the sensitive information to which they became privy, Levi reminds us that these were the minority of Kapos. Who then became a Kapo? He responds to the claim "that we are all victims or murderers" by indicating that while he was not a guiltless victim, he was also not a murderer. To confuse the two is "a moral disease [...] or a sinister sign of complicity" (DS 49). It would also be to make the moral distinction easy. To say we are all murderers becomes trite. His entry into this particular question of ethics is risky and courageous—how do we raise a moral question of those in the gray zone? Indeed, how do we even admit that such a gray zone exists? Near the end of this chapter, Levi says this: "I ask that we meditate on the story of 'the crematorium ravens' with pity and rigor, but that the judgment of them be suspended" (*DS* 61). After retelling the story of Rumkowski, a president of the Lodz ghetto who kept all in line and then himself ultimately wound up in the gas chamber, Levi says,

> All this [his own demise—like every other Jew] does not exonerate Rumkowski from his responsibilities. That a Rumkowski should have emerged from Lodz's affliction is painful and distressing. Had he survived his own tragedy [...] no tribunal would have absolved him, nor, certainly can we absolve him on a moral plane. But there are extenuating circumstances: an infernal order such as National Socialism exercises a frightful power of corruption, against which it is difficult to guard oneself. It degrades its victims and makes them similar to itself, because it needs both great and small complicities. (*DS* 68)

The brilliance of Levi's analysis is that at the end of the day, he offers no clear explanation. There is no reason, no set of reasons, that one can use to explain why this happened, that can be used to predict who will become a Kapo and who will stand strong against that temptation. What does this mean for ethics? What does this mean for the Enlightenment? For reason? Levi observes that to resist the pressure and power of a force like National Socialism requires a "truly solid moral armature," and he poses this question to his readers: How strong is ours? How would each of us behave if driven by necessity and at the same time lured by seduction? (*DS* 68). How, indeed? He ends this chapter by simply reminding us of our fragility and the fragility of morality, that we are all in the ghetto and that outside of this ghetto the train is waiting.

Forgiveness

Although the relationship between Levinas's two bodies of writings—those classified as philosophy and those classified as writings on Judaism—are not blended without tension, each often does serve to illuminate difficult themes in the other. We see this illumination in the theme of forgiveness which has recently become prominent in humanities disciplines from German studies to philosophy to literature. While participating in the Colloquium of French Jewish Intellectuals, Levinas delivered a talmudic commentary on the possibility of forgiveness and the question of justice. The commentary, published in 1963 as "Toward the Other," begins with a discussion of the Jewish holiday, Yom Kippur, and what the Day of Atonement means within the context of Judaism. Levinas then offers an extended discussion of forgiveness—its possibility and its limits. He supplements the traditional rabbinic discussion of forgiveness by turning to the question of justice. The two themes are related, although that relationship is frequently overlooked. The commentary is complex but it sheds light on how Levinas understands the impossibility of justice and the ways in which some moral transgressions leave a mark on a society for generations to come.

We can begin the discussion by looking at what Levinas writes in the foreword to *Difficult Freedom*:

> The Other's hunger—be it of the flesh, or of bread—is sacred; only the hunger of the third party limits its rights; *there is no bad materialism other than our own.* This first inequality defines Judaism. A difficult condition. An inversion of the apparent order. An inversion that is always on the point of recommencing. It is this which gives rise to the ritualism that leads the Jew to devote himself to service with no thought of reward, to accept a burden carried out at his own expense, a form of conduct involving both risks and perks. This is the original and incontestable meaning of the Greek word *liturgy*. (*DF* xiv, emphasis added)

This statement echoes his discussion at the conclusion of his talmudic reading "Toward the Other." That commentary, though it ostensibly focused on Judaism's views of atonement and forgiveness, could also be a discussion about the complexity and potential horror of justice.[8] In this commentary, Levinas offers an analysis of repentance and forgiveness in response to the question of German guilt for the Holocaust.

After a long discussion of the passage from the Mishna and its corresponding commentary in the Gemara, Levinas turns to the story where Rav Hanina refuses to forgive Rab for thirteen years in a row. Levinas reminds us that on the surface what is at stake in this discussion is not only the wrong that Rab committed against Rav Hanina, but also that Rab recognizes his fault and that he asks Rav Hanina for forgiveness. The offended party can grant forgiveness when the offender becomes conscious of the wrong.[9]

Levinas recalls that the first difficulty with making amends is the good will of the offended party to grant forgiveness. But in the commentary we have been assured of this, so why does he continue to refuse? We have, it seems, another difficulty, and Levinas points us to something more complex in this process of making amends. He asks if the offender is capable of measuring the extent of his wrongdoing. Do we know the limits of our ill will? And do we therefore truly have the capacity *to ask* for forgiveness? (25). That is, what if the offending party is not aware of the wrong for which she needs to ask forgiveness? What if the offending party is asking for forgiveness for the incorrect wrong? And if psychoanalysis has taught us anything it is that we are often unaware of our deep motivations—we are often opaque to ourselves.

The interpretation of Rav Hanina's dream, mentioned at the end of the talmudic passage, discloses precisely this point about Rab's unconscious motivations:

The dream revealed Rab's secret ambitions, beyond the inoffensive gesture at the origin of the incident. Rab, without knowing it, wished to take his master's place. Given this, Rav Hanina could not forgive. How is one to forgive if the offender, unaware of his deeper thoughts, cannot ask for forgiveness? As soon as you have taken the path of offenses, you may have taken a path with no way out. (*NTR* 25)

But the story does not end here with this optimistic comment on our relationships with others. There is yet another layer.

Levinas complicates an already complex talmudic passage by introducing discussions of atonement and forgiveness from sources that are not included in the talmudic conversation. For help with his task, he turns to 2 Samuel, which tells of the three-year famine during the time of King David. When David asks God about this famine he receives this response: "This was because of Saul and the city of blood and because he put the Gibeonites to death" (*NTR* 26). There is nothing in the story about the Gibeonites that indicates any violence was done to them directly. Nonetheless, David sends for the Gibeonites and hears their complaints. "Saul made their presence on the land of Israel impossible—they want neither gold nor silver. They have no hatred toward the children of Israel. Instead, they want seven of Saul's descendants to be handed over to them to be put to death" (*NTR* 26). David listened to them. He took two sons from Rizpah, daughter of Aiah (Saul's concubine), and five sons from Michal (Saul's daughter), but he took pity on Mephibosheth, Jonathan's son. The seven descendants of Saul were then nailed to a rock and left to die. Rizpah stayed with the corpses, covering their bodies and protecting them from the animals that would attack them (*NTR* 26).

Levinas calls our attention to the "savage greatness" of the text, which he tells us is about the necessity of *talion*, "which the shedding of blood brings about whether one wants it or not" (*NTR* 26).[10] He then adds: "The greatness of the [Hebrew Bible] consists in remaining sensitive to spilled blood, in being incapable of refusing this justice to whoever cries for vengeance, in feeling horror for the pardon granted by proxy when the right to forgive belongs only to the victim" (*NTR* 26). To sort through this difficult passage, he turns to the talmudic commentary on this story and finds that David would not have waited three years to find out the cause of the famine.[11] In his searching, David finds that the community is not itself corrupt. There is neither idolatry nor debauchery; no one is breaking promises, there are no empty speeches, no welcoming committees without welcome. David thus concludes that the famine is not the result of their way of life, and thus must be a political wrong. He asks God what the cause of the famine is and gets the strange double answer: there had been a wrong committed to the Gibeonites, who were destroyed by Saul, and a wrong done to Saul when he was not granted a royal burial (*NTR* 26–27).

The Talmud imagines the wrong Saul did to the Gibeonites, even though this wrong is not mentioned in the Bible. And the Talmud recounts that the wrong was indirect. When Saul executed the priests of the city of Nov, the Gibeonites who served them were left with no means of subsistence. Applying this point to the question of German guilt, which was part of that year's colloquium theme, Levinas repeats the midrash which affirms that "the crime of extermination begins before the murders take place, that oppression and economic uprooting already indicate its beginnings, that the laws of Nuremburg already contain the seeds of the horrors of the extermination camps and the 'final solution'." And he adds,

the Midrash also affirms that there is no fault which takes away the merit: there is simultaneously a complaint against Saul and the recalling of his rights. Merits and faults do not enter into an anonymous bookkeeping, either to annul each other or to increase one another. They exist individually. That is, they are incommensurable, and each requires its own settlement. (*NTR* 27)

Levinas presents three questions in response to this story. The first is a question about David's pity toward Mephibosheth, which results in the latter's life being spared. Is this not an exception and thus an injustice? Levinas cites the Talmud, which reassures us that David was not being partial when he selected the victims. Rather, the Holy

Ark had separated Saul's guilty sons from those who were innocent. Levinas takes from this text the lesson that recognizing the role of an objective principle does not exclude the role of the individual. There can be no justice without mercy. His second question asks after the right to punish children for the faults of their parents. His answer: "it is better that a letter of the Torah be damaged than that the name of the Eternal be profaned" (*NTR* 27). It is less dreadful

> to punish children for the faults of their parents than to tolerate impunity when the stranger is injured [...] The respect for the stranger and the sanctification of the name of the Eternal are strangely equivalent. And all the rest is dead letter. All the rest is literature. The search for the spirit beyond the letter, that is Judaism itself. (*NTR* 27–28)

Finally, Levinas's third question recalls the Torah's strict prohibition to leave human corpses exposed for so many months. Does this not profane the image of God? For Levinas, the answer is similar to the one above—the tension lies in where the profanation of God's image would lie. It would be just as much a profanation not to respond to the cry for justice and thus, in this instance, it is better that a letter of the Torah be damaged than that God's image be profaned by not responding to the call of the stranger for justice, which for Levinas, is the real meaning of the Torah (*NTR* 28).

The story of David that Levinas recalls tells of the difficulty and the pain that justice carries. David is unable not to respond to the call of those victims who cry out for justice, even if that justice is cruel. Yet, to complicate matters yet again, Levinas refers to the Gemara passage that claims the Gibeonites were not part of the children of Israel but of the rest of the Amoreans. The Talmud adds that David would have been the one to exclude them from the community of Israel. "To belong to Israel, one must be humble [place something or someone higher than oneself] one must know pity and be capable of disinterested acts. The Gibeonites excluded themselves from Israel" (*NTR* 28).

What lessons, then, does Levinas think this story teaches us? Under the Occupation, the Jews learned that there were those "whose hearts do not open before their neighbor runs a mortal risk, just as there are people whose generosity turns away from men fallen to the level of hunted animals," but they also learned that there were "souls full of humility, pity, and generosity—souls of Israel beyond Israel. The Gibeonites who lacked pity put themselves outside Israel" (*NTR* 28). We can see the roots of Levinas's now familiar asymmetrical obligation made famous in *Totality and Infinity* in his reading of the talmudic story. This story of David

> teaches that one cannot force men who demand retaliatory justice to grant forgiveness. It teaches that Israel does not deny this imprescriptible right to others. But it teaches us above all that if Israel recognizes this right, it does not ask for it itself and that to be Israel is not to claim it. (*NTR* 29)

We see his view repeated even in commentaries on others. For example, in his homage to the French philosopher Vladimir Jankélévitch, Levinas writes the following:

> [Jankélévitch's ethics] take the form of a worrying about the other, a spending without counting, a generosity, a goodness, love, obligation toward others. A generosity without recompense, a love unconcerned with reciprocity; duty performed without 'salary' of a good-conscience-for-a-duty-performed [...] All duties are incumbent upon me, all rights first due to the others. That is the dis-inter-estment of duration and a summary (if possible!) of Jankélévitch's ethics [...] *It is as if Jankélévitch were an astonishing magician, able to divine the words of the Talmud!*[12]

My point in bringing this talmudic reading into this discussion is that it makes clear that Levinas (and Jankélévitch insofar as Levinas interprets him in this manner) adheres to the view that the Other must come first, even if it means not only the possibility of self-destruction but also that this is not something I can expect from the Other in return. It is something that Levinas can *expect* from Judaism, from Jews, and from Israel but which he cannot expect from others.

Gender, Forgiveness and 2 Samuel

The entirety of Levinas's commentary on forgiveness, "Toward the Other," is precisely about the difficulty of forgiveness and that there are some Germans, namely Martin Heidegger, who cannot be forgiven. To ignore the atrocities and violence done to others that may occasion a refusal to forgive if not a demand for justice is to commit yet another violence to the victims of those acts. David did not only what he was asked to do by the Gibeonites but also what the law and morality require of an obligation to a stranger. Rizpah did what she was required to do—not to think of herself but her children and the children of others. In doing so, she satisfies the requirement of mercy—not to further the bloodshed that she might request in exchange for the bloodshed of her sons. Hence Levinas's reference to the "savage greatness" of the text becomes clear. But he also reminds us, as I mentioned above, that the Hebrew Bible demands that we remain "sensitive to spilled blood, in feeling incapable of refusing this justice to whoever cries for vengeance, in feeling horror for the pardon granted by proxy when the right to forgive belongs only to the victim" (*NTR* 26).

Providing a gloss on this particular part of Levinas's commentary, Laurence Edwards repeats Levinas's observation that "we are left with the image of this woman, this mother, this Rizpah Bat Aiah, who for six months watches over the corpses" (*NTR* 29). Like the reading offered by the Christian theologian Cheryl Exum, in her essay simply titled, "Rizpah," Edwards compares Rizpah to Antigone when he writes, "Echoes of Antigone—it so often seems to be women who perform the duty of mourning in the wake of masculine justice."[13] But unlike Exum, Edwards acknowledges the role of justice within the larger narrative. Indeed, Edwards's fleeting comment on Rizpah as the mourning mother comes near the end of a long discussion on the problem of justice—justice is both demanded but cannot be perfectly realized.[14] It is both too much and not enough. Edwards, in fact, notes Levinas's use of the 2 Samuel story to extend his original talmudic discussion on the problem of imperfect justice—a discussion in which he raises questions of "justice, reconciliation, and the impossibility of always finding neat endings."[15] Levinas's juxtaposition of these texts do not get us any closer to satisfying answers, but nor is this Levinas's intention. Rather, we must sit with the difficulty of a justice that is necessary and insufficient, moral, and violent. It is not clear to me that Rizpah is this parallel figure, even if Edwards only means to point out that women are often left to clean up the mess of a so-called masculine version of justice.

Edwards's essay echoes Levinas's own attempts to reveal the tension with regard to the Gibeonites. While it is the case that the Gibeonites are excluded from the community of Israel because they demanded blood, the laws that govern how one treats the stranger compelled David to act as he did. A terrible wrong had been done to the Gibeonites, and David was required to respond to their request. Rizpah's role in this narrative is an interesting one. It does not undo the other actions, but rather is an extension of them. Her action, to sit with the corpses and protect them, not only responds to the prohibition in Deuteronomy to leave corpses uncovered but also only makes sense within the context of the question of justice. The corpses are left uncovered because God wants everyone to see what happens when one violates the stranger. The corpses would otherwise have been buried. The very act of the corpses being left uncovered is itself part of a complicated narrative about justice. Rizpah's act is not really an act of mercy—it is not for her to be merciful. This was for the Gibeonites to do. Rather, Rizpah's act is an act of generosity, of self-abnegation.

My intention is not to discount Rizpah as a mother, or even as a woman. Indeed, recalling Levinas's own statement above about the work of mourning that women perform, Levinas himself might be emphasizing the gendered roles involved in justice. In "Damages Due to Fire," Levinas makes the explicit connection between the Hebrew word for mercy, *rahamin*, and its Hebrew root *rahem*, which means uterus. He makes the further connection that mercy is derived from the womb—thus making a more compelling image of his use of maternity, the maternal body, as the ethical relation par excellence in his most mature work *Otherwise than Being, or Beyond Essence*. But my point is that for Levinas mercy makes sense only in light of justice—even so-called masculine justice. He has always proclaimed that justice and mercy go hand in hand. They cannot be separated. Forgiveness only makes sense if an act is so horrific that forgiveness seems unlikely if not impossible.

In Exum's reading, Rizpah is the only morally worthy character, but I think this reading is not only different from the ones offered by Edwards and Levinas, for example, but different because theirs are informed by Judaism—and thus try to make sense of the complexity of justice that permeates the narrative. Additionally, I would argue in contrast that to make this claim actually undermines the difficult nature of justice that David faced and why Rizpah's action was an extension of his. Without the *moral* complexity of David's actions, Rizpah's actions are simply those of a caring mother and have nothing to do with the larger, more complex narrative— one that is necessary for her self-abnegation to be powerful. The commentators who interpret the ending of the draught as a response solely to Rizpah's actions are simply wrong in their inability to see Rizpah's actions as part of David's. It is not that Rizpah's actions were sufficient; rather, it is that as horrifying as they were, David's actions were also necessary. Her actions complete the other side of the Gibeonites' need for *talion*—an act that Levinas declares to be more vengeance than justice, since the act seems to be more for themselves than for another—and in so doing her actions, the extension of David's, reunite the houses of David and Saul.

If the commentary further emphasizes that the Other must come first, it also reveals the problem with justice. Some deeds are so bad, so horrific, that their effects will reverberate through the generations to come. We will feel those ill effects just as we reap the benefits from the past and hope to pass those benefits to the generations not yet born. Certainly murder is one of those sins, but there are others.[16] Levinas stands firm in his view that the Talmud is a continual commentary on the spilled blood of the Hebrew Bible, that it continually asks after the victim, the question of justice and the impossibility of a responsibility that ever ends or is ever done.

At the same time that Levinas delivers his talmudic reading, Jankélévitch also published an essay on the possibility of forgiveness. Jankélévitch's theory of forgiveness is complex and later became a tremendous influence on Jacques Derrida's own analysis of the possibility and impossibility of forgiveness. Because of the recent trends in this area, it is worth considering both Jankélévitch and then Derrida. Jankélévitch wrote his book *Forgiveness* during the 1960s when the debate about whether to forgive the Nazis raged in France. Like Kierkegaard's indictment of Christianity in nineteenth-century Denmark, expressed in *Fear in Trembling*, Jankélévitch worries that forgiveness has been bandied around so easily that it has now become meaningless. We forgive everything and everyone. So here is how he sums up the problem. If the act can be understood—if a person can explain why he or she committed a particular transgression or harmed us in some way, there is no need to forgive, precisely because a reason or an explanation has been given for the wrongdoing. Forgiveness is needed precisely at the moment where understanding ends, not where it begins. Forgiveness for Jankélévitch must have three features: it must be gratuitous, unselfishly motivated; it must be an event that changes my relationship with another person; and it must express the relationship between the victim and the wrongdoer. That is, it must be expressed spontaneously with what appears to be no motivation at all, almost like an act of grace. His point, like Kierkegaard's, is to illustrate just how difficult the real act of forgiveness is and that the easy way it is currently dispensed renders it absurd and diminishes the wrongs that have been done.

But Jankélévitch has a second account of forgiveness that is, shall we say, less forgiving. In this account, "Should we Pardon Them?," a more developed version of an earlier essay published under the title, "L'Imprescriptible" (The Unforgiveable), Jankélévitch examines the question of whether in 1965 the Nazis should be forgiven for the crimes committed at Auschwitz. Is twenty years enough time, he asks? Is it only about time? He states that the criteria that surround juridical law do not apply here. The question of forgiveness is asked in a different register from the legal one. Where his book *Forgiveness* takes on a distinctly non-Jewish tone and instead picks up the tenor of the Protestant philosophers like Kant, this essay is decidedly more Jewish. Focusing specifically on the crimes of Auschwitz, Jankélévitch examines what made the crimes against the Jews unique. Unlike other relations between people that seem to operate at the level of basic respect and the implicit understanding that each has the fundamental right to exist, such is not the case for the Jew, who Jankélévitch explains needs to justify his existence on a daily basis. His explanation then moves to how this view of the Jew translated into how the Jew was treated in the camps and then ultimately put to death. The crime, Jankélévitch states, was not motivated by villainous motives. Rather, he says, "the extermination of the Jews is the product of pure wickedness, of *ontological* wickedness, of the most diabolical and gratuitous wickedness that history has ever known" ("Pardon?" 556). The crime was exorbitant, and the criminals who commit crimes like these are monsters. And in response to this analysis, he says this:

> When an act denies the essence of a human being as a human being, the statutory limitations that in the name of morality would lead one to absolve that act in itself contradict morality. Is it not contradictory and even absurd to call for a pardon in this case? To forget this gigantic crime against humanity would be a new crime against the human species. ("Pardon?" 556)

Jankélévitch concludes that there are indeed acts that are unforgiveable, and crimes against humanity are *imprescriptible* ("Pardon?" 556). Time has no hold on them. It is not a question of time.

Beginning with Jankélévitch's analysis in this particular account, Derrida argues in his extended essay "On Forgiveness" that forgiveness is required at the moment when we find that which cannot be forgiven. That is, taking the two accounts of forgiveness that Jankélévitch offers, we find this: forgiveness by definition is not about understanding, for if we understood, if there was a reason offered, forgiveness would not be required. Forgiveness, then, is like an act of grace, bestowed precisely where reason cannot exist. In *Forgiveness*, then, there seems to be no limit to forgiveness, assuming that the victim is able to grant it. However, Jankélévitch admits that the position he argues in the essay, that there are in fact acts that are unforgiveable, appears to contradict the book. Nonetheless, Derrida picks up on these two pieces and argues that forgiveness is required precisely where the act appears unforgiveable. For if we can argue that the act requires forgiveness, the reasoning behind this would actually render the act no longer in need of forgiveness. It is precisely those acts that we appear not to be able to forgive that demand it. But for Jankélévitch, as soon as one can no longer punish the criminal with a punishment proportionate to his crime, and the punishment becomes almost indifferent, it is a matter of the inexpiable—he says, also—the irreparable. From the inexpiable or the irreparable, Jankélévitch concludes the unforgivable.

For Jankélévitch:

1. Forgiveness must rest on human possibility.
2. This human possibility is the correlate to the possibility of punishment, to punish according to the law.

But just as Wiesel concluded about God, at the end of the day, Jankélévitch concludes that forgiveness died in the death camps. For Derrida this reply is unsatisfactory and the aporia of forgiveness remains.

Returning to Arendt

In the final chapter of *Eichmann in Jerusalem*, Arendt argues that Eichmann should be put to death, not because it is a fitting punishment, since there is no fitting punishment, but because it would signify his removal from the moral community. In contrast to Jankélévitch, forgiving the unforgiveable would make no sense to Arendt since forgiveness would only apply to that which is comprehensible. Indeed one review of Jankélévitch's book, *Forgiveness*, argues that while he is concerned with the relationship between victim and perpetrator, he does not comment on what forgiveness would look like for the bystander who does nothing. Indeed, it is the bystander, and the bureaucrat who does not actually pull the trigger of a gun, with whom Arendt is concerned. In several essays published in the wake of "controversy" surrounding her views in *Eichmann in Jerusalem*, Arendt clarifies several of her positions and argues even more vehemently for a personal responsibility the lack of which is no excuse for committing an evil act in order to prevent one's possible death.

In her 1964 essay, "Personal Responsibility Under Dictatorship," she takes up the response to her book that took her to task for what looked like "blaming the victim."[17] Early in the essay she confesses, "I had somehow taken it for granted that we all still believe with Socrates that it is better to suffer than to do wrong" (*RJ* 18). Using Mary McCarthy's observation, Arendt draws the distinction between force and temptation. "If somebody points a gun at you and says, 'Kill your friend or I will kill you,' he is *tempting* you, that is all" (*RJ* 18). She acknowledges both that the "force" of the *temptation* to save one's own life and also the possible legal excuse for having done so, but for Arendt, this act cannot be excused ever on moral terms. There is no moral justification for it—ever. She reminds her readers that the claim "you can't know what it was like" is also the defense that Eichmann used in response to the accusation that he had alternatives. Arendt offers a twofold response: first, what does it mean even to talk about right and wrong if the issue has already been pre-judged. And second, if we remove historical events from moral discourse, what do we have left but future hypotheticals? How could we even bring someone—anyone—to trial if it is true that "the past cannot be judged by those who were not there"? Arendt addresses this view about not being able to judge by speculating, "behind the unwillingness to judge lurks the suspicion that one is a free agent, and hence the doubt that one is responsible or could be expected to answer for what he has done" (*RJ* 19). Embedded in the question, "Who am I to judge?" is the belief that we are all equally bad—"and those who try, or pretend that they try, to remain halfway decent are either saints or hypocrites, and in either case should leave us alone" (*RJ* 19). Thus, ironically, the attempt to find a "rationale" for what Hitler did, to trace his actions back to Plato, for example, is a way of alleviating guilt or responsibility since it simply attributes to his actions some kind of pre-determinism. It is a way of white-washing both history and Hitler.

What is most interesting about the analysis that Arendt provides is the difference between the obvious moral wrongs of one group versus the not so obvious and surprising wrongs of another, and it is in the distinction that we learn something important about Arendt's approach to Eichmann and Nazi Germany and something profound about how to understand what went morally wrong during that time. She writes the following:

> What mattered in our early, nontheoretical education in morality was never the conduct of the true culprit of whom even then no one in his right mind could expect other than the worst. Thus we were outraged, but not morally disturbed, by the bestial behavior of the storm troopers in the concentration camps and the torture cellars of the secret police, and it would have been strange indeed to grow morally indignant over the speeches of the Nazi bigwigs in power, whose opinions had been common knowledge for years [...] I think we were also prepared for the consequences of ruthless terror and we would gladly have admitted that this kind of fear is likely to make cowards of most men. All of this was terrible and dangerous

but it posed no moral problems. The moral issue arose only with the phenomenon of "coordination," that is, not with fear inspired hypocrisy but with this very early eagerness not to miss the train of History, with this, as it were, honest overnight change of opinion that befell a great majority of public figures in all walks of life and all ramifications of culture, accompanied as it was, by an incredible ease with which lifelong friendships were broken and discarded. In brief, what disturbed us was the behavior not of our enemies but of our friends who had done nothing to bring this situation about. They were not responsible for the Nazis, they were only impressed by the Nazi success and unable to pit their own judgment against the verdict of History as they read it. Without taking into account the almost universal breakdown, not of personal responsibility, but of personal *judgment* in the early stages of the Nazi regime, it is impossible to understand what actually happened. (*RJ* 23–24)

Her description of this other group of people brilliantly lays bare not only the problem with our moral language but also the problem with how to talk about punishment. In what ways can the normal system of punishment begin to apply to the war criminal? They were not people who under "normal" circumstances committed crimes. They were not petty thieves, for example. They were not people who once having returned to their homes would be expected to commit crimes again. Society needs no further protection from them. And the view that they can be improved in prison does not make sense. Moreover, the crimes are so vast that it is not clear imprisonment would ever match what they did. And yet, they cannot be let go; they cannot go without being punished. Arendt concludes, "[H]ere we are, demanding and meting out punishment in accordance with our sense of justice, while on the other hand, this same sense of justice informs us that all previous notions about punishment and its justifications have failed us" (*RJ* 26).

After drawing a distinction between feeling guilty and personal responsibility, Arendt proceeds to focus on the meaning of the latter. In so far as we participate in public institutions, from universities to advertising, we are all in some way implicated in the effects of the larger regime in which we live. We all follow the rules laid out for us. What concerns Arendt is the group of people whose judgment obstructed their view of personal responsibility. The "lesser evil" excuse has no purchase for her. How does one even calculate such a claim? Citing the Talmud, she claims that while politics and moral philosophy (with the exception of Kant) make a space for dirty hands, it is religious thought that does not compromise on this point: "If they ask you to sacrifice one man for the security of the community, don't surrender him; if they ask you to give one woman to be ravished for the sake of all women, don't let her be ravished" (*RJ* 36).[18] That is, while it is acceptable and even required to transgress most of the commandments within Judaism in order to save one's own life, committing murder in order to do so is strictly prohibited. Additionally, Arendt notes, it is not the vast numbers of people that were killed nor even that we might call this particular act a genocide that is so alarming. Rather, it is the complete inversion of the moral command not to kill. The new law was "thou shalt kill," not thy enemy, but innocent people.

> And these deeds were not committed by outlaws, monsters, or raving sadists, but by the most respected members of respectable society. Finally, it must be realized that although these mass murderers acted consistently with a racist or anti-Semitic, or at any rate demographic ideology, the murderers and their direct accomplices more often than not did not believe in these ideological justifications; for them, it was enough that everything happened according to the "will of the Fuhrer," was the law of the land. (*RJ* 42)

In other words, these acts were not done because people actually believed they should be done but rather because they believed that this is just the way things were supposed to be. Morality, Arendt says, was revealed to have collapsed into its original meaning—a set of mores, like table manners, that were followed by a group of people and at that moment had lost any significance connoting right and wrong in any meaningful way.

How then do we explain the non-participants? Quite simply, Arendt observes, those who refused to participate were those whose conscience did not function in an automatic way (*RJ* 44):

> They asked themselves to what extent they would be able to live in peace with themselves after having committed certain deeds; and they decided that it would be better to do nothing, not because they would then be changed for the better but because only on this condition could they go on living with themselves at all. Hence, they also chose to die when they were forced to participate. To put it crudely, they refused to murder, not so much because they still held fast to the command, "Though shalt not kill," but because they were unwilling to live together with a murderer—themselves. (*RJ* 44)

To end this chapter, then, I simply want to point out that in contrast to how I opened this chapter with a question about the limits of philosophy, indeed, the limits of reason, Arendt places evermore emphasis on reason and judgment, on thinking, for our capacity and our responsibility to consider what is right and wrong independently of the forces that try to claim otherwise, and especially in contexts where those actions are considered legal and possibly even required.[19] Indeed, for Arendt, it was not that there was too much reason that allowed Nazi Germany to flourish, but precisely not enough. But I worry that the education that will deliver such a thinking, or thoughtful person, the education that informs Arendt's belief, is not the education prevalent today.

Concluding Remarks

Why study modern Jewish philosophy? Well, part of me would like to say because it's interesting! But I realize that you might not find that answer satisfying. My hope is that through the course of reading this book, one can not only still see the relevance of modern Jewish philosophy to contemporary themes and concerns but also see reading Jewish philosophy in the same way that one would see reading in all of the humanities—there is great joy in reading material that asks questions of us, that invites us to think differently, and that offers us new ways to consider age-old questions. If, as I mentioned in the Introduction, we think of modern Jewish philosophy as critique, as raising questions about the philosophy alongside which it developed, whose view it at once appropriated and rejected, there is a way in which these late modern thinkers—post-modern thinkers, if you rather—ask us similarly to take stock of the world in which we live. From Mendelssohn who asks what the proper boundary is between religious and state authority to Buber who asks after the appropriate response to Nazi violence, to Levinas who asks us to reconsider the way modernity has fashioned the ethical subject, to Heschel who believes the prophets can still speak to us—interrupt us and guide us.

Heschel turned to the prophets because they still had something to say that was relevant to his life in the twentieth century. For him, this relevance was found in how the prophets connected to his concerns about the Vietnam War. For us, it might be the war in Afghanistan, the question of the veil in France, or simply a question about the social contract. Indeed, the most recent presidential election in the United States raised these questions exactly—Mitt Romney was asked if his religion would dictate his decisions as President of the United States. What role does religion play in governance? It is a question almost idiosyncratic to the modern period when a secular life outside of religion is imagined. Mendelssohn asked this question two hundred and fifty years prior, but the question is still not only not settled but it also has become muddied. We can learn from the questions that Mendelssohn raised and we can learn from the way those questions reverberate through the modern period generating rich discussions as the philosophers struggle to find answers.

My aim in this book has been to present and structure the material that I teach in my classes so that the threads that connect these thinkers to each other can be seen. The question that Mendelssohn was asked—"Why is he still Jewish?" is a question posed today, even if in slightly different language. That someone could ask during the 2000 presidential campaign if Joe Lieberman, an observant Jew, would be available should there be an emergency on the Sabbath indicates not only ignorance about Judaism, but also reveals the doubts people still hold about whether someone who subscribes to this religion could govern the United States. Interestingly, a similar question has not been posed to a presidential candidate who admits to be Christian, even though working on the Sabbath—Sunday (for most Christians, though not all)—is also forbidden. When Jesus answered that he would violate the Sabbath to save a life, he was (not surprisingly) answering the same way a Jew would answer.

My aim as a teacher is always to give my students as many tools as I can so that they leave college with a large toolbox and as many different kinds of tools as they can carry with them. My hope is that all students of philosophy and not only students of Jewish philosophy will find this book helpful. Although it might not initially occur to students in mainstream philosophy classes that any thinker in the Jewish philosophy canon could offer them useful tools, over my many years of teaching, my students have indicated otherwise. They consistently tell me that the most exciting part of the course was a text in Jewish philosophy or a close reading of a biblical text using a Jewish philosopher's interpretation. They also admit that these are texts they would most likely not have been exposed to because they would probably not take a course in Jewish studies, if they were in a university or college that even had such a program. They would not initially see the relevance or they would believe that a course in Jewish studies is only for Jewish students, and so on. If philosophy really is the love of wisdom, then that search ought to be expanded, and we ought to search for it in places we never imagined we would, even as we also recognize its limits. What I found in my own study of Jewish philosophy is a discovery of philosophy's own limits. By considering what philosophy cannot do, we are more able to allow philosophy to do what it does best. But we can only do this, if we also enlarge the philosophical tent so that thinkers who are not considered part of the traditional Western canon are included.

Let me end the same way I began—with an anecdote. I recently taught a two-week intensive course to five students enrolled in a unique summer scholars program for humanities majors—in this case, four students were philosophy majors and one was a double-major in film and English. I picked the theme The Enlightenment and Its Limits, with the idea that we would circle back to the Enlightenment at the end and discuss the recent reappropriation of traditional enlightenment values in order to advance arguments in support of the humanities and a humanities education. We began with the essays by eighteenth-century German philosophers that articulated an answer to the question, "What is Enlightenment?" My students, who had entered this class prepared to write on Nietzsche, race theory, gender, and so forth—all circulating around critiques of the Enlightenment, surprised themselves at how much they loved these essays that struggled to find an adequate answer to questions such as the following: What is education? What is enlightenment?

How important is freedom of the press? Is education dangerous? Who should have access to it?

But the question they found the most interesting and the most compelling was the one posed by Moses Mendelssohn in his essay: What is the relationship between moral and scientific progress? Mendelssohn, they thought, articulated the problem precisely by recognizing that societies often describe themselves as enlightened or advanced when really they simply have really good technology, but they lack the moral wisdom to know how to use it—and when not to use it. One student, entering his senior year in the fall, exclaimed every day for the next two weeks, "I still cannot believe I am only hearing Mendelssohn's name for the first time in this course and if I had not taken the spring course with you, I might not have been included in this course and then I would never have heard his name!" He felt ripped off, to put it bluntly, that an entire set of thinkers had been "kept from him." And to be clear, none of my five students is Jewish. They found the line drawn from Mendelssohn to Arendt and Ardorno, to Levi, to Levinas compelling for asking them to think about philosophy and ethical questions differently than they had done previously. And they believed by the end of the two weeks, they had been exposed to a new and exciting way of thinking about the same questions their philosophy major has been asking them to consider. Thus, while I can provide one hundred reasons for studying modern Jewish philosophy, I think the single most important one is the impact it had on my students.

Notes

Introduction: What is Jewish Philosophy?

1   Fackenheim uses the term "Orthodox" though we might consider that use anachronistic—it is odd to use the term before the Haskalah, or Jewish Enlightenment when separations in Judaism began to emerge.

2   It is difficult still to point to philosophers who have turned to his writings on Judaism, however, Robert Bernasconi, a prominent scholar of Levinas's philosophy, is one such person. In a lecture course in Italy (2003) and more recently in his public lecture at the eastern division of the American Philosophical Association (2011), Bernasconi announced to the audience that he thought it was imperative to read Levinas's essays on Judaism. If one looks at the majority of Bernasconi's writings up to that point, they do not include Levinas's writings on Judaism. The same can be said for several other Levinas scholars: e.g., Adriaan Peperzak and Simon Critchley.

3   Edmund Husserl, "Philosophy as a Rigorous Science," in *Phenomenology and the Crisis of Philosophy*, trans. Quentin Lauer (New York: Harper and Row, 1965), 71–147.

Chapter 1: Mendelssohn and the Enlightened Mind

1   http://www.english.upenn.edu/~mgamer/Etexts/kant.html (accessed January 20, 2012).

2   Immanuel Kant, "An Answer to the Question: What is Enlightenment?," translated by James Schmidt, in *What is Enlightenment? Eighteenth-Century Answers and Twentieth-Century Questions*, edited by James Schmidt (Berkeley, CA: University of California Press, 1996), 61.

3   *Moses Mendelssohn: The Sage of Modernity*, Shmuel Feiner, translated by Anthony Berris (New Haven: Yale University Press, 2010), 38.

4   This distinction is reminiscent of Rousseau's distinction in his educational treatise, *Emile, or On Education*. In this book, Rousseau tells his readers that he is concerned with the education of Emile as a man, not a citizen, because it is only if the education of Emile as a man is effective that Emile can function properly as a citizen. Additionally, in this case, the education of Emile as a man was also gendered—Rousseau did not mean "man" in the neutered general sense that the

term often connotes. Rather, he meant man, qua male. Insofar as this distinction is reminiscent of Rousseau, other of Mendelssohn's distinctions are also reminders of Aristotle's *Nicomachean Ethics*. I am assuming that for much of the time period this book covers, "man" and "men" refers to man and men, thus, I am leaving as is for ease of reference.

5   John Locke, "A Letter Concerning Toleration," translated by William Popple. http://www.constitution.org/jl/tolerati.htm (accessed January 20, 2012).

6   It should be noted that the term "toleration," as used in this letter, does not carry the positive connotation that we attribute to it now. We frequently deploy the term broadly to connote something stronger than merely allowing others who are different from us to live among us as they wish. For Locke, "toleration" was the minimal requirement for this kind of "co-habitation." This minimal requirement might be best explained by Locke's observation of religious hypocrisy: those who claim faith and love as the foundation of Christianity nonetheless use force and violence to convert others to Christianity. He wonders how it can be justified that those who are not yet fully Christian—that is, those who do not behave according to fundamental Christian values—even by their own definition, can be allowed to convert others. Thus, for Locke, mere toleration might be all that can be expected.

7   Mendelssohn is writing at a time when modern social contract theory has first taken root. For the most influential of these social contract theorists, see Thomas Hobbes, *Leviathan*; John Locke, *Two Treatises on Government*; Jean-Jacques Rousseau, *The Social Contract* and also his *Discourse on Inequality*.

8   See John Locke, *Two Treatises*.

9   Cf. Emmanuel Levinas, "Loving the Torah more than God," in *Entre-Nous*, trans. Barbara Harshav and Michael B. Smith (New York: Columbia University Press, 1998).

10 Susan E. Shapiro, "The Status of Women and Jews in Moses Mendelssohn's Social Contract Theory: An Exceptional Case," *The German Quarterly* (Winter 2009): 373–94.

11 Michah Gottlieb, editor, *Moses Mendelssohn: Writings on Judaism, Christianity, and the Bible* (Boston: Brandeis University Press 2011), 77.

12 See Spinoza, *Tractatus Theologico-Politicus*.

13 See Leibniz, *Monadology*.

Chapter 2: From Modern to Post-modern

1   Several sources helped with the collection of this information. See the entry on Hermann Cohen from the Stanford Encyclopedia of Philosophy: http://plato. stanford.edu/entries/cohen/#LifWor. See also Andrea Poma, *The Critical Philosophy of Hermann Cohen*, trans. John Denton (Albany: SUNY Press, 1997); Steven Schwarzschild, "The Tenability of Hermann Cohen's Construction of the Self," *Journal of the History of Philosophy* 13, no. 3 (1975); William Kluback, *The Legacy of Hermann Cohen*, Brown Judaic Studies (Atlanta: Scholars Press, 1989); and Emil Fackenheim, *Jewish Philosophers and Jewish Philosophy*, ed. Michael L. Morgan (Bloomington: Indiana University Press, 1996).

2   As a side note, the role that happiness, along with other emotions, plays in Kantian ethics has been a source of much scholarship. Cohen was writing long before this scholarship came to be. His point, however, that pleasure is not the end of ethics, is well taken.

3   Cf. Cohen's distinction between religion and mythology with the contrast drawn by the German critical theorists, Theodor Adorno and Max Horkheimer, in their essay, "The Concept of Enlightenment." In this essay, Adorno and Horkheimer make a similar point—mythology is characterized by lacking self-reflection. Thus, enlightenment, based on reason, views itself in contrast to mythology, yet through its own dogmatic assertions and insistence on a universality that reduces everything to calculation, enlightenment has become just as unreflective.

4   Hannah Arendt, "Jew as Pariah: A Hidden Tradition," *Jewish Social Studies*, vol. 6, no. 2 (April 1944): 99–122.

5   Morris Kaplan notes that in her biography of Rahel Varnhagen, "Arendt insisted that the great mistake of European Jewry and its friends was to treat as a social question what was inherently a political question about citizenship." Circling back to the concerns Mendelssohn raised in the divorce case, we can see a similar concern raised by Arendt, but from a different perspective. The stigmas that are attached to 'intermarriages' by both Jewish and non-Jewish communities (particularly Christian) were for her similar to the effects of anti-miscegenation laws that restricted marriages between white and non-white people in the American south. These laws, for whatever else they did, also served to maintain racial inequality. Similarly, restrictions on intermarriage regarding religion, she argued, also "[maintained] Jewish difference and subordination." See Morris B. Kaplan, "Refiguring the Jewish Question: Arendt, Proust, and the Politics of Sexuality," in *Feminist Interpretations of Hannah Arendt*, edited by Bonnie Honig (University Park, PA: Penn State Press, 1995), 109.

6   In Jerome Kohn and Ron H. Feldman. *The Jewish Writings: Hannah Arendt*. New York: Schocken Books, 2007. First published in German in 1932, the year Hitler was elected.

7   My gratitude to Zachary Braiterman for helping me clarify this point.

Chapter 3: Jewish Existentialism

1   See Bernard Martin's biography of Shestov. http://www.angelfire.com/nb/shestov/intro.html (accessed December 1, 2012).

2   "[Shestov's] exclusive concentration on the character of the individual's existence in this world, the 'adogmatic' nature of his teachings, and the aphoristic style of his writing placed him outside any trends or schools of Russian thought." See Taras Zakydalsky, in the Editor's Introduction, *Russian Studies in Philosophy*, vol. 44, no. 4 (Spring 2006): 3–4.

3   Emmanuel Levinas, Review of Leon Chestov's *Kierkegaard and the Existentialist Philosophy* translated by James McLachlan. http://www.angelfire.com/nb/shestov/sk/levinas.html (accessed November 30, 2012).

4   See Shestov, *Athens and Jerusalem*, edited and translated by Bernard Martin (Ohio University Press, 1966). http://www.angelfire.com/nb/shestov/aaj/aj_0.html (accessed December 1, 2012).

5   V. F. Asmus, "Existential Philosophy: Intentions and Results," translated by Taras Zakydalsky, *Russian Studies in Philosophy*, vol. 44, no. 4 (Spring 2006): 5–35.

6   Nahum Glatzer, *Franz Rosenzweig: His Life and Thought* (Indianapolis: Hackett Publishing, 1998), 27.

7   See Rosenzweig, *On Jewish Learning*, ed. N. N. Glatzer (Madison: University of Wisconsin Press, 1995).

8   For a few sources, see the following: Richard A. Cohen, *Elevations: The Height of the Good in Rosenzweig and Levinas* (Chicago, IL: University of Chicago Press, 1994); Robert Gibbs, *Correlations in Rosenzweig and Levinas* (Princeton: Princeton University Press, 1992); Martin Kavka, *Jewish Messianism and the History of Philosophy* (Cambridge, UK: Cambridge University Press, 2004), especially chapter 4; Hilary Putnam, *Jewish Philosophy as a Guide to Life* (Bloomington: Indiana University Press, 2009).

9   These next few pages are an expanded version of a discussion in Claire Elise Katz, *Levinas and the Crisis of Humanism* (Bloomington, IN: Indiana University Press, 2013).

10   Here, Rosenzweig means, in the language that still contains the plethora of meanings not yet removed by translation.

11   For a remarkable discussion of Rosenzweig's writings on Jewish education, see Martin Kavka, "What Does it Mean to Receive the Tradition?: Jewish Studies in Higher Education," *Cross Currents* (Summer 2006). http://www.crosscurrents.org/kavkasummer2006.htm.

12   Rosenzweig's view of Jewish education is inspiring, and not unlike the way we understand a classical liberal arts education—as enflaming the mind and transforming those engaged in the process. His essays reflect his own concerns regarding Jewish assimilation, though he could not have anticipated how the world would change for the Jews.

13   Kavka, "What Does it Mean to Receive Tradition?," 192.

14   Nahum Glatzer, "The Frankfurt Lehrhaus," *Leo Baeck Institute Yearbook* (1956), 105–22.

15   Franz Rosenzweig, *God, Man, and the World: Lectures and Essays*, ed. and trans. from the German by Barbara E. Galli (Syracuse: Syracuse University Press, 1998).

16   See Galli's Introduction to Franz Rosenzweig's "The New Thinking", edited and translated from the German by Alan Udoff and Barbara E. Galli (Syracuse: Syracuse University Press, 1999).

17   As some scholars note, *The Star* is hermetic and esoteric, lending itself to being a pedagogically ineffective text. My thanks to Zak Braiterman for encouraging me to use stronger language to describe the difficulty associated with reading—and teaching—*The Star*.

18   See Lev Shestov's lovely essay "Martin Buber," originally published in *Put* no. 39 (June 1933). http://www.angelfire.com/nb/shestov/sar/buber.html (accessed December 13, 2012).

19   Zachary Braiterman, *Shapes of Revelation: Aesthetics and Modern Jewish Thought* (Palo Alto: Stanford University Press, 2007), 37. See Braiterman's longer discussion where he takes up the difference between dead Form and living Gestalt (37–40).

20   Buber, "Dialogue," in *The Martin Buber Reader: Essential Writings*, ed. Asher D. Biemann (New York: Palgrave, 2002), 190.

21   "Letter from Martin Buber to Gandhi." http://www.jewishvirtuallibrary.org/jsource/History/BuberGandhi.html (accessed November 1, 2012).

22   Buber, *Between Man and Man*, trans. Ronald Gregor Smith (New York: Macmillan, 1965), 104–17.

23   Buber, *Pointing the Way: Collected Essays*, trans. from the German by Maurice Friedman (London: Humanities Press International, 1957), 161–76.

24   Leora Batnitzky, "Dependency and Vulnerability: Jewish and Feminist Existentialist Constructions of the Human," in *Women and Gender in Jewish Philosophy*, edited by Hava Tirosh-Samuelson (Bloomington: Indiana Universtiy Press, 2004), 127–52.

Chapter 4: Emmanuel Levinas and Abraham Joshua Heschel

1   *Face to Face with Levinas,* edited by Richard A. Cohen (Albany: State University of New York Press, 1986), 17.

2   A word about dates for Levinas: I have yet to find more than two sources that cite any set of dates for Levinas's activities in exactly the same way. *The Cambridge Companion to Levinas,* for example, notes that his directorship of the ENIO began in 1945. Other credible sources note the year as 1946 and still others cite this as 1947. There are similar discrepancies regarding the date he began working at the Alliance Universelle Israélite in the 1930s. I have done the best I can to substantiate the dates I have listed.

3   What follows in this section is an abbreviated version of a longer discussion from Claire Elise Katz, *Levinas and the Crisis of Humanism* (Indiana University Press, 2013).

4   Levinas, "Some Reflections on the Philosophy of Hitlerism," trans. Seán Hand, *Critical Inquiry* no. 17: 63–71.

5   Levinas wrote this essay only five years after attending the 1929 Davos debate between Heidegger and Cassirer. It is thought that Heidegger "won" the debate—though that declaration has come to mean many things, ranging from his position being more persuasive at showing the problems in Cassirer's view to being the philosophy that was the most influential. Certainly, we can say the latter is true, and yet, much of Levinas's essays indicate that he laments this outcome. Although he did not think Cassirer's humanism went far enough, he came to see that Heidegger's anti-humanism was far more dangerous. For an excellent, nearly line-by-line, analysis of the Davos debate, see Peter Gordon, *Continental Divide: Heidegger, Cassirer, Davos* (Cambridge: Harvard University Press, 2010).

6   Levinas makes a similar point in "L'inspiration religieuse de l'Alliance," published in the same year that he published *On Escape.* Blending themes from both the essay on "Hitlerism" and *On Escape,* Levinas refers to Hitlerism as an incomparable event that Judaism must cross. The moral and physical challenges that Hitlerism presents go straight to the very core of Judaism. Additionally, Hitlerism presented an anti-Semitism of a different kind, one in which the plight of simply being Jewish became a fatality. "The Jew cannot escape being Jewish. The Jew is ineluctably riveted [*rivé*] to his Judaism." See Levinas, "L'inspiration religieuse de l'Alliance," *Paix et Droit* 15, no. 8 (October 1935): 4 (translations are mine). Thus, it is interesting to note that while Levinas describes "being enchained" or riveted more generally—or as part of the general human condition—he makes a specific point about the Jew being "enchained" or "riveted" to his Judaism as a result of Hitler's version of anti-Semitism, which tied Judaism to a race.

7   Levinas, *Difficult Freedom,* trans. Sean Hánd (Baltimore: Johns Hopkins University Press, 1990). *Difficile Liberté* (Paris: Albin Michel, 1976).

8   Levinas, *Difficult Freedom,* 236. Unfortunately, Hegel's characterization of the Jews has influenced not only non-Jews but also Jews themselves. For more on anti-Semitism in both Hegel and Nietzsche see Yirmiyahu Yovel, *Dark Riddle: Hegel, Nietzsche, and the Jews* (University Park, PA: Pennsylvania State University Press, 1998).

9   To connect the point back to Mendelssohn, see his "Open Letter to Deacon Lavater of Zurich," Moses Mendelssohn, "Reply to Johann Caspar Lavater

(1769)," trans. Richard Levy, *From Absolutism to Napoleon, 1648–1815*, vol. 2 of *German History in Documents and Images*. Source of original German text: Moses Mendelsohn, *Gesammelte Schriften, Jubiläumsausgabe* [*Collected Writings. Anniversary Edition*], eds I. Elbogen, J. Guttmann und E. Mittwoch. Berlin: Akademie-Verlag, 1930, pp. 7–17. General website: http://germanhistorydocs.ghi-dc.org/Index. cfm?language=english. Website to document: http://germanhistorydocs.ghidc. org/sub_doclist_s.cfm?s_sub_id=28&sub_id=329&section_id=8 (accessed April 2, 2012).

10 Levinas, *On Escape*, trans. Bettina Bergo (Stanford: Stanford University Press, 2003), 50.

11 Again, to connect this point back to Mendelssohn, see Matt Erlin, "Reluctant Modernism: Moses Mendelssohn's Philosophy of History," *Journal of the History of Ideas* 63, no. 1 (January 2002): 83–104.

12 See Levinas, *Time and the Other*, trans. Richard Cohen (Pittsburgh: Duquesne University Press, 1987); and *Totality and Infinity*, trans. Alphonso Lingis (Pittsburgh: Duquesne University Press, 1969). See also, Claire Elise Katz, *Levinas, Judaism, and the Feminine: The Silent Footsteps of Rebecca* (Bloomington: Indiana University Press, 2003).

13 See Levinas, *Otherwise than Being; or, Beyond Essence*, trans. Alphonso Lingis (The Hague: Martinus Nijhoff, 1981).

14 See Levinas, *Otherwise than Being*, 67. Translation altered: "Psychisme comme un corps maternel" (*AE*, 107).

15 Nietzsche, *Thus Spoke Zarathustra*, prologue, part 4, in *The Portable Nietzsche*, trans. Walter Kaufmann (New York: Penguin, 1982). Quoted in Levinas, *Humanism of the Other*, trans. Nidra Poller (Urbana: University of Illinois Press, 2003), 45.

16 "Levinas's Political Judgment: The *Esprit* articles 1934–1983," Howard Caygill, *Radical Philosophy* 104 (November–December 2000), 6–15; 6.

17 Thomas Friedman, "The Beirut Massacre: The Four Days," *New York Times*, September 26, 1982. http://www.nytimes.com/1982/09/26/world/the-beirut-massacre-the-four-days.html?pagewanted=all (accessed June 12, 2012).

18 Abraham Joshua Heschel, *The Prophets* (New York: Harper Perennial Modern Classics Readers, 2001). Readers might think it odd to pair the hasidic thinker, Abraham Joshua Heschel with Emmanuel Levinas. However, there are several points of intersection between these two men. The first is that each sees Judaism as a path to bring about social justice. Their writings are strikingly similar on several themes: for example, Judaism having lost its way and become focused too much on ritual and not the meaning behind the ritual and the role of prayer as that which alerts us to injustice and positions us to do something about it. Finally, they both wrote about Judaism and education. When I was in the archives of the Alliance Israélite Universelle (AIU), I came across a letter, dated March 29, 1962, written by Morris Laub, the director of the World Council of Synagogues. It was addressed to Jules Braunschvig, the vice-president of the AIU. The letter invited Emmanuel Levinas to the convention of the World Council of Synagogues, to be held in Jerusalem, May 1962, in order to be a discussant for the paper on Jewish education that Abraham Joshua Heschel would be presenting. The letter mentioned that having met Levinas at the Paris conference that previous year, they believed he was the perfect person to participate in this capacity. The reply by Jules Braunschvig indicates that Levinas would be unable to attend because he needed to be in Paris at that time to oversee the move of the ENIO to its

new building. See the Alliance files during the years that Levinas was the director of the ENIO. (These are unpublished documents. See the folders containing Levinas's correspondence while he was directing the ENIO—these folders are dated 1961 and 1962.)

19 Heschel, *The Prophets*, xviii. In a biographical note about Heschel, we find him struggling to find an academic home where he fits in both intellectually and spiritually. His colleagues at the Jewish Theological Seminary did not welcome his belief that academics also have a responsibility to be activists for social causes. The JTS faculty later lamented this disagreement with Heschel and conceded that they should have followed his lead. At this present time, Heschel's concern rings all too true.

20 Heschel, *The Prophets*, xxi.

21 Ibid., xxvii.

22 Ibid., xxvi.

23 Susannah Heschel, "Looking Back, Looking Forward: A Forum," *The Nation*, December 2, 2004. http://www.thenation.com/doc.mhtml?i=20041220&s=forum (accessed October 1, 2007).

24 A. J. Heschel, *The Prophets*, xxix.

25 Levinas, "Education and Prayer," in *Difficult Freedom: Writings on Judaism*, trans. Seán Hand (Baltimore: Johns Hopkins University Press, 1990); first published as "Philosophie et Prière," dans "Bulletin intérieur du Consistoire Central des Israélites de France," 1964, juillet, 196–7, exposition on pp. 57–59 (dedicated to the "Assises du judaïsme français" of June 1964). Reprinted in *Difficile Liberté: essays sur le judaïsme* (Paris: Éditions Alban Michel, 1976). I am grateful to Georges Hansel for finding the citation for the original French publication. Revealing his continued struggle with the tension and the relationship between reason and revelation, philosophy and religion, Levinas originally titled this essay, "*Philosophie et Prière*." He introduces this essay with the following assertion: "Prayer is one of the most difficult subjects for a philosopher, as it is for a believer" (*DF*, 269).

26 Emmanuel Levinas, "On Religious Language and the Fear of God" in *Beyond the Verse: Talmudic Readings and Lectures*, trans. Gary D. Mole (Bloomington: Indiana University Press, 1994).

27 In A. J. Heschel, *Moral Grandeur and Spiritual Audacity*, ed. Susannah Heschel (New York: Farrar, Straus and Giroux, 1997).

28 Heschel, *Moral Grandeur*, 101.

29 Ibid.

30 Ibid., 110.

31 Ibid., 111.

32 The simplest definition of *kavanah* would be mindset or disposition, the direction of the heart, meaning here that the prayer is recited not as a simple mouthing of the words but with the person's full attention and the person's heart directed at what the prayer means.

33 Ibid., 112.

34 Ibid., 114.

35 Let me also state here that without question, my own relationship to Judaism and its prayers is unorthodox—both literally and figuratively. My Reform upbringing by two socially activist and intellectually minded grandparents informs my relationship to Judaism as a religion that at its heart promotes social justice, requires us to respond to those who are most needy among us, and encourages

our minds to be critically engaged. I do not doubt that this informs my own interpretation of Judaism. That is, I understand Judaism as a relationship to God that mirrors precisely what one is asked when one recites the Sh'ma—to approach it with all one's mind, heart, and body. Thus, this engagement with Judaism, God, and the Sh'ma are neither mindless nor are they indicative of blind faith. Rather, this relationship requires one to be fully engaged.

36 Heschel, *The Prophets*, xviii.

Chapter 5: The Limits of Philosophy

1 *Jewish Philosophers and Jewish Philosophy*, edited by Michael L. Morgan (Bloomington, IN: Indiana University Press, 1996), 129–36.

2 I appreciate the distinction that Fackenheim is trying to make, and indeed, "Holocaust" implies a sense of martyrdom that we would want to reject. My concern is that I am not sure that even a burnt sacrifice negates the possibility that the act is still a murder. It should be noted that in *Fear and Trembling*, Søren Kierkegaard's philosophical examination of the biblical story of the binding of Isaac, Kierkegaard raises precisely this question about sacrifice and murder by asking after the possibility of a teleological suspension of the ethical. Even if it were true in some sense that Abraham had been commanded by God to sacrifice his son Isaac, the public expression of this act would still have been murder. I do not mean to digress, but if anything to drive the point a little harder.

3 Kohn, Jerome and Ron H. Feldman, 2007, *The Jewish Writings: Hannah Arendt* (New York: Schocken Books), 453–61.

4 Arendt's analysis of Eichmann is based primarily on testimony at the trial. She published this work without the benefit of fifty more years of documents, analysis, interviews, and so forth. It should be noted however that with the release of many, many documents—some in German archives, some in Israel, Eichmann's anti-Semitism appears less disputed. In her 2011 book, *The Eichmann Trial*, Deborah Lipstadt reveals that Eichmann was in fact deeply anti-Semitic. Using archive material that was unavailable to Arendt, Lipstadt also puts to rest Eichmann's claim that he was simply following orders when he admits in a memoir he wrote during the trial that he had exempted several Jews from deportation. On what grounds could he have done this—what would allow him not to follow orders in these instances? And if he did not follow orders at these times, then why anytime?

5 There is considerable controversy surrounding the status of Wiesel's trilogy, which includes *Night*. Bookstores long stocked Wiesel's books in the fiction section, thus raising questions about who the narrator is: Do we call him Elie or Wiesel, the latter indicating that the book is a memoir or autobiographical account. In recent interviews both the publisher and Wiesel himself indicate that the book is indeed a memoir and bookstores have begun relabeling the book as non-fiction.

6 From Deuteronomy 6:6-9:

> 6 And these words, which I command thee this day, shall be upon thy heart;
> 7 and thou shalt teach them diligently unto thy children, and shalt talk of them when thou sittest in thy house, and when thou walkest by the way, and when thou liest down, and when thou risest up.

8 And thou shalt bind them for a sign upon thy hand, and they shall be for frontlets between thine eyes.

9 And thou shalt write them upon the door-posts of thy house, and upon thy gates.

7 The literal meaning of this term is "Muslim." From the documents at the Yad Vashem website, we find one explanation for this term: that the weakness and near death state led to the prisoners succumbing to a prone position, not unlike the image of a "Muslim prostrating himself on the ground in prayer." http://www1.yadvashem.org/odot_pdf/Microsoft%20Word%20-%206474.pdf (accessed October 12, 2012).

8 Levinas, "Toward the Other," in *Nine Talmudic Readings*, trans. Annette Aronowicz (Bloomington: Indiana University Press, 1990).

9 How can one hold that faults committed by a man against another are not forgiven him by the Day of Atonement when it is written (1 Samuel 2): "If a man offends another man, Elohim will reconcile" (cited in Levinas's *Nine Talmudic Readings* 18). The Gemara ultimately rejects Rabbi Joseph bar Helbe's argument and inserts the phrase, "and *appeases him*" so that the line reads like this: "If a man commits a fault toward another man and *appeases him*, God will forgive."

10 From Genesis 9:6, "Whoever sheds the blood of man, by man shall his blood be shed." In general this is a view of retaliatory justice, or exchanging like injury for like injury—what has come to be interpreted as an "eye for an eye," although the rabbinic commentary on this particular phrase indicates that an "eye for an eye" is not to exchange like for like, literally, but rather the punishment should fit the crime, and should not exceed it. Additionally, individual justice or personal revenge is prohibited, and holding a grudge is discouraged if not outright prohibited (Lev. 19:17-18).

11 Levinas refers to the Talmud, Tractate *Yebamot*, 58b–59a.

12 Emphasis added. See Levinas, *Outside the Subject*, trans. Michael B. Smith (Palo Alto, CA: Stanford University Press, 1993), 87.

13 Laurence L. Edwards, "'Extreme Attention to the Real': Levinas and Religious Hermeneutics," *Shofar: An Interdisciplinary Journal of Jewish Studies* 26, no. 4 (Summer 2008), 36–53.

14 Ibid., 47.

15 Ibid.

16 Leora Batnitzky, "Jewish Vengeance, Christian Compassion?—or the misunderstanding that won't go away," *Character: A Journal of Everyday Virtues* (September 1, 2006). http://incharacter.org/archives/justice/jewish-vengeance-christian-compassion-or-the-misunderstanding-that-wont-go-away/ (accessed August 23, 2010).

17 Hannah Arendt, "Personal Responsibility Under Dictatorship," in *Responsibility and Judgment*, edited by Jerome Kohn (New York: Schocken, 2003). I would like to thank Matthew Wester for reading this chapter and recommending that I look at the collection of essays in this book.

18 The Talmudic passage in which this view is found is Sanhedrin 74a, which states: "Transgress and suffer not death, he may transgress and not suffer death, excepting idolatry, incest, [which includes adultery] and murder."

19 See also Arendt's essay, "Thinking and Moral Considerations," in *Responsibility and Judgment*.

References, Sources and Suggested Reading

Preface

References

Baehr, Peter and Daniel Gordon, "From the Headscarf to the Burqa: The Role of Social Theorists in Shaping Laws Against the Veil." *Economy and Society*, forthcoming.

Chanter, Tina, 1994. *Ethics of Eros: Irigaray's Rewriting of the Philosophers.* New York: Routledge.

———, 2001a. *Time, Death, and the Feminine: Levinas with Heidegger.* Stanford: Stanford University Press.

———, 2001b. *Feminist Interpretations of Emmanuel Levinas*, ed. Rereading the Canon series. University Park, PA: Pennsylvania State University Press.

Cohen, Hermann, 1971. *Reason and Hope: Selections from the Jewish Writings of Hermann Cohen*, trans. and ed. Eva Jospe. Cincinnati: Hebrew Union College Press.

———, 1995. *Religion of Reason Out of the Sources of Judaism*, trans. Simon Kaplan. Atlanta: Scholars Press.

Critchley, Simon, 1992. *The Ethics of Deconstruction: Derrida and Levinas.* London: Blackwell.

Gordon, Daniel. 2008. "Why Is There No Headscarf Affair in the United States?" *Historical Reflections* 34, no. 3 (Winter): 37–60.

Honig, Bonnie, 2009. *Emergency Politics: Paradox, Law, Democracy.* Princeton: Princeton University Press.

Katz, Claire Elise, 2001. "Reinhabiting the House of Ruth: Exceeding the Limits of the Feminine in *Totality and Infinity*." In *Feminist Interpretations of Emmanuel Levinas*, Tina Chanter, ed., 145–170. University Park, PA: Pennsylvania State University Press.

———, 2003. *Levinas, Judaism, and the Feminine: The Silent Footsteps of Rebecca.* Bloomington: Indiana University Press.

———, 2013. *Levinas and the Crisis of Humanism.* Bloomington: Indiana University Press.

Levinas, Emmanuel. 1946. "La réouverture de l'Ecole Normale Israélite Orientale." Cahiers l'Alliance Israélite Universelle no. 9 (July): 1–2.

———, 1969. *Totality and Infinity*, trans. Alphonso Lingis. Pittsburgh: Duquesne University Press.

———, 1990. *Difficult Freedom: Essays on Judaism*, trans. Seán Hand. Baltimore, MD: Johns Hopkins University Press.

———, 1991. "Some Reflections on the Philosophy of Hitlerism," trans. Seán Hand. *Critical Inquiry* no. 17: 63–71. "Quelques Réflexions sur la Philosophie de L'Hitlérisme." *Esprit* 2 (1934): 199–208.

———, 1994. *Nine Talmudic Readings*, trans. Annette Aronowicz. Bloomington: Indiana University Press.

———, 1998. *Otherwise Than Being or Beyond Essence*, trans. Alphonso Lingis. Pittsburgh: Duquesne University Press.

———, 2003. *On Escape*, trans. Bettina Bergo. Palo Alto, CA: Stanford University Press.

Mendelssohn, Moses, 1983. *Jerusalem*. Waltham, MA: Brandeis University Press.

Peperzak, Adriaan, 1993. *To the Other: An Introduction to the Philosophy of Emmanuel Levinas*. West Lafayette, IN: Purdue University Press.

Perpich, Diane, 2008. *The Ethics of Emmanuel Levinas*. Palo Alto, CA: Stanford University Press.

Rosenzweig, Franz, 1995. *On Jewish Learning*, ed. N. N. Glatzer. Madison: University of Wisconsin Press.

Sandford, Stella, 2000. *The Metaphysis of Love: Gender and Transcendence in Levinas*. London: Continuum.

Introduction: What is Jewish Philosophy?

Philosophers of the Enlightenment

Bacon, F., 1620. *The New Organon (Novum Organum)*, ed. Lisa Jardine and Michael Silverthorne. Cambridge, UK: Cambridge University Press, 2000.

Descartes, R., 1641. *Meditations on First Philosophy*, ed. John Cottingham. Cambridge, UK: Cambridge University Press, 1996.

Diderot, D., 1751–72. *Encyclopedia: Selections*, ed. Stephen J. Grendzier. New York: Harper and Row, 1967.

Hobbes, T., 1651. *Leviathan*, ed. R. Tuck. Cambridge, UK: Cambridge University Press, 1991.

Hume, D., 1739–40. *A Treatise of Human Nature*, ed. L. A. Selby-Bigge, 2nd edn, revised by P. H. Nidditch. Oxford: Clarendon, 1975.

———, 1748. *Enquiry Concerning Human Understanding*. In *Enquiries Concerning Human Understanding and Concerning the Principles of Morals*, ed. L. A. Selby-Bigge, 3rd edn, revised by P. H. Nidditch. Oxford: Clarendon, 1975.

———, 1779. *Dialogues Concerning Natural Religion*, 2nd edn, ed. R. Popkin. Indianapolis: Hackett, 1980.

Kant, I., 1781, 2nd edn, 1787. *Critique of Pure Reason*, trans. and ed. P. Guyer and A. Wood. Cambridge, UK: Cambridge University Press, 1998.

———, 1784. "What is Enlightenment?" In *Foundations of the Metaphysics of Morals* and *What is Enlightenment*, trans. L. W. Beck. New York: Liberal Arts Press, 1959.

Lessing, G. E., 1766. *Laocoön: An Essay on the Limits of Painting and Poetry*, trans. E. A. McCormick. Indianapolis: Bobbs-Merrill, 1962.

Locke, J., 1690. *An Essay Concerning Human Understanding*, ed. P. H. Nidditch. Oxford: Clarendon, 1975.

———, 1690. *Locke's Two Treatises of Government*, ed. Peter Laslett. Cambridge, UK: Cambridge University Press, 1960.

———, 1690. *The Reasonableness of Christianity, as delivered in Scripture*, ed. G. W. Ewing. Chicago: Regnery, 1965.

Montesquieu, Baron de (Charles-Louis de Secondat), 1748. *The Spirit of the Laws*, trans. T. Nugent. New York: Dover, 1949.

Pope, A., 1733. *An Essay on Man*, ed. M. Mack. New Haven, CT: Yale University Press, 1951.

Rousseau, J. J., 1762. *Emile, or On Education*, trans. A. Bloom. New York: Basic Books, 1979.

———, 1762. *On the Social Contract*, trans. M. Cranston. New York: Viking Penguin, 1988.

Spinoza, B., 1677. *Ethics*, vol. 1 of *The Collected Writings of Spinoza*, trans. E. Curley. Princeton: Princeton University Press, 1985.

———, 1677. *Theological-Political Treatise*, trans. S. Shirley. Indianapolis: Hackett, 2001.

Voltaire (Francois-Marie d'Arouet), 1734. *Philosophical Letters (Letters on the English Nation, Letters on England)*, ed. L. Trancock. New York: Penguin, 2002.

———, 1752. *Philosophical Dictionary*, ed. T. Besterman. London: Penguin, 2002.

Critical Response to the Enlightenment

Adorno, Theodor W. and Max Horkheimer, 1947. *Dialectic of Enlightenment*, trans. Edmund Jephcott, ed. Gunzelin Schmid Noerr. Palo Alto, CA: Stanford University Press, 2002.

Berlin, Isaiah, 1997. *The Proper Study of Mankind*, ed. Henry Hardy and Roger Hausheer. New York: Farrar, Straus, Giroux.

Cassirer, Ernst, 1932. *The Philosophy of the Enlightenment*, trans. Fritz C. A. Koelln and James P. Pettegrove. Boston: Beacon, 1955.

Gay, Peter, 1966–69. *The Enlightenment: An Interpretation*. New York: Knopf.

Israel, Jonathan, 2001. *Radical Enlightenment: Philosophy and the Making of Modernity 1650–1750*. Oxford: Oxford University Press.

Schmidt, James, ed., 1996. *What is Enlightenment? Eighteenth-Century Answers and Twentieth-Century Questions*. Berkeley, CA: University of California Press.

Spinoza

James, Susan, 2012. *Spinoza on Philosophy, Religion, and Politics: The Theological-Political Treatise*, Oxford: Oxford University Press.

LeBuffe, Michael, 2010. *From Bondage to Freedom: Spinoza on Human Excellence*. Oxford: Oxford University Press.

Melamed, Yitzhak, and Michael A. Rosenthal, eds, 2010. *Spinoza's Theological-Political Treatise: A Critical Guide*. Cambridge, UK: Cambridge University Press.

Nadler, Steven, 1999. *Spinoza: A Life*. Cambridge, UK; New York: Cambridge University Press.

———, 2002. *Spinoza's Heresy*. Oxford: Oxford University Press.

———, 2006. *Spinoza's Ethics: An Introduction*. Cambridge, UK: Cambridge University Press.

———, 2011. *A Book Forged in Hell: Spinoza's Scandalous Treatise and the Birth of the Secular Age*. Princeton: Princeton University Press.

Ravven, Heidi, and Leonard E. Goodman, eds, 2002. *Jewish Themes in Spinoza's Philosophy*. Albany: SUNY Press.

Sharp, Hasana, 2011. *Spinoza and the Politics of Renaturalization*. Chicago, IL: University of Chicago Press.

Yovel, Yirmiyahu, 1989. *Spinoza and Other Heretics*, 2 vols. Princeton: Princeton University Press.

———, ed., 1991. *God and Nature: Spinoza's Metaphysics*. Leiden: Brill.

———, ed., 1994. *Spinoza on Knowledge and the Human Mind*. Leiden: Brill.

———. ed., 1999. *Desire and Affect: Spinoza as Psychologist*. New York: Little Room Press.

Yovel, Yirmiyahu and Gideon Segal, eds, 2004. *Spinoza on Reason and the "Free Man."* New York: Little Room Press.

What is Jewish Philosophy?

Hughes, Aaron W. and Elliot R. Wolfson, eds, 2009. *New Directions in Jewish Philosophy*. Bloomington, IN: Indiana University Press.

Ochs, Peter and Nancy Levene, eds. *Textual Reasonings: Jewish Philosophy and Text Study at the end of the Twentieth Century*. London: SCM Press, 2002; Grand Rapids: Eerdmans, 2003.

Samuelson, Norbert, 2008. *Jewish Faith and Modern Science: On the Death and Rebirth of Jewish Philosophy*. Lanham, MD: Rowman and Littlefield.

Tirosh-Samuelson, Hava, ed., 2005. *Women and Gender in Jewish Philosophy*. Bloomington: Indiana University Press.

Chapter 1: Mendelssohn and the Enlightened Mind

Other Works by Mendelssohn in English

Phaedo; or, On the Immortality of the Soul, an excerpt can be found here: http://www.schillerinstitute.org/fid_91-96/941_phaedon.html

1997. *Philosophical Writings*, trans. D. O. Dahlstrom. Cambridge, UK: Cambridge University Press.

Suggested Reading

Altmann, Alexander, 1973. *Moses Mendelssohn: A Biographical Study*. University of Alabama Press.

Arkush, Allan, 1994. *Moses Mendelssohn and the Enlightenment*. Albany: SUNY Press.

Cassirer, E., 1951. *The Philosophy of the Enlightenment*. Princeton: Princeton University Press.

Foucault, Michel, 1984. "What is Enlightenment?" ("Qu'est-ce que les Lumières?"), in *The Foucault Reader*, ed. Paul Rabinow, New York: Pantheon Books, 32–50.

Hobbes, Thomas. *Leviathan*. http://www.gutenberg.org/catalog/world/readfile?fk_files=2522681.

Horkheimer and Adorno, 2002. *The Dialectic of Enlightenment: Philosophical Fragments*, trans. Edmund Jephcott. Palo Alto, CA: Stanford University Press, 1–34.

Locke, John. *Two Treatises of Government*. http://oregonstate.edu/instruct/phl302/texts/locke/locke2/2nd-contents.html.

Morgan, Michael, 1989. "Mendelssohn's Defense of Reason in Jerusalem." *Judaism: A Quarterly Journal of Jewish Life and Thought* 38 (4): 449–59.

Rousseau, Jean-Jacques. *Social Contract*. http://www.constitution.org/jjr/socon.htm.

Schmidt, James, 1996. *What is Enlightenment? Eighteenth-Century Answers and Twentieth-Century Questions*. Berkeley: University of California Press.

Chapter 2: From Modern to Post-modern

Major Works by Cohen in English

1971. *Reason and Hope: Selections from the Jewish Writings of Hermann Cohen*, trans. Eva Jospe. New York: Norton and Norton.

1995. *Religion of Reason: Out of the Sources of Judaism*, trans. Simon Kaplan. Atlanta, GA: Scholars Press.

Suggested Reading

Kant, Immanuel, *Religion within the Limits of Reason Alone*.
———, *Groundwork for a Metaphysics of Morals*.
———, *Critique of Pure Reason*.

Kepnes, S., 2007. *Jewish Liturgical Reasoning*. Oxford: Oxford University Press.

Kluback, W., 1884. *Hermann Cohen: The Challenge of a Religion of Reason*. Atlanta, GA: Scholars Press.

Poma, A., 1997. *The Critical Philosophy of Hermann Cohen*, trans. John Denton. Albany: SUNY Press.

Rashkover, Randi, 2005. *Revelation and Theopolitics: Barth, Rosenzweig, and the Politics of Praise*. London: Continuum. (See especially the chapter on Cohen).

Major Works by Arendt

1944. "The Jew as Pariah: A Hidden Tradition." *Jewish Social Studies*, vol. 6, no. 2 (April): 99–122.

1965. *Eichmann in Jerusalem: A Report on the Banality of Evil*. New York: Viking.

1965. *On Revolution*. New York: Viking.

1968. *Between Past and Future*. New York: Penguin.

1973. *The Origins of Totalitarianism*. New York: Harcourt Brace Jovanovich.

Sources and Recommended Reading

Benhabib, S., 1996. *The Reluctant Modernism of Hannah Arendt*. London: Sage Publications.

Bernstein, R., 1996. *Hannah Arendt and the Jewish Question*. Cambridge: Polity Press.

D'Entreves, Maurizio Passerin, 2006. Entry on Hannah Arendt. *Stanford Encyclopedia of Philosophy*. http://plato.stanford.edu/entries/arendt/ (accessed December 6, 2012).

Honig, B., ed., 1995. *Feminist Interpretations of Hannah Arendt*. University Park, PA: Pennsylvania State University Press.

Isaac, J., 1992. *Arendt, Camus, and Modern Rebellion*. New Haven: Yale University Press.

Kohn, Jerome and Ron H. Feldman, 2007. *The Jewish Writings: Hannah Arendt*. New York: Schocken Books.

Magid, Shaul, 2013. "The 'Ethnic Jew' and Judaism in America according to Felix Adler, Josephine Lazarus, and Mordecai Kaplan." In William Plevan, ed. *Personal Theology: Essays in Honor of Neil Gillman*. Brighton, MA: Academic Studies Press.

Taminiaux, J., 1997. *The Thracian Maid and the Professional Thinker: Arendt and Heidegger*. Albany: State University of New York Press.

Villa, D., 1996. *Arendt and Heidegger: The Fate of the Political*. Princeton: Princeton University Press.

———, 1999. *Politics, Philosophy, Terror: Essays on the Thought of Hannah Arendt*. Princeton: Princeton University Press.

———, ed., 2000. *The Cambridge Companion to Hannah Arendt*. Cambridge: Cambridge University Press.

Young-Bruehl, E., 1982. *Hannah Arendt: For Love of the World*. New Haven: Yale University Press. Second edition, 2004.

Chapter 3: Jewish Existentialism

Suggested Reading for Existentialism

Barrett, W., 1962. *Irrational Man: A Study in Existential Philosophy* (1958). Garden City: Doubleday.

Camus, A., 1955. *The Myth of Sisyphus and Other Essays*, trans. Justin O'Brien. New York: Knopf.

———, 1988. *The Stranger*, trans. Matthew Ward. New York: Knopf.

Kaufmann, W., 1968. *Existentialism from Dostoevsky to Sartre*. Cleveland: Meridian Books.

Kierkegaard, S., 1983. *Fear and Trembling*, trans. Howard V. Hong and Edna H. Hong. Princeton: Princeton University Press.

Nietzsche, F., 1975. *Thus Spoke Zarathustra*. In *The Portable Nietzsche*, trans. Walter Kaufmann. New York: Viking Press.

Sartre, Jean-Paul. 1955. *No Exit, and Three Other Plays*. New York: Vintage Books.

———, 1959. *Nausea*, trans. Lloyd Alexander. New York: New Directions.

———, 1988. *What is Literature?* (1948). Cambridge MA: Harvard University Press.

———, 2007. *Existentialism is a Humanism*, trans. Carol Macomber. New Haven: Yale University Press.

Shestov, Lev. 1969. *Kierkegaard and the Existential Philosophy*, trans. Elinor Hewitt. Athens: Ohio University Press.

Tillich, P., 2000. *The Courage to Be*. New Haven: Yale University Press.

Unamuno, M., 1954. *The Tragic Sense of Life*, trans. J. E. Crawford Flitch. New York: Dover.

Wahl, J., 1949. *A Short History of Existentialism*, trans. Forrest Williams and Stanley Maron. New York: Philosophical Library.

Major Works by Shestov

1966. *Athens and Jerusalem*, ed. and trans. Bernard Martin. Ohio University Press. http://www.angelfire.com/nb/shestov/aaj/aj_0.html (accessed December 1, 2012).

1969. *Kierkegaard and the Existential Philosophy*, trans. Elinor Hewitt. Athens: Ohio University Press.

Suggested Reading

Asmus, V. F., 2006. "Existential Philosophy: Its Intentions and Results," trans. Taras Zakydalsky. *Russian Studies in Philosophy*, vol. 44, no. 4 (Spring): 5–35.

Finkenthal, Michael, 2010. *Lev Shestov: Existential and Religious Thinker*. New York: Peter Lang Publishing.

Kornblatt, Judith Deutsch, 2003. "The Apotheosis of Exile: Jews and the Russian Religious Renaissance (The Case of Lev Shestov)." *Symposium: A quarterly Journal in Modern Literature*, vol. 57, issue 3: 127–36.

Levinas, Emmanuel. Review of Leon Chestov's *Kierkegaard and the Existentialist Philosophy*, trans. James McLachlan. http://www.angelfire.com/nb/shestov/sk/levinas.html (accessed November 30, 2012).

Zakydalsky, Taras, 2006. Editor's Introduction. *Russian Studies in Philosophy*, vol. 44, no. 4 (Spring): 3–4.

Major Works by Buber in English

1937. *I and Thou*, trans. Ronald Gregor Smith. Edinburgh: T. and T. Clark, 2nd edn. New York: Scribner, 1958. 1st Scribner Classics edn. New York: Scribner, 2000, c.1986.

1952, 1977. *Eclipse of God*. New York: Harper and Bros. Publ. 2nd edn. Westport, CT: Greenwood Press.

1965. *Between Man and Man*, trans. Ronald Gregor-Smith; with an introduction by Maurice Friedman. London, New York: Routledge.

1967. *On Judaism*, ed. Nahum Glatzer and trans. Eva Jospe and others. New York: Schocken.

1968. *On the Bible: Eighteen Studies*, ed. Nahum Glatzer. New York: Schocken.

1970. *I and Thou*, a new translation with a prologue, "I and you," and notes by Walter Kaufmann. New York: Scribner.

1974. *Pointing the Way*, trans. Maurice Friedman. New York: Harper, 1957. 2nd edn. New York: Schocken.

Suggested Reading

Cohen, Adir, 1983. *The Educational Philosophy of Martin Buber*. East Brunswick, NJ: Associated University Presses.

Friedman, Maurice, 1981. *Martin Buber's Life and Work: The early years, 1878–1923*. New York: Dutton.

Hodes, Aubrey, 1972. *Encounter with Martin Buber*. London: The Penguin Press.

Horwitz, Rivka, 1978. *Buber's Way to I and Thou: An Historical Analysis*. Heidelberg.

Vermes, Pamela, 1988. *Buber*. New York: Grove Press.

Major Works by Rosenzweig in English

1953. *Understanding the Sick and the Healthy: A View of World, Man, and God*, ed. and trans. Nahum N. Glatzer. New York: Noonday Press.

1971. *Judaism Despite Christianity: The "Letters on Christianity and Judaism" Between Eugen Rosenstock-Huessy and Franz Rosenzweig*, ed. Eugen Rosenstock-Huessy and trans. Dorothy Emmet. New York: Schocken.

1971. *The Star of Redemption*, trans. William W. Hallo. New York: Holt, Rinehart, and Winston.

1998. *God, Man, and the World: Lectures and Essays*, ed. and trans. Barbara E. Galli. Syracuse, NY: Syracuse University Press.

2000. *Cultural Writings of Franz Rosenzweig*, ed. and trans. Barbara E. Galli. Syracuse, NY: Syracuse University Press.

2000. *Philosophical and Theological Writings*, trans. and ed. with notes and commentary, by Paul W. Franks and Michael L. Morgan. Indianapolis: Hackett.

2005. *The Star of Redemption*, trans. Barbara E. Galli. Madison: University of Wisconsin Press.

Suggested Reading

Batnitzky, Leora, 2000. *Idolatry and Representation: The Philosophy of Franz Rosenzweig Reconsidered*. Princeton: Princeton University Press.

Benjamin, Mara H., 2009. *Rosenzweig's Bible: Reinventing Scripture for Jewish Modernity*. Cambridge, UK; New York: Cambridge University Press.

Bernstein, Jeffrey, "Rosenzweig's Tragedy and the Spectacles of Strauss: The Question of German-Jewish History" in *The German Tragic*, ed. Steven Dowden and Thomas Quinn. Camden House, forthcoming.

Braiterman, Zachary, 2007. *The Shape of Revelation: Aesthetics and Modern Jewish Thought*. Stanford: Stanford University Press.

Cohen, Richard A., 1994. *Elevations: The Height of the Good in Rosenzweig and Levinas*. Chicago, IL: University of Chicago Press.

Galli, Barbara, 2002. *Franz Rosenzweig and Jehudah HaLevi: Translating, Translations, and Translators*. Montreal: McGill-Queens University Press.

Gibbs, Robert, 1992. *Correlations in Rosenzweig and Levinas*. Princeton: Princeton University Press.

Glatzer, Nahum, ed., 1998. *Franz Rosenzweig: His Life and Thought*, with a new foreword by Paul Mendes-Flohr. Indianapolis: Hackett Publishing.

Gordon, Peter Eli, 2003. *Rosenzweig and Heidegger: Between Judaism and German Philosophy*. Berkeley: University of California Press.

Mendes-Flohr, Paul, ed., 1988. *The Philosophy of Franz Rosenzweig*. University Press of New England for Brandeis University Press.

Mosès, Stéphane, 1992. *System and Revelation: The Philosophy of Franz Rosenzweig*, trans. Catherine Tihanyi. Detroit: Wayne State University Press.

Pollock, Benjamin, 2009. *Franz Rosenzweig and the Systematic Task of Philosophy*. Cambridge, UK; New York: Cambridge University Press.

Putnam, Hilary, 2008. *Jewish Philosophy as a Guide to Life: Rosenzweig, Buber, Levinas, Wittgenstein*. Bloomington: Indiana University Press.

Samuelson, Norbert M., 1999. *A User's Guide to Franz Rosenzweig's* The Star of Redemption. Richmond, VA: Curzon.

Wolfson, Elliot R., 1997. "Facing the Effaced: Mystical Eschatology and the Idealistic Orientation in the Thought of Franz Rosenzweig." *Zeitschrift fUr neuere Theologiegeschichte* 4: 39–81.

———, 2010. "Light does Not Talk but Shines: Apophasis and Vision in Rosenzweig's Theopetic Temporality," in Hughes, Aaron and Elliot Wolfson, eds. *New Directions in Jewish Philosophy*. Bloomington: Indiana University Press.

Chapter 4: Emmanuel Levinas and Abraham Joshua Heschel

Major Works by Levinas in English

1969. *Totality and Infinity: An Essay on Exteriority*, trans. Alphonso Lingis. Pittsburgh, PA: Duquesne University Press.

1978. *Otherwise than Being or Beyond Essence*, trans. Alphonso Lingis. Dordrecht and Boston, MA: Kluwer Academic Publishers.

1987. *Time and the Other*, trans. Richard A. Cohen. Pittsburgh, PA: Duquesne University Press.

1990. *Nine Talmudic Readings*, trans. Annette Aronowicz. Bloomington: Indiana University Press.

1991. *Difficult Freedom: Essays on Judaism*, trans. Seán Hand, London: Athlone.

1994. *Beyond the Verse: Talmudic Readings and Lectures*, trans. Gary D. Mole. Bloomington: Indiana University Press.

1994. *In the Time of the Nations*, trans. Michael B. Smith. Bloomington: Indiana University Press.

1997. *Proper Names*, trans. Michael B. Smith. Stanford: Stanford University Press.

1999. *New Talmudic Readings*, trans. Richard A. Cohen. Pittsburgh, PA: Duquesne University Press.

2000. *Entre Nous: On Thinking-of-the-Other*, trans. Barbara Harshav and Michael B. Smith. New York: Columbia University Press.

2003. *Humanism of the Other*, trans. Nidra Poller, Introduction by Richard A. Cohen. Urbana and Chicago: Illinois University Press.

Major Works by Heschel in English

1976. *God in Search of Man: A Philosophy of Judaism*. New York: Farrar, Straus and Giroux.
1997. *Moral Grandeur and Spiritual Audacity: Essays*, ed. Susannah Heschel. New York: Farrar, Straus, and Giroux.
2001. *The Prophets*. New York: Harper Perennial Modern Classics Readers.
2002. *The Sabbath: Its Meaning for Modern Man*. New York: Farrar Straus Giroux.

Suggested Reading

Ajzenstat, Oona, 2001. *Driven Back to the Text: The Premodern Sources of Levinas's Postmodernism*. Pittsburgh, PA: Duquesne University Press.
Batnitzky, Leora, 2006. *Leo Strauss and Emmanuel Levinas: Philosophy and the Politics of Revelation*. Cambridge, UK; New York: Cambridge University Press.
Bergo, Bettina, 1999. *Levinas Between Ethics and Politics: For the Beauty that Adorns the Earth*. The Hague, the Netherlands: Martinus Nijhoff Publishers.
Bloechl, Jeffrey, 2000. *Liturgy of the Neighbor: Emmanuel Levinas and the Religion of Responsibility*. Pittsburgh, PA: Duquesne University Press.
Caygill, Howard, 2002. *Levinas and the Political*. New York: Routledge.
Chanter, Tina, 2001. *Time, Death and the Feminine: Levinas with Heidegger*. Stanford: Stanford University Press.
Cohen, Richard A., 1994. *Elevations: The Height of the Good in Rosenzweig and Levinas*. Chicago, IL: University of Chicago Press.
——, 2001. *Ethics, Exegesis and Philosophy: Interpretation after Levinas*. Cambridge, UK; New York: Cambridge University Press.
Critchley, Simon, 1992. *The Ethics of Deconstruction: Derrida and Levinas*. Oxford: Blackwell. 2nd edn. Edinburgh University Library, 1999.
——, 1999. *Ethics Politics Subjectivity: Essays on Derrida, Levinas and Contemporary French Thought*. London: Verso.
Derrida, Jacques, 1980. "Violence and Metaphysics," in *Writing and Difference*, trans. Allan Bass. Chicago, IL: University of Chicago Press.
——, 1991. "At this Very Moment in this Work Here I Am," in *Re-Reading Levinas*, eds Robert Bernasconi and Simon Critchley. Bloomington: Indiana University Press.
——, 1999. *Adieu to Emmanuel Levinas*, trans. Pascale-Anne Brault and Michael Naas. Stanford: Stanford University Press.
Drabinski, John E., 2011. *Levinas and the Postcolonial: Race, Nation, Other*. Edinburgh, Scotland: Edinburgh University Press.
Fagenblat, Michael, 2010. *A Covenant of Creatures: Levinas's Philosophy of Judaism*. Stanford: Stanford University Press.
Gibbs, Robert, 1992. *Correlations in Rosenzweig and Levinas*. Princeton: Princeton University Press.
——, 2000. *Why Ethics? Signs of Responsibilities*. Princeton: Princeton University Press.
Gordon, Peter Eli. 2010. *Continental Divide: Heidegger, Cassirer, Davos*. Cambridge: Harvard University Press.
Hand, Seán, 2009. *Emmanuel Levinas*. London; New York: Routledge.

Handelman, Susan A., 1991. *Fragments of Redemption: Jewish Thought and Literary Theory in Benjamin, Scholem, and Levinas*. Bloomington: Indiana University Press.

Katz, Claire E., 2003. *Levinas, Judaism and the Feminine: The Silent Footsteps of Rebecca*. Bloomington: Indiana University Press.

Kavka, Martin, 2004. *Jewish Messianism and the History of Philosophy*. Cambridge, UK; New York: Cambridge University Press.

Malka, Salomon, 2006. *Emmanuel Levinas: His Life and Legacy*, trans. Michael Kigel and Sonia M. Embree. Pittsburgh, PA: Duquesne University Press.

Peperzak, Adriaan, 1993. *To the Other: An Introduction to the Philosophy of Emmanuel Levinas*. West Lafayette, IN: Purdue University Press.

———, 1997. *Beyond: The Philosophy of Emmanuel Levinas*. Evanston, IL: Northwestern University Press.

Perpich, Diane, 2008. *The Ethics of Emmanuel Levinas*. Stanford: Stanford University Press.

Putnam, Hilary, 2008. *Jewish Philosophy as a Guide to Life: Rosenzweig, Lévinas, Wittgenstein*. Bloomington: Indiana University Press.

Robbins, Jill, 1991. *Prodigal Son/Elder Brother: Interpretation and Alterity in Augustine, Petrarch, Kafka and Levinas*. Chicago, IL: University of Chicago Press.

———, 1999. *Altered Reading: Levinas and Literature*. Chicago, IL: University of Chicago Press.

Wolfson, Elliot, 2009. *Language, Eros, Being: Kabbalistic Hermeneutics and Poetic Imagination*. Oxford: Oxford University Press.

Wyschogrod, Edith, 2000. *Emmanuel Levinas: The Problem of Ethical Metaphysics*. The Hague, Netherlands: Martinus Nijhoff Publishers, 1974; 2nd edn, Fordham University Press.

Chapter 5: The Limits of Philosophy

Major Works

Arendt, Hannah, 1963. *Eichmann in Jerusalem: A Report on the Banality of Evil*. New York: Penguin.

———, 2003. *Responsibility and Judgment*, ed. Jerome Kohn. New York: Schocken.

Derrida, Jacques, 2001. *On Cosmopolitanism and Forgiveness*. London: Routledge.

Fackenheim, Emil, 1996. *Jewish Philosophers and Jewish Philosophy*, ed. Michael L. Morgan. Bloomington: Indiana University Press.

Jankélévitch, Vladimir, 1996. "Should we Pardon Them?" *Critical Inquiry* 22, no. 3 (Spring): 552–72.

———, 2005. *Forgiveness*, trans. Andrew Kelley. Chicago, IL: University of Chicago Press.

Levi, Primo, 1989. *The Drowned and the Saved*. New York: Simon and Schuster.

———, 1996. *Survival in Auschwitz*. New York: Touchstone.

Levinas, Emmanuel, 1990. *Nine Talmudic Readings*, trans. Annette Aronowicz. Bloomington: Indiana University Press.

Wiesel, Elie. 1960. *Night*. New York: Bantam Books.

Suggested Reading

Arendt, Hannah, 1944. "The Jew as Pariah: A Hidden Tradition." *Jewish Social Studies*, vol. 6, no. 2 (April): 99–122.

——, 1965. *Eichmann in Jerusalem: A Report on the Banality of Evil.* New York: Viking.

——, 1965. *On Revolution.* New York: Viking.

——, 1968. *Between Past and Future.* New York: Penguin.

——, 1973. *The Origins of Totalitarianism.* New York: Harcourt Brace Jovanovich.

Bernstein, Jeffrey, 2008. "Aggadic Moses: Spinoza and Freud on the Traumatic Legacy of Theological-Political Identity." *Idealistic Studies* 38: 1–2.

Braiterman, Zachary, 1998. *(God) After Auschwitz.* Princeton: Princeton University Press.

Derrida, Jacques, 2001. *On Cosmopolitanism and Forgiveness.* London: Routledge.

Frankl, Victor, 2006. *Man's Search for Meaning.* Boston, MA: Beacon Press.

Hatley, James, 2000. *Suffering Witness: The Quandary of Responsibility After the Irreparable.* Albany: SUNY Press.

Hughes, Aaron and Elliot Wolfson, eds, 2009. *New Directions in* Jewish Philosophy. Bloomington: Indiana University Press.

Jonas, Hans, 1996. Mortality and Morality: A Search for Good After Auschwitz, ed. Lawrence Vogel. Evanston, IL: Northwestern University Press.

Kohn, Jerome and Ron H. Feldman, 2007. *The Jewish Writings: Hannah Arendt.* New York: Schocken Books.

Murphy, Jeffrey, 2004. Getting Even: Forgiveness has its Limits. Oxford: Oxford University Press.

Spiegelman, Art, 1986. *Maus I: A Survivor's Tale: My Father Bleeds History.* Pantheon: 1986.

Verdeja, Ernesto, 2005. Review of Vladimir Jankélévitch, *Forgiveness* (University of Chicago Press, 2005). http://www.h-net.org/reviews/showrev.php?id=10842 (accessed February 22, 2013).

Wiesel, Elie, 2008. *The Night Trilogy: Night, Dawn, Day.* New York: Hill and Wang.

Wiesenthal, Simon, 1998. *The Sunflower: On the Possibilities and Limits of Forgiveness.* New York: Schocken.

Index